FATHER FACTS
FIFTH EDITION

TABLE OF CONTENTS

Tables & Figures*

Some of the tables provided here contain data from multiple sources. When citing specific numerical data within a table, be sure to visit the referenced source for accuracy.

FOREWARD
by Roland C. Warren
President, National Fatherhood Initiative

"Father Facts" got its start in the early 1990's as a one-page photo copy of some pertinent data on the effects of father absence on children. From those humble, black-and-white beginnings, and four subsequent bound editions, Father Facts has evolved into the substantial volume you hold in your hands today -- over 175 pages of graphs, data, and essays on father absence and its broad impact on our society and our children.

While the size and format may have changed, the message has remained the same, and it is as resoundingly clear as ever – kids need their dads. As you peruse the data in this, the fifth edition of Father Facts, we are confident that you will come to the same conclusion.

Indeed, Father Facts seeks to provide community workers, elected leaders, judges, clergy, policy makers, opinion leaders, scholars, and the public with a comprehensive and up-to-date overview of the social science research being conducted on family structure, father absence and its implications, and the effects of father involvement on the well-being of children and society.

Like previous editions of Father Facts, this edition categorizes the data by subject. It starts with an overall demographic look at today's families, follows up with a section on the effects of father absence across a variety of measures, and ends with a section on the effects of father involvement on a similar range of measures of child and societal well-being.

New to this edition of Father Facts is a set of two essays on the cultural environment surrounding fatherhood at the beginning of the 21st century. The essays, on music and media, provide thought-provoking ideas on how fatherhood is affected by our culture, and what this means as we look ahead at the challenges facing the institution of fatherhood.

The combination of hard data and thought provoking essays should provide you with the information and inspiration you need to ramp up your efforts to connect dads to kids, or, if you are a dad, to capitalize on your efforts to be the best dad that you can be for your children.

The evolution of Father Facts over the past 12 years reflects an evolution in NFI's approach to accomplishing its mission of improving the well-being of children by increasing the proportion of children growing up with involved, responsible, and committed fathers.

When NFI began its work in 1994, its primary goal was to educate the public about how widespread the problem of father absence had become, and to inspire people about the irreplaceable role that fathers play in the lives of their children. While this is still central to NFI's work, NFI has become focused on moving the public from "inspiration to implementation." Once an organization is inspired, NFI wants to provide the best resources to help them most effectively serve the needs of fathers. Once a father is inspired, NFI wants to provide him with state-of-the-art tools to help him become involved in his children's lives.

Accordingly, each of the topics that Father Facts addresses – education, crime, poverty, teen pregnancy – corresponds roughly to a programming area that NFI has developed to address the needs of fathers and organizations in all sectors of society.

With its Community-based, Faith-based, Corrections, Healthcare, Work-Family Balance, and Military programming, NFI provides the curricula, resources, and technical assistance that organizations and individuals from a variety of settings need to help our nation's children.

Additionally, NFI has formed strategic alliances and partnerships with organizations at the nexus of children and families to create new ways to connect fathers to their children, heart to heart.

This formula reflects NFI's "three-e" strategy of educate, equip, and engage.

With this strategy, NFI heads into its second decade with a clear vision of how to capitalize on the knowledge that Father Facts brings. And as more and more organizations and individuals are empowered by this knowledge, the lives of our nation's children will improve as they receive the love, nurture, and guidance of involved, responsible, and committed fathers.

DAD

is a verb.
like catch and hug and listen.
it is not just something you are.
it is something you do.
like laugh and read and play.
are you doing anything more important?
have you been a dad today?

National
Fatherhood
Initiative
www.fatherhood.org

who are you spending your quality time with?

have you been a dad today?

National Fatherhood Initiative®
www.fatherhood.org

ESSAY
Media & The State of Fatherhood
by Jamin Warren

If you want to know the state of fatherhood in the media consider the blurb from one of FOX's now-cancelled reality shows "Who's Your Daddy?":

"After a lifetime of separation, does the bond between parent and child remain? A reunion show like no other, WHO'S YOUR DADDY? provides a woman, who was given up for adoption as an infant, with an extraordinary opportunity to meet the birth father who also has been searching for her. But wait, there's a twist. Before meeting her dad, the young woman will be presented with eight men, all claiming to be her father, and she must determine which one really is. And to keep her real dad from revealing himself from the start, there is $100,000 at stake for his daughter. She will have opportunities to interview and observe the men, narrowing the field. If she guesses right, the prize will be hers. If she guesses wrong, the imposter will win the money."

The utter tackiness of the concept should have sabotaged the show before it aired. (Not to mention the potential discord between the child who fails to choose her father from a crowd of imposters and lose $100,000.) We've entered a post-abandonment generation; the initial shock of father absence that dawned during the out-of-wedlock bonanza of the 90s has dulled. Now, the trials of separation are ripe for a FOX reality television show.

The representation of fatherhood on television has been a part of NFI's mission since it launched its study on the portrayal of dads in 1999. After NFI's discovery that dads were 8 times more likely to be shown in a negative light when compared to moms, critics have pointed to the loss of dad as a respectable television icon.

John Tierney of The New York Times heralded the arrival of "the Doofus Dad." "Where did we fathers go wrong?," he writes in his Father's Day piece in 2005. "We spend twice as much time with our kids as we did two decades ago, but on television we're oblivious ("Jimmy Neutron"), troubled ("The Sopranos"), deranged ("Malcolm in the Middle") and generally incompetent ("Everybody Loves Raymond")." The L.A. Times' Paul Brownfield came to a similar conclusion the year before: "He is being recycled, network season after network season, as a hapless, benign man-child, tolerated (if he hasn't been abandoned) by the wife and the butt of one-liners from child actors who tell jokes as if they've spent July and August at some kind of Friars Club summer camp." Stephanie Cook Broadhurst of the Christian Science Monitor sees a new motif for prime-time: "the Joe sitcom." She writes: "His couch is sacred. He's a little pudgy and not terribly bright. He's a "guys' guy" who works a lunch-pail job and likes to drink beer and eat bratwurst. He claims he's always right - but in the end, it's his comely, intelligent wife who wins the battles."

Are TV writers merely getting lazy or is there a universal network allergy to responsible dads? To avoid patent alarmism, we should understand that the reality is slightly more complicated.

Consider FOX's 2005 season line-up. Homer Simpson leads one of the longest running shows on television. His clone, Peter Griffin of animated series The Family Guy, enjoys a comfortable prime-time spot on the same network. Although he is stellar real-life dad (He filmed a documentary called KidSmartz), Bryan Cranston's role as Malcolm's dad on Malcolm in the Middle portrays him as an impotent, impossible dad in a wholly dysfunctional family. Kurtwood Smith's character, Red, on That 70's Show might be the least laudable of the group. Hornery, dismissive, and occasionally violent, Red is hardly a paragon of fatherly excellence.

But fathers like Jason Bateman from Arrested Development, Bernie Mac, and Hank Hill break from their FOX contemporaries' model. Bateman, who won a Golden Globe in 2004, is a dedicated, involved father who holds his family together when his dad is sent to prison. He actually contrasts the two mothers (Lucille and

Lindsay) on the show as the model for a responsible parent. Bernie Mac is a stern disciplinarian but supports his kids. Hank Hill is deeply committed to wife, son, and niece, even though he experiences occasional lapses. Overall, these three men certainly fit the mold for involved, responsible, and committed fathers.

Unfortunately, FOX's varied paternal landscape is rare. For every Bernie Mac or Jason Bateman, there's a Ray Romano, George Lopez, or Damon Wayans. They are bumbling dads with a beautiful wives and they are clueless and impotent at home. The preponderance of this image of dad led critic Paul Brownfield to note: "Today, every sitcom father, no matter his race, appears to be the same white man standing in the same living room in the same plaid shirt."

Professors Katherine Young and Paul Nathanson of McGill University in Montreal came to a similar conclusion. After studying how men were portrayed in US pop culture over the past decade, they found that men in films, ads, and on TV fit three main archetypes: evil villains, juvenile buffoons, or brave men with a feminine side or who had been redeemed by a woman.

Why the shift? John Tierney of the Times points to three major changes that have birthed the new image of "doofus dad." First, sit-coms cater to women's interest. Sit-coms have become a primarily female domain, as four out of five sit-com watchers are female. Second, women are bringing home second paychecks, so the easily type-cast housemom no longer exists in ubiquity as it once did. Third, dumb dads make men laugh too. Three-quarters of sit-com scripts are written by men and 90% of all Simpsons scripts are submitted by men.

So if men are in control of the output, what's the problem? Wouldn't they know best if the image of dumb dad is hurting them? Poor images of fathers become problematic for several reasons.

While we have traded the father-first patriarchy of the 60s for more equal modes of family management, creating a new, destructive identity for families is hardly helpful. Television helps create the expectations that children have about what fathers should look like. There is no guarantee that they will internalize those images, but sit-coms and their ilk normalize modern conceptions of the family. Prof. Young argues, "When you have a constant barrage of images that are negative of men and boys, there are going to be problems. Boys will act it out if that's what society says they are." William Douglas and Beth Olson found similar results in their study of family relationships in TV comedies. Children have little experience with family structures, so portrayals of family can be highly influential in their social development. Again, this effect is not insured; however, let's not be naïve about the consequences of deluging the airwaves with the same scenes of disaffected fatherhood.

Moreover, TV dads often have poor relationships with their wives. Depictions of high-conflict marriages on television are perhaps more pernicious, because they explode the tensions of all marriages and make them the subject of ridicule. While Homer or Peter Griffin's outrageous exploits are often too crazy to imitate in real life, poor marital quality is more of a reality. When Ray Romano trades his wife's expensive diamond ring in for a cheaper knock-off, the ensuing drama resonates with every couple that's ever fought. But there's rarely any true resolution. Ray will be the same insensitive husband in the next episode when he does something stupid to irritate his wife. The Sisphyean intractability of the dumb dads misrepresents the nature of marital conflict as both male-driven and impossible. TV dads will continue to wallow in an endless cycle of irresponsibility, anguish, and apology.

The chief problem with "doofus dads" is context. Currently, there are more than 24 million children living without a father in the home. As many of these children are subjected to different images of fatherhood, they will have to make a key decision as to the type of father they would like to become. However, without a involved, responsible and committed father in their lives, they will have no image with which to compare their own conceptions. I never thought that Homer Simpson was a good dad, because I knew that my father would never choke me every day, abandon my mother at a marriage retreat to go fishing, or gain 70 lbs. to qualify for worker's compensation. My father was always supportive and fulfilled every obligation to be a good dad and would never dream of emulating Homer's behaviors.

We should be realistic. There should be no expectation that every portrayal of fatherhood should fit the ideal mold of flawless fatherhood. That is an unfair artistic warrant. Nor is there a complete lack of good dads on TV. In addition to the handful of FOX fathers, dads like John Schneider of Smallville and Terry Crews from the popular Everybody Hates Chris are good examples of responsible fatherhood. Even Homer has his moments of pop brilliance despite his numerous ridiculous foibles.

The goal should not be a return to the alleged halcyon TV days of the 60s. Nor should we forget that fathers and mothers have the heaviest influence on their children, despite whatever images are portrayed on TV. But why should we make the already treacherous road of fatherhood more perilous? Why should fathers have to battle television over their own legacy? Abandoning a father's unquestioned authority from past shows was certainly a step in the right direction, but adopting a new orthodoxy where fathers are villains, buffoons, or worse does no good for anyone. Cheap laughs are hardly an adequate substitute. As viewers, we should demand more protection for the fathers we hold dear.

Sources

Fox.com. "Fox Special: Who's Your Daddy." Accessed 13 Jan. 2006 <http://www.fox.com/schedule/showinfo/daddy/wyd_101.htm>

John Tierney. "The Doofus Dad." *The New York Times* 18 June 2005: A13.

Paul Brownfield. "Deadpan Dads; Help Mr. C! Today's sitcom fathers may be clad in plaid, but they're colorless and weak." *The Los Angeles Times* 19 Sept. 2004: E1.

Stephanie Cook Broadhurst. "Joe Sitcom; In a trend that's reached Homeric (as in Simpson) proportions, lovable shlubs have taken over TV." *Christian Science Monitor* 7 Mar. 2003: 13. Broadhurst, 13.

William Douglas and Beth Olson. "Subversion of the American family?; An examination of children and parents in television families." *Communication Research 23* (Feb. 1996): 73-99.

ESSAY
A Dad's (and Mom's) History of Hip-Hop
by Martha Bayles and Jamin Warren
Submitted to the National Fatherhood Initiative

When rapper Jay-Z announced that he was retiring from the world of hip-hop and releasing his magnum opus, The Black Album, fans and critics waited with expectant breath for a classic. The Brooklyn rapper did not disappoint. Not only did the release deliver some of the best singles in 2003, such as "Change Clothes" and "Encore", Jay-Z also revealed an important snippet from his early childhood. On "December 4th," he raps:

> *Now I'm just scratchin' the surface*
> *'Cause what's buried under there*
> *Was a kid torn apart once his pop disappeared*
> *I went to school got good grades*
> *Could behave when I wanted*
> *But I had demons deep inside*
> *That would raise when confronted*
> *Hold on*
> *Now all the teachers couldn't reach me*
> *And my momma couldn't beat me*
> *Hard enough to match the pain of my pop not seeing me, so*
> *With that disdain in my membrane*
> *Got on my pimp game*
> *F**k the world my defense came*

It is no surprise that the Brooklyn rapper pointed to the loss of his father as life-changing. The pain of parting with a father and the subsequent difficulty in becoming a man in his absence are not unique experiences. Currently, there are more than 24 million American children growing up without their fathers.

Jay-Z views his father's disappearance as his first step towards hip-hop. Again, this is no surprise. Such a significant change in the structure of families could not go unnoticed. Former editor of *The Source*, Bakari Kitwana, identifies the generation of youngsters from 1964 to 1984 as the core demographic known as the hip-hop generation. Coincidentally, that same time period saw the first significant flight of black fathers from their households and their children. Between 1960 and 1970,

the percentage of children living in a household without a father increased by 40%; in the following decade, it increased by the same percentage. By 2004, two-thirds (65.8%) of all black children were being raised in the absence of their biological father. More than any other cultural expression, hip-hop communicates that experience.

Hip hop is universally taken to be a form of expression whose roots run deep in North America. In other words, many people think hip-hop came out of the same Afro-American musical tradition as funk, soul, R&B, swing, gospel, blues, jazz, spirituals, and ragtime – all the musical styles created by black people living in the United States.

But hip-hop didn't come out of this musical tradition, it came out of a spoken-word tradition brought to New York by Caribbean immigrants. It emerged during the late 1970s, when the most popular discos in the black and Latino neighborhoods of Manhattan and the Bronx featured DJs from Jamaica and Barbados.

Back then the disco DJ's job was to switch back and forth between two LPs on two turntables, playing track after track to fuel nonstop dancing. With Joseph Saddler, a Barbados-born immigrant also known as Grandmaster Flash, this switching became a minor art form. As he recalls, "I mastered punch phrasing – taking certain parts of a record where there's a vocal or drum slap or a horn. I would throw it out and then bring it back, keeping the other turntable playing." Flash was not a musician in the sense of singing or playing. But he was a talented percussionist, working with turntables the way another performer might work with a drum kit.

The development of the "rap" element was also due to the Caribbean influence. In the islands, most people could not afford record players, and the elite controlled radio. This left popular music in the hands of DJs who traveled the countryside with huge record collections and souped-up "sound systems," competing for business by "dubbing," or removing the vocal part of a record and substituting their own voices. But when a Caribbean DJ added his own voice, it wasn't to sing, it was to talk. In particular, it was to talk in the stylized manner known as "toasting."

To North Americans, "toasting" suggests a brief tribute over a glass of champagne. But Jamaican toasting was improvised poetry, with roots running back through the calypso of Trinidad to the griots of West Africa, who could recite clan histories, offer praise songs, and insult prominent people with such skill that the better toasters made a handsome living just keeping their mouths shut, hiding their rapier tongues.

This history demonstrates how the first American rappers showed a marked tendency toward boasting and insult, echoing such North American practices as "signifying," "sounding," and "playing the dozens." But early rap also displayed its Caribbean roots by serving as a voice of political protest: today, Grandmaster Flash and his group, the Furious Five, are remembered for raps focusing on topics few Americans wanted to face in the late '70s (or now): inner-city poverty, gang violence, cocaine abuse, fatherless families.

For example, "The Message," recorded in 1982, describes a young boy "in the ghetto, living second rate," admiring "all the number book-takers, thugs, pimps, pushers, and the big money-makers," then ending up committing suicide in prison. This and other cautionary verses are followed by the refrain: "Don't push me 'cause I'm close to the edge / I'm tryin' not to lose my head / It's like a jungle sometimes, it makes me wonder / How I keep from going under."

Hip-hop is often compared with the blues, and here the comparison is quite apt. Musically, hip-hop is nothing like the blues, but lyrically, this refrain captures the essence of the blues: a cold-eyed reckoning with the facts, accompanied by a stubborn determination "to keep from going under."

Despite its Caribbean origins and the many changes it has gone through over the last three decades, hip-hop still carries the voice of the black community. Chuck D, the frontman for the popular group Public Enemy, once said that hip-hop was the black man's CNN. At its heart, Chuck's statement reflected this deep connection. Hence, when black fathers began to disappear in large numbers, hip-hop registered that disappearance in its verses and images – for better or worse.

In June 2005, a 30-something math teacher named Derek Phillips organized a "Black Fatherhood Summit" in a Harlem church for the members of a self-help group called Real Dads Network. Of all the topics that could have been discussed, one stood out: the image of African-American men in rap. Speaker after speaker expressed dismay at the way stars like Nelly, the Game, Snoop Dogg, and 50 Cent depict young black men as either embittered losers moping on the street corner (or cell block) or extravagant winners living large in surreal mansions or tropical paradises, surrounded by compliant, disposable young women who do not expect men to accept any kind of responsibility, least of all that of fatherhood.

With few notable exceptions, most of the best and most popular rappers of the last twenty years have been raised in fatherless homes. Agnes Carter raised her son Jay-Z alone when his father left the Carter home when Jay was 11. Loretta Wallace also raised her son, the Notorious B.I.G. (aka Christopher Wallace), without his father.

The tremendous struggles that these single mothers faced raising their children alone merited them an esteemed place in hip-hop. They boast a gilded legacy in hip-hop and serve as sources of authority, sympathy, and inspiration. Mothers are rappers' confidantes.

Fathers receive less favorable treatment. Los Angeles rapper/poet Tupac Shakur, who exalted his mother on tracks like "Dear Mama," was hardly merciful when speaking of his father. On "Papa'z Song," Tupac fires:

> *Had to play catch by myself, what a sorry sight*
> *A pitiful plight, so I pray for a starry night*
> *Please send me a pops before puberty*
> *The things I wouldn't do to see a piece of family unity*
> *Moms always work, I barely see her*
> *I'm startin' to get worried without a pops I'll grow to be her*
> *It's a wonder they don't understand kids today*
> *So when I pray, I pray I'll never grow to be that way*
> *And I hope that he answers me*
> *I heard God don't like ugly well take a look at my family*
> *A different father every weekend*
> *Before we get to meet him they break up before the week ends*

I'm gettin' sick of all the friendships
As soon as we kick it he done split and the whole s**t ends quick
How can I be a man if there's no role model?
Strivin' to save my soul I stay cold drinkin' a forty bottle
I'm so sorry...

For Tupac, a history has been severed. In the next verse, his disappointment turns to rage: "So don't even start with that "wanna be your father" s**t/Don't even bother with your dollars I don't need it / I'll bury moms like you left me all alone G / Now that I finally found you, stay the f**k away from me."

Queens rapper 50 Cent, aka Curtis Jackson, lost his mother, a cocaine dealer, when he was eight, and never knew his father. So when asked by Toure of Rolling Stone about his father, the rapper gave this blunt appraisal: "Let's give him a warning in this article. Don't you even crawl you're a** out this way. I don't want to know the n***a…"

Having no father in the home and seeking to become a man, Tupac did what many young boys in his situation would do: He sought out the only older male figures available. Shakur told MTV: "I didn't have a father, but I had pimps and drug dealers and robbers and killers telling me what I should do." For Jay-Z, the pain of his father's absence filled him with anger and pushed towards selling drugs. On "Dear Mama," Shakur narrates a similar tale:

Now ain't nobody tell us it was fair
No love from my daddy
'Cause the coward wasn't there
He passed away and I didn't cry
'Cause my anger wouldn't let me feel for a stranger
They say I'm wrong and I'm heartless, but all along
I was lookin' for a father he was gone
I hung around with the thugs
Even though they sold drugs
They showed a young brother love
I moved out and started really hangin'

Of course, not all father-son relationships in hip-hop are marked with strife and separation. Queens rapper,

Nas, has always prided himself on self-improvement and eschewed the luxurious lifestyles of rap peers. In 2004, Nas released the outstanding "Closing the Gap" which features his father, jazz trumpeter Olu Dara. As suggested by the title, Nas feels connected with his father through music, and that connection is manifested in lyrics like: "Hey-Hey-Hey -- My poppa was not a Rollin' Stone / He been around the world blowin' his horn, still he came home."

Chicago rapper, Common, has a similarly positive relationship with his dad. He has featured his father prominently on several of his songs, allowing him to deliver the benedictions on "Like Water For Chocolate" and "Be". Fellow Chicagoan, multi-platinum rapper/producer Kayne West, was pictured in a profile in *Time* with both of his parents. Although West has highlighted father absence in songs like "Gold Digga" from his sophomore release Late Registration, his verses are hardly autobiographical with respect to his dad, as his relationship with his father differs from the norm of his peers. To date, Kanye has not released verse that slanders his father.

But unfortunately, the vast majority of rappers feel a mixture of painful loss and angry disdain towards the fathers who abandoned them. Yet in some cases, it is striking how much rappers still want to be responsible father figures to their own children. For example, back in 1991 Boston rapper Ed O.G. rapped, "Be a father to your child." More than a decade later, former Crip and rapper, The Game, echoed that refrain with Busta Rhymes on the final track of his platinum album The Documentary. Greeting the birth of The Game's son, Busta rapped:

I hope you grow up to become that everything you can be
That's all I wanted for young'n, like father, like son
For in the end I hope you'll only turn out better than me
I hope you know I love you young'n, like father, like son

As an art form with deep roots in Black America, hip-hop will continue to express the pain of fatherlessness, as well as the hope of a new generation that they can break the cycle. At the same time, hip-hop as global entertainment will continue to trade in cartoonish images of black men as "players" and hustlers interested only in "bling" and "booty," with black women as their silent, disposable playthings. Which influence will be more powerful?

The question is of the highest importance, because this art form is not going away. It will continue to teach, inspire, and persuade young people in the black community and beyond. Perhaps the best thing listeners can do is express their opinion, because underneath the hardened facades, diamond-encrusted teeth, and surgically-enhanced bodies of hip-hop artists, are young men and women seeking an answer to the question, "What does it mean to be a man?" They are not the only ones who need to find the answer.

FATHER FACTS
STATISTICS

I. Trends in Father Absence

"Over the past four decades, fatherlessness has emerged as one of our greatest social problems. We know that children who grow up with absent fathers can suffer lasting damage. They are more likely to end up in poverty or drop out of school, become addicted to drugs, have a child out of wedlock or end up in prison. Fatherlessness is not the only cause of these things, but our nation must recognize it as an important factor."

PRESIDENT GEORGE W. BUSH, SPEAKING AT NATIONAL FATHERHOOD INITIATIVE'S 4TH ANNUAL NATIONAL SUMMIT ON FATHERHOOD IN WASHINGTON, D.C., JUNE 7, 2001.

"If I had to summarize my deepest conviction in this whole area of the family, it would be that every child has a birthright to grow up with her mother and father who love the child and love each other. Far too many of our children are denied that birthright. And we see so much childhood pain, and so many social problems, stemming from that basic denial of what children need."

DAVID BLANKENHORN QUOTED IN THE JACKSON CLARION-LEDGER, AUGUST 1, 2004.

"The single biggest social problem in our society may be the growing absence of fathers from their children's homes because it contributes to many other social problems... Without a father to help guide, without a father to care, without a father to teach boys to be men, and teach girls to expect respect from men, it's harder."

FORMER PRESIDENT BILL CLINTON, FROM SPEECH AT THE UNIVERSITY OF TEXAS, AUSTIN, OCTOBER 16, 1993.

"Promoting responsible fatherhood is the critical next phase of welfare reform and one of the most important things we can do to reduce child poverty."

FORMER VICE PRESIDENT AL GORE, SPEAKING AT THE NATIONAL FATHERHOOD INITIATIVE'S 3RD ANNUAL NATIONAL SUMMIT ON FATHERHOOD IN WASHINGTON, D.C., JUNE 2, 2000.

Attitudes About Fatherhood and Father Absence

In 1999, 72.2% of those polled in a national survey (n=928) agreed that "the physical absence of the father from the home is the most significant problem facing America." This figure is up from 69.9% of respondents in 1992, but down from 79.1% in 1996.

Source: Survey conducted by the Gallup Organization for the National Center for Fathering, as quoted in *Today's Father*, vol. 7 (2-3), 1999: 16.

Seven in 10 adults believe a child needs a home with both a father and a mother to grow up happy.

Source: Gallup, George. "Report on the Status of Fatherhood in the United States." *Emerging Trends, 20* (September 1998): 3-5. Published by the Princeton Religion Research Center, Princeton, NJ.

According to a national survey of 2,000 adults, only 22% agreed that fathers who are "affectionate and loving" toward their kids are "very common."

Source: Farkas, Steve, and Jean Johnson. "Kids These Days: What Americans Really Think About the Next Generation." New York: *Public Agenda*, 1997: 39.

76% of single dads under age 45 and 81% of single moms under age 45 believe that they are as good or better a parent on their own as they would be with the other parent also in the home. Overall, 88% of dads and 82% of moms think they are as good or better a father/mother than their own father/mother.

Source: Roper Starch Worldwide, as reported in *Parenting*, November 1998: 120.

In a poll of 1,031 adults, 28 percent of respondents said their fathers were more influential in their upbringing, while 53 percent credited their mothers as more influential, and 15 percent said both parents influenced them equally.

Source: Chambers, Chris. "Mothers Still Perceived as Having More Dominant Influence Than Fathers, but Dads Don't Seem to Mind." Princeton, NJ: Gallup News Service: June 16, 2000.

According to a 1996 Gallup Poll, 90.9 percent of Americans feel "it is important for children to live in a home with both their mother and father."

Source: Gallup Poll, 1996. National Center for Fathering. "Father Figures." *Today's Father, 4.1* (1996): 8.

> Seven in 10 adults believe a child needs a home with both a father and a mother to grow up happy.

Father Absence
Children's Living Arrangements

Of the 73.2 million children under 18 years old living in the United States in 2004, 67.7 percent (49.6 million) were living with two parents, 27.9 percent (20.4 million) were living with a single parent, and 4.3 percent (3.1 million) were living with neither parent.

Source: U.S. Census Bureau. *Current Population Survey Reports*. "Household Relationship and Living Arrangements of Children Under 18 Years, by Age, Sex, Race, Hispanic Origin: 2004; All Races, White only, Black only, and Hispanic only." Table C2. Published July 29, 2005. <http://www.census.gov/population/socdemo/hh-fam/cps2004/tabC2-all.csv>

In 2001, 59 percent of children lived with married, biological parents. This was a decrease from 62 percent that had been constant since 1991.

Source: Krieder, Rose M. and Jason Fields. *Living Arrangements of Children: 2001*. Current Population Reports, P70-104. Table 1. Washington, D.C.: US Census Bureau, 2005; Fields, Jason. *The Living Arrangements of Children: Fall 1996*. Current Population Reports, P70-74. Washington, D.C.: U.S. Census Bureau, 2001; Furukawa, Stacy. *The Diverse Living Arrangements of Children: Summer 1991*. Current Population Reports, P70-38. Washington, D.C.: U.S. Census Bureau, 1994.

Of the nation's 46.2 million families with own children in 2004, 68.3 percent were headed by two married parents, 25.3 percent by female householders, and 6.3 percent by male householders.

Source: U.S. Census Bureau. *America's Families and Living Arrangements: 2004*. "Family Households, by Type, Age of Own Children, Educational Attainment, and Race and Hispanic Origin of Householder: 2004." Table F1. Accessed August 26, 2005. <http://www.census.gov/population/socdemo/hh-fam/cps2004/tabF2-all.csv>

Living Arrangements of Children Under 18 Years, by Percentage, 1960 to 2004

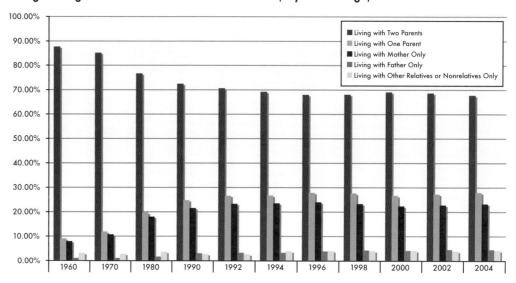

Living Arrangements of Children Under 18 Years, by Number, 1960 to 2004

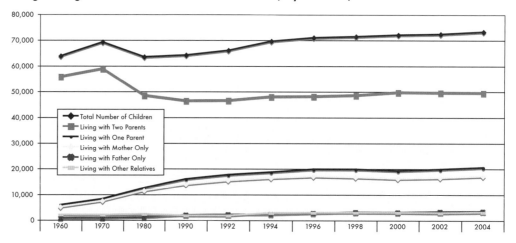

FATHER FACTS, 5TH EDITION • © 2007 National Fatherhood Initiative

Living Arrangements of Children Under 18 Years, Data Table, 1960 to 2004

	Total	Living with Two Parents	Living with One Parent	Living with Mother Only	Living with Father Only	Living with Other Relatives
1960	63,727	55,877	5,829	5,105	724	2,021
		87.70%	9.10%	8.00%	1.10%	3.20%
1970	69,162	58,939	8,199	7,452	748	2,024
		85.20%	11.90%	10.80%	1.10%	2.90%
1980	63,427	48,624	12,466	11,406	1,060	2,337
		76.70%	19.70%	18.00%	1.70%	3.70%
1990	64,137	46,503	15,867	13,874	1,993	1,768
		72.50%	24.70%	21.60%	3.10%	2.80%
1992	65,965	46,638	17,578	15,396	2,182	1,749
		70.70%	26.60%	23.30%	3.30%	2.70%
1994	69,508	48,084	18,591	16,334	2,257	2,806
		69.20%	26.80%	23.50%	3.30%	4.00%
1996	70,908	48,224	19,752	16,993	2,759	2,932
		68.00%	27.90%	24.00%	3.90%	4.10%
1998	71,377	48,642	19,777	16,634	3,143	2,959
		68.10%	27.70%	23.30%	4.40%	4.10%
2000	72,012	49,795	19,220	16,162	3,058	2,997
		69.10%	26.70%	22.40%	4.20%	4.20%
2002	72,321	49,666	19,770	16,473	3,297	2,885
		68.70%	27.30%	22.80%	4.60%	4.00%
2004	73,205	49,603	20,474	17,072	3,402	3,129
		67.80%	28.00%	23.30%	4.60%	4.30%

Source: U.S. Census Bureau. "Living Arrangements of Children Under 18 Years Old: 1960 to Present." Table CH-1. Internet Release Date September, 21 2006.

Family Groups by Presence of Own Children Under 18, 1970 to 2004

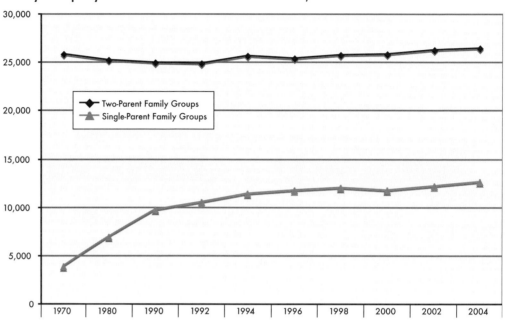

	Total		White		Black		Hispanic	
	Two-Parent Family Groups	Single-Parent Family Groups	Two-Parent Family Groups	Single-Parent Family Groups	Two-Parent Family Groups	Single-Parent Family Groups	Two-Parent Family Groups	Single-Parent Family Groups
1970	25,823	3,808	23,477	2,638	2,071	1,148	-	-
	87.20%	12.80%	89.90%	10.10%	64.30%	35.70%	-	-
1980	25,231	6,920	22,628	4,664	1,961	2,114	1,626	568
	78.50%	21.50%	82.90%	17.10%	48.10%	51.90%	74.10%	25.90%
1990	24,921	9,749	21,905	6,389	2,006	3,081	2,289	1,140
	71.90%	28.10%	77.40%	22.60%	39.40%	60.60%	66.80%	33.20%
1992	24,879	10,499	21,909	6,938	1,948	3,216	2,473	1,298
	70.30%	29.70%	75.90%	24.10%	37.70%	62.30%	65.60%	34.40%
1994	25,598	11,410	22,310	7,335	1,978	3,636	2,786	1,583
	69.20%	30.80%	75.30%	24.70%	35.20%	64.80%	63.80%	36.20%
1996	25,361	11,717	22,178	7,769	1,942	3,493	2,858	1,702
	68.40%	31.60%	74.10%	25.70%	35.70%	64.30%	62.70%	37.30%
1998	25,709	11,948	22,237	8,077	2,111	3,493	3,233	1,789
	68.30%	31.70%	73.40%	26.60%	37.70%	62.30%	64.40%	35.60%
2000	25,771	11,725	22,241	7,838	2,135	3,395	3,625	1,878
	68.70%	31.30%	73.90%	26.10%	38.60%	61.40%	65.90%	34.10%
2002	26,271	12,201	22,381	8,169	2,179	3,456	3,936	2,114
	68.29%	31.71%	73.26%	26.74%	38.67%	61.33%	65.06%	34.94%
2004	26,377	12,624	22,499	8,506	2,160	3,684	4,273	2,300
	67.63%	32.37%	73.13%	26.87%	36.96%	63.04%	65.01%	34.99%

*Family groups with children include families who maintain their own household and those who live in the home of a relative; numbers in thousands. Includes people who are divorced, never-married, married but not living with spouse, and widowed. Source: U.S. Census Bureau. "All Parent/Child Situations, by Type, Race, and Hispanic Origin of Householder or Reference Person: 1970 to Present; All Races, White only, Black only, and Hispanic only." Table FM-2. Internet Release Date September, 21 2006. <http://www.census.gov/population/socdemo/hh-fam/fm2.pdf>

In a 1999 nationally representative survey of 42,000 households, it was found that 64 percent of children were living with their two biological (or adoptive) parents. One-quarter (25 percent) lived in a single-parent household, 8 percent lived in a blended family, and 4 percent lived absent both biological parents.

Source: Vandivere, Sharon, Kristin Moore, and Martha Zaslow. "Children's Family Environment: Findings from the National Survey of America's Families." *Snapshots of America's Families II.* Washington, D.C.: Urban Institute, 2000.

Recent Trends in Family Structure

Although the percentage of children living in single parent families has not changed since 1996, the proportion by race has shifted. White single parent families increased 3 percent, black single parent families decreased 6 percent, and Hispanic families decreased 3 percent.

The percentage of children living in single mother families by race increased from 15% to 17% for white children, decreased from 50% to 48% for black children, and stayed at 24% for Hispanic children.

It should also be noted that the percentage of black children living with neither parent increased from 7.9% to 9.5% of all black children.

Source: Krieder, Rose M. and Jason Fields. *Living Arrangements of Children: 2001.* Current Population Reports, P70-104. Table 1. Washington, D.C.: US Census Bureau, 2005.

Between 1995 and 2000, the proportion of children younger than 18 living with a non-cohabiting single mother declined from 19.9 percent to 18.4 percent — a statistically significant drop of 1.5 percentage points, or 8 percent. This represents a change from the trend seen ten years earlier. Between 1985 and 1990, the proportion of children living with a single mother remained at essentially the same level.

Source: Dupree, Allen, and Wendell Primus. Declining Share of Children Lived With Single Mothers in the Late 1990s. Washington, D.C.: Center on Budget and Policy Priorities, 2001.

The proportion of children living with two married parents (including stepparents) remained stable between 1995 and 2000, at about 70 percent. In 2004, the number had dipped slightly to 67 percent. This differs from the trend a decade earlier, when the share of children living with two married parents declined.

Additionally, the proportion of black children living with two married parents increased from 34.8 percent in 1995 to 38.9 percent in 2000—a substantial rise.

Source: Dupree, Allen, and Wendell Primus. *Declining Share of Children Lived With Single Mothers in the Late 1990s.* Washington, D.C.: Center on Budget and Policy Priorities, 2001; U.S. Census Bureau. *America's Families and Living Arrangements:* 2004. "Living Arrangements of Children Under 18 Years and Marital Status of Parents, by Age, Sex, Race, and Hispanic Origin and Selected Characteristics of the Child for All Children: 2004." Table C3. Accessed August 26, 2005. < http://www.census.gov/population/socdemo/hh-fam/cps2004/tabC3-all.csv>

Number of Children in Various Family Arrangements, 2004

	Total	White	Black	Hispanic*
Total	73,205	55,902	11,424	13,752
Living with Two Parents	49,603	41,550	3,972	8,886
Living with One Parent	20,474	12,518	6,415	4,220
Living with Single Mother	17,072	10,050	5,758	3,489
Living with Single Father	3,402	2,468	657	731
Living with Neither Parent	3,129	1,834	1,037	646
Living with Grandparents	1,504	826	586	246
Living with Other Relatives	796	449	265	235
Living in Other Arrangement	829	560	186	166

*Persons of Hispanic origin may be of any race.

Source: US Census Bureau. Living arrangements of children, Tables CH-1 to CH-4. Internet Release Date September 21, 2006. <http://www.census.gov/population/www/socdemo/hh-fam.html>

Between 1995 and 2004, the number of unmarried couples with children under 15 years old increased by 38 percent, from 1.3 million to 1.9 million.

Between 1997 and 1999, the percentage of children in single-parent families decreased from 27 to 25 percent, while the percentage living with two parents increased by more than one percentage point. By 2004, however, the number had returned to 28 percent for children in single-parent families and the percentage of children in two-parent households had returned to 1997 levels.

Source: Vandivere, Sharon, Kristin Moore, and Martha Zaslow. "Children's Family Environment: Findings from the National Survey of America's Families." Figure 2. *Snapshots of America's Families II*. Washington, D.C.: Urban Institute, 2000; U.S. Census Bureau. Current Population Surveys. "Living Arrangements of Children Under 18 Years Old: 1960 to Present." Table CH-1. Published June 29, 2005. <http://www.census.gov/population/socdemo/hh-fam/ch1.pdf>

While all racial and ethnic groups saw a decrease in the proportion of children living with a non-cohabiting single mother from 1995 to 2000, the greatest decline occurred among black children (a drop from 47.1 to 43.1 percent). Among Hispanics, the proportion fell from 24.6 percent to 21.3 percent, while the proportion among white children declined slightly (12.8 percent to 12.0 percent).

Source: Dupree, Allen, and Wendell Primus. *Declining Share of Children Lived With Single Mothers in the Late 1990s*. Washington, D.C.: Center on Budget and Policy Priorities, 2001.

Excluding cohabiting single mothers, the percentage of children living in single-mother families dropped from 21.3 percent in 1997 to 19.2 percent in 1999.

Source: Acs, Gregory, and Sandi Nelson. "Honey, I'm Home." *Changes in Living Arrangements in the Late 1990s*. Table 2. Assessing the New Federalism, Series B, No. B-38. Washington, D.C.: The Urban Institute, 2001.

Between 1997 and 1999, the share of single mothers living alone (as a percentage of all families with children) dropped by 1.8 percentage points, while the share of cohabiting single mothers grew by 1.5 percentage points.

Source: Acs, Gregory, and Sandi Nelson. "Honey, I'm Home." *Changes in Living Arrangements in the Late 1990s*. Assessing the New Federalism, Series B, No. B-38. Washington, D.C.: The Urban Institute, 2001.

Between 1995 and 2004, the number of unmarried couples with children under 15 years old increased by 38 percent, from 1.3 million to 1.9 million.

Source: U.S. Census Bureau. *America's Families and Living Arrangements*. Current Population Reports, P20-537. Table 8. *Characteristics of Unmarried Partners and Married Spouses by Sex*: 2003. Washington, D.C.: U.S. Census Bureau, 2004; U.S. Census Bureau. *America's Families and Living Arrangements*: 2004. "Opposite Sex Unmarried Partner Households by Presence of Own Children Under 18, and Age, Earnings, Education, and Race and Hispanic Origin of Both Partners: 2004." Table UC3. Accessed August 26, 2005. <http://www.census.gov/population/socdemo/hh-fam/cps2004/tabUC3-all.csv>

The number of children in single-father families with children grew by 55 percent over the 1990s, from 2.0 million to 3.1 million. By 2004, the number stood at 3.4 million. However, only 4.6 percent of all children live with single fathers, and single mothers still outnumber single fathers more than five to one.

Source: U.S. Census Bureau. *Current Population Reports*, P20-537. Table CH-1. *Living Arrangements of Children Under 18 Years Old: 1960 to Present*. Table FM-2. All Parent/Child Situations, by Type, Race, and Hispanic Origin of Householder or Reference Person: 1970 to Present. Washington, D.C.: U.S. Census Bureau, 2001; U.S. Census Bureau. *America's Families and Living Arrangements: 2004*. "Household Relationship and Living Arrangements of Children Under 18 Years, by Age, Sex, Race, Hispanic Origin: 2004" Table C3. Accessed August 26, 2005. < http://www.census.gov/population/socdemo/hh-fam/cps2004/tabC2-all.csv>

The Facts of Father Absence

In America, 24.35 million children (33.5 percent) live absent their biological father.

Source: Krieder, Rose M. and Jason Fields. *Living Arrangements of Children*: 2001. Current Population Reports, P70-104. Table 1. Washington, D.C.: US Census Bureau, 2005.

Of students in grades 1 through 12, 39 percent, or 17.7 million, live in homes absent their biological father.

Source: Nord, Christine Winquist, and Jerry West. *Fathers' and Mothers' Involvement in Their Children's Schools by Family Type and Resident Status*. Table 1. (NCES 2001-032). Washington, D.C.: U.S. Department of Education, National Center for Education Statistics, 2001.

Over a quarter of all American children (28 percent, or 19.4 million) live in homes without a biological, adoptive, or stepfather present.* Over 17 million children (23.0 percent) live in mother-only families. This is up from 16.1 million children (22.4%) in 2000.

*does not include children living with widowed mothers.

Source: U.S. Census Bureau. *Current Population Surveys*. "Living Arrangements of Children Under 18 Years Old: 1960 to Present." Table CH-1. Published June 29, 2005. <http://www.census.gov/population/socdemo/hh-fam/ch1.pdf>

Among teens, only 67 percent live with their biological fathers, compared with 91 percent who live with their biological mothers. In urban areas, the percentage of teens who live with their biological fathers drops to only 57 percent.

Source: Gallup, George. "Report on Status of Fatherhood In the United States." *Emerging Trends, 20* (September 1998): 3-5. Published by the Princeton Religion Research Center, Princeton, NJ.

In America, 24.35 million children (33.5 percent) live absent their biological father.

Number of Children Under 18 Years Living with Mother Only, by Marital Status, 1960 to Present

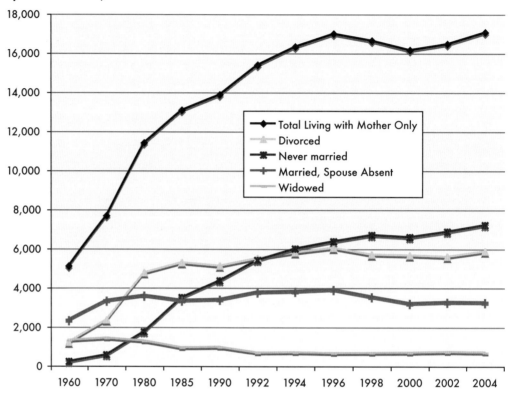

Percentage of Children Under 18 Years Living with Mother Only, by Marital Status, 1960 to Present

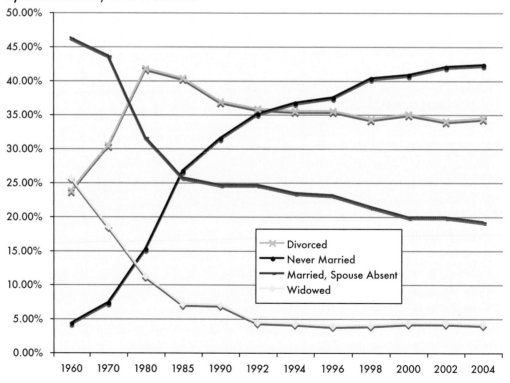

Children Under 18 Years Living with Mother Only, by Marital Status, Data Table, 1960 to Present

	Total	Divorced	Never Married	Married, Spouse Absent	Widowed
1960	5,105	1,210	221	2,363	1,311
		23.70%	4.30%	46.20%	25.60%
1970	7,678	2,338	565	3,351	1,421
		30.40%	7.30%	43.60%	18.50%
1980	11,406	4,766	1,745	3,610	1,286
		41.70%	15.20%	31.60%	11.20%
1985	13,081	5,280	3,496	3,367	939
		40.30%	26.70%	25.70%	7.10%
1990	13,874	5,118	4,365	3,416	975
		36.90%	31.50%	24.60%	7.00%
1992	15,396	5,507	5,410	3,790	688
		35.80%	35.10%	24.60%	4.40%
1994	16,334	5,799	6,000	3,838	696
		35.50%	36.70%	23.40%	4.20%
1996	16,993	6,039	6,365	3,927	662
		35.50%	37.50%	23.10%	3.90%
1998	16,634	5,704	6,700	3,558	671
		34.30%	40.30%	21.40%	4.00%
2000	16,162	5,655	6,591	3,224	692
		35.00%	40.80%	19.90%	4.30%
2002	16,472	5,593	6,872	3,287	720
		34.00%	42.00%	19.90%	4.30%
2004	17,072	5,870	7,218	3,281	704
		34.40%	42.30%	19.20%	4.10%

Source: U.S. Census Bureau. "Children Under 18 Living With Mother Only, By Marital Status of Mother, 1960 to Present." Table CH-5. Internet Release Date September, 21 2006. <http://www.census.gov/population/socdemo/hh-fam/ch5.pdf>

Number of Children Living in Father-Absent Homes, 1960 to 2004

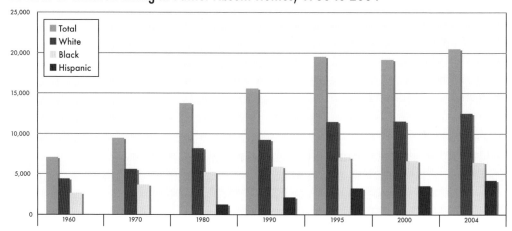

Percentage of Children Living in Father-Absent Homes, 1960 to 2004

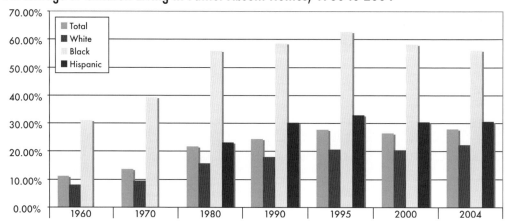

Children Living in Father-Absent Homes, Data Table, 1960 to 2004

	Total	White	Black	Hispanic
1960	7,126	4,444	2,641	-
	11.20%	8.10%	31.00%	-
1970	9,475	5,638	3,702	-
	13.70%	9.60%	39.30%	-
1980	13,743	8,200	5,239	1,260
	21.70%	15.70%	55.90%	23.10%
1990	15,641	9,249	5,885	2,174
	24.40%	18.00%	58.70%	30.30%
1995	19,517	11,489	7,097	3,236
	27.80%	20.80%	62.80%	32.90%
2000	19,159	11,531	6,642	3,546
	26.60%	20.40%	58.20%	30.50%
2004	20,474	12,518	6,415	4,220
	28.00%	22.30%	56.20%	30.70%

*Includes children living in homes without a biological, adoptive, or step-father. Source: U.S. Census Bureau. "Household Relationship and Living Arrangements of Children Under 18 Years, by Age, Sex, Race, Hispanic Origin: 2004; All Races, White only, Black only, and Hispanic only." Table C2. Published July 29, 2005. <http://www.census.gov/population/www/socdemo/hh-fam/cps2004.html>

Father Absence by Race and Ethnicity

Sixty-three percent of black children, 35 percent of Hispanic children, and 28 percent of white children are living in homes absent their biological father. The percentage of black children decreased three percentage points since 1996.
Source: Krieder, Rose M. and Jason Fields. *Living Arrangements of Children: 2001.* Current Population Reports, P70-104. Table 1. Washington, D.C.: US Census Bureau, 2005; Fields, Jason. The Living Arrangements of Children: Fall 1996. Current Population Reports, P70-74. Internet Table 1. Washington, D.C.: U.S. Census Bureau, 2001.

In 2001, 65 percent of white children, 29 percent of black children, and 58 percent of Hispanic children lived with both of their married, biological (or adoptive) parents. All of these percentages were down slightly since 1996.
Source: Krieder, Rose M. and Jason Fields. *Living Arrangements of Children: 2001.* Current Population Reports, P70-104. Table 1. Washington, D.C.: US Census Bureau, 2005; Fields, Jason. *The Living Arrangements of Children: Fall 1996.* Current Population Reports, P70-74. Washington, D.C.: U.S. Census Bureau, 2001.

For teenagers (12- to 17-year-olds), the proportion living with their biological married parents is 62 percent for whites, 25 percent for blacks, and 49 percent for Hispanics.
Source: Nelson, Sandi, Rebecca L. Clark, and Gregory Acs. *Beyond the Two-Parent Family: How Teenagers Fare in Cohabiting Couple and Blended Families.* Assessing the New Federalism, Series B, No. B-31. Washington, D.C.: The Urban Institute, 2001.

Half of black children (51 percent) live with single mothers, compared to one in four Hispanic children (25 percent) and one in six white children (18 percent).
Source: U.S. Census Bureau. *America's Families and Living Arrangements.* Current Population Reports, P20-553. Table C3. Washington, D.C.: U.S. Census Bureau, 2004.

Of the 24 million children in father-absent homes, 64.7 percent are white, 30.5 percent are black, and 17.9 percent are Hispanic.* The number of black children in father-absent homes decreased 1.5 percentage points and the number of Hispanic children in father-absent households has increased 3 percentage points since 1996.
Source: Krieder, Rose M. and Jason Fields. *Living Arrangements of Children: 2001.* Current Population Reports, P70-104. Table 1. Washington, D.C.: US Census Bureau, 2005. * Persons of Hispanic origin may be of any race.

Eighty percent of African-American children can now expect to spend at least a significant part of their childhood years living apart from their fathers.
Source: "Report of Final Natality Statistics, 1996," *Monthly Vital Statistics Report 46, no. 11, Supplement* (Washington, D.C.: U.S. Department of Health and Human Services, June 30, 1998); see also *Turning the Corner on Father Absence in Black America: A Statement From the Morehouse Conference on African-American Fathers*, Atlanta, GA: Morehouse Research Institute & Institute for American Values (June 1999): 4.

63 percent of black children, 35 of Hispanic children, and 28 percent of white children are living in homes absent their biological father.

Eighty percent of African-American children can now expect to spend a significant part of their childhood years living apart fom their fathers.

Living Arrangements of White Children Under 18 Years, by Number, 1960 to 2004

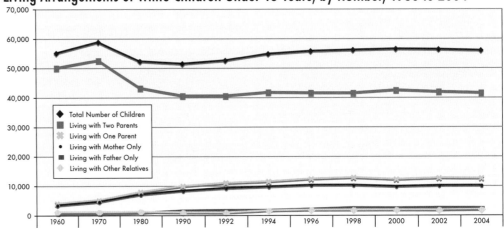

Living Arrangements of White Children Under 18 Years, by Percentage, 1960 to 2004

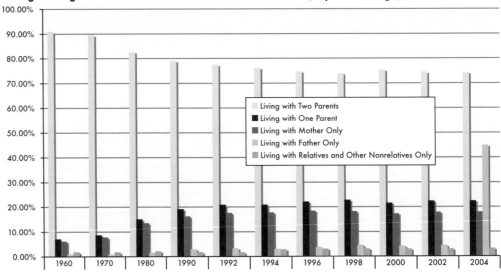

FATHER FACTS, 5TH EDITION • © 2007 National Fatherhood Initiative

Living Arrangements of White Children Under 18 Years, Data Table, 1960 to 2004

	Total	Living with Two Parents	Living with One Parent	Living with Mother Only	Living with Father Only	Living with Other Relatives
1960	55,077	50,082	3,932	3,381	551	1,062
		90.90%	7.10%	6.10%	1.00%	1.90%
1970	58,970	52,624	5,109	4,581	528	1,058
		89.50%	8.70%	7.80%	0.90%	1.80%
1980	52,242	43,200	7,901	7,059	842	1,141
		82.70%	15.10%	13.50%	1.60%	2.20%
1990	51,390	40,593	9,870	8,321	1,549	928
		79.00%	19.20%	16.20%	3.00%	1.80%
1992	52,493	40,635	10,971	9,250	1,721	887
		77.40%	20.90%	17.60%	3.30%	1.70%
1994	54,795	41,766	11,433	9,724	1,710	1,574
		76.20%	20.90%	17.70%	3.10%	2.90%
1996	55,714	41,069	12,335	10,239	2,096	1,770
		74.70%	22.10%	18.40%	3.80%	3.20%
1998	56,124	41,547	12,772	10,210	2,562	1,799
		74.00%	22.80%	18.20%	4.60%	3.20%
2000	56,455	42,497	12,192	9,765	2,427	1,766
		75.30%	21.60%	17.30%	4.30%	3.10%
2002	56,276	41,944	12,600	10,052	2,548	1,732
		74.50%	22.40%	17.90%	4.50%	3.10%
2004	55,902	41,550	12,518	10,050	2,468	1,835
		74.30%	22.40%	18.00%	4.90%	3.30%

Source: U.S. Census Bureau. "Living Arrangements of White Children Under 18 Years Old: 1960 to Present." Table CH-2. Internet Release Date September, 15 2004. <http://www.census.gov/population/socdemo/hh-fam/tabCH-2.xls>

Living Arrangements of Hispanic Children Under 18 Years, by Number, 1970 to 2004

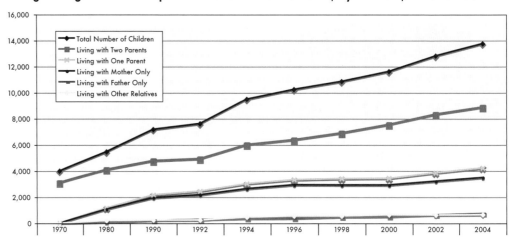

Living Arrangements of Hispanic Children Under 18 Years, by Percentage, 1970 to 2004

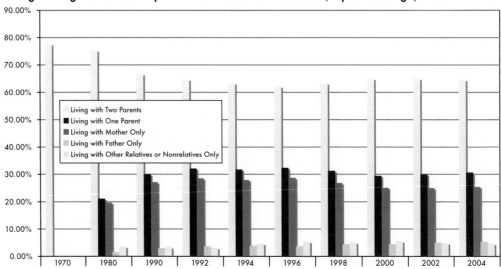

Living Arrangements of Hispanic Children Under 18 Years, Data Table, 1970 to 2004

	Total	Living with Two Parents	Living with One Parent	Living with Mother Only	Living with Father Only	Living with Other Relatives
1970	4,006	3,111	-	-	-	-
		77.70%	-	-	-	-
1980	5,459	4,116	1,152	1,069	83	191
		75.40%	21.10%	19.60%	1.50%	3.50%
1990	7,174	4,789	2,154	1,943	211	231
		66.80%	30.00%	27.10%	2.90%	3.30%
1992	7,619	4,935	2,447	2,168	279	237
		64.80%	32.10%	28.50%	3.70%	3.10%
1994	9,496	6,022	3,019	2,646	373	455
		63.40%	31.80%	27.90%	3.90%	4.70%
1996	10,251	6,381	3,321	2,937	384	549
		62.20%	32.40%	28.70%	3.70%	5.40%
1998	10,863	6,909	3,397	2,15	482	551
		63.40%	31.30%	26.80%	4.40%	5.10%
2000	11,613	7,651	3,425	2,919	506	637
		65.10%	29.50%	25.10%	4.40%	5.50%
2002	12,817	8,338	3,853	3,212	641	626
		65.10%	30.00%	25.00%	5.00%	4.90%
2004	13,752	8,886	4,220	3,489	731	647
		64.60%	30.70%	25.40%	5.30%	4.70%

Source: U.S. Census Bureau. "Living Arrangements of Hispanic Children Under 18 Years Old: 1970 to Present." Table CH-4. Internet Release Date September, 21 2006.: <http://www.census.gov/population/socdemo/hh-fam/ch4.pdf>

Living Arrangements of Black Children Under 18 Years, by Number, 1960 to 2004

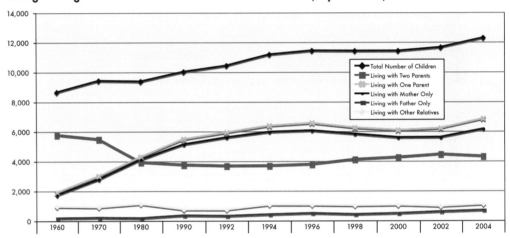

Living Arrangements of Black Children Under 18 Years, by Percentage, 1960 to 2004

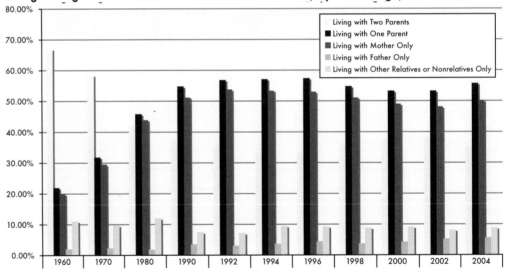

Living Arrangements of Black Children Under 18 Years, Data Table, 1960 to 2004

	Total	Living with Two Parents	Living with One Parent	Living with Mother Only	Living with Father Only	Living with Other Relatives
1960	8,650	5,795	1,897	1,723	173	959
		67.00%	21.90%	19.90%	2.00%	11.10%
1970	9,422	5,508	5,109	4,581	213	1,058
		58.50%	31.80%	29.50%	2.30%	9.70%
1980	9,375	3,956	4,297	4,117	180	1,122
		42.20%	45.80%	43.90%	1.90%	12.00%
1990	10,018	3,781	5,485	5,132	353	752
		37.70%	54.80%	51.20%	3.50%	7.50%
1992	10,427	3,714	5,934	5,607	327	749
		35.60%	56.90%	53.80%	3.10%	7.20%
1994	11,177	3,722	6,384	5,967	417	1,063
		33.30%	57.10%	53.40%	3.70%	9.50%
1996	11,434	3,816	6,560	6,056	504	1,058
		33.40%	57.40%	53.00%	4.40%	9.30%
1998	11,414	4,137	6,254	5,830	424	1,015
		36.20%	54.80%	51.10%	3.70%	8.90%
2000	11,412	4,286	6,080	5,596	484	1,046
		37.60%	53.30%	51.10%	4.20%	9.20%
2002	11,646	4,481	6,210	5,605	605	955
		38.40%	53.30%	48.10%	5.20%	8.20%
2004	12,277	4,340	6,841	6,153	688	1,095
		35.40%	55.70%	50.10%	5.60%	8.90%

Source: U.S. Census Bureau. "Living Arrangements of Black Children Under 18 Years Old: 1960 to Present." Table CH-3. Internet Release Date September, 21 2006. <http://www.census.gov/population/socdemo/hh-fam/ch3.pdf>

Predictors of Father Absence

In an analysis of data from both waves of the National Survey of Families and Households, a national probability sample of over 13,000 households, it was found that the most important determinant of whether a father lived with his children was marital status at the time of the child's birth. Fully 80% of men who were married to the child's mother at the child's birth were living with all of their biological children, compared to only 22.6% of men who were not in a co-residential union relationship with the child's mother at the time of the child's birth.

Source: Clarke, L., E.C. Cooksey, and G. Verropoulou. "Fathers and Absent Fathers: Sociodemographic Similarities in Britain and the United States." *Demography, 35* (1998): 217-228.

Marital status is the strongest predictor of father presence/ father absence.

In a study of 799 families from the National Survey of Families and Households, fathers in two-parent biological families reported spending more time with their children and having higher family cohesion than did fathers in all other types of family structures.

Source: Lansford, Jennifer E., Rosario Ceballo, Antonia Abbey, and Abigail J. Stewart. "Does Family Structure Matter? A Comparison of Adoptive, Two-Parent Biological, Single-Mother, Stepfather, and Stepmother Households." *Journal of Marriage and the Family, 63* (August 2001): 840-851.

Marital status is the strongest predictor of father presence/father absence. Compared to children born within marriage, children born to cohabiting parents are three times more likely to experience father absence, and children born to unmarried, non-cohabiting parents are four times as likely to have an absent father.

Source: Clarke, L., E.C. Cooksey, and G. Verropoulou. "Fathers and Absent Fathers: Sociodemographic Similarities in Britain and the United States." *Demography, 35* (1998): 217-228.

Single-Parent Families
The Facts about Single-Parent Families

Seven in 10 parents in America agree that "to be a single parent has got to be the most stressful thing in the world," with 51% saying they agree strongly. This opinion is held by majorities of parents of all marital statuses, races, and incomes.

Source: Farkas, Steve, Jean Johnson, and Ann Duffett. *A Lot Easier Said Than Done: Parents Talk About Raising Children in Today's America.* New York, NY: Public Agenda, 2002: 32.

Of the 20.4 million children living with a single parent in 2003, 83.4 percent (17.1 million) were living with their mother; 16.6 percent (3.4 million) were living with their father. The percentage of single mothers has decreased as a proportion of single-parent families from 87.8% in 1994 to 84.4% in 1999.

Source: U.S. Census Bureau. *Current Population Survey Reports.* "Living Arrangements of Children Under 18 Years Old: 1960 to Present." Table CH-1. Published June 29, 2005. < http://www.census.gov/population/socdemo/hh-fam/ch1.pdf>

The proportion of single mothers who have never been married stopped its rise in 2003, falling slightly to 41.7%. The number had been rising over the previous decade from 33% in 1990 to 43% in 2000. A majority of single mothers with children under six years old are divorced or separated.
Source: U.S. Census Bureau. *America's Families and Living Arrangements: 2004*. Current Population Survey Report. "One-Parent Family Groups with Own Children Under 18, by Marital Status, and Race and Hispanic Origin of the Reference Person: 2004." Table FG6. Accessed August 25, 2005. <http://www.census.gov/population/socdemo/hh-fam/cps2004/tabFG6-all.csv> ; U.S. Census Bureau. *America's Families and Living Arrangements*. Current Population Reports, P20-553. Table C3. Washington, D.C.: U.S. Census Bureau, 2004; Fields, Jason, and Lynn M. Casper. *America's Family and Living Arrangements: March 2000*. Current Population Reports, P20-537. Table 4. Washington, D.C.: U.S. Census Bureau, 2001; Bryson, Ken, and Lynn Casper. *Household and Family Characteristics: March 1997*. Current Population Reports, P20-509. Washington, D.C.: U.S. Census Bureau, 1998.

In 2004, of children living with only their mothers, 42 percent were living with never-married mothers, 49 percent with divorced or separated mothers, and 4 percent with widowed mothers. Of children living with only their fathers, 35 percent were living with never-married fathers, 54 percent with divorced or separated fathers, and 5 percent with widowed fathers.
Source: U.S. Census Bureau. *America's Families and Living Arrangements: 2003*. Current Population Reports, P20-553. Table C3. Washington, D.C.: U.S. Census Bureau, 2004.

Of single mothers, 43 percent are never-married, 52 percent are divorced or separated, and 4 percent are widowed. Of single fathers, 39 percent are never-married, 56 percent are divorced or separated, and 4 percent are widowed.
Source: U.S. Census Bureau. *America's Families and Living Arrangements: 2004*. Current Population Survey Report. "One-Parent Family Groups with Own Children Under 18, by Marital Status, and Race and Hispanic Origin of the Reference Person: 2004." Table FG6. Accessed August 25, 2005. <http://www.census.gov/population/socdemo/hh-fam/cps2004/tabFG6-all.csv>

In 2004, single-parent families comprised 28 percent of all households with children, up from 27 percent in 2000, 24 percent in 1990, 20 percent in 1980, and 11 percent in 1970.
Source: U.S. Census Bureau. "Families by Presence of Own Children Under 18: 1950 to Present." Table FM-1. Released June 29, 2005. <http://www.census.gov/population/socdemo/hh-fam/fm1.pdf>

Of women currently entering their childbearing years, half will experience female headship at some point in their childbearing years, compared to one-third of women a generation ago. Nearly 80% of black women will be the family head at some point in their childbearing years.
Source: Moffitt, Robert A. and Michael S. Rendall. "Cohort Trends in the Lifetime Distribution of Female Family Headship in the United States, 1968-1985." *Demography, 32* (August 1995): 407-423.

Number of Children Living in Single-Parent Families, 1960 to 2004

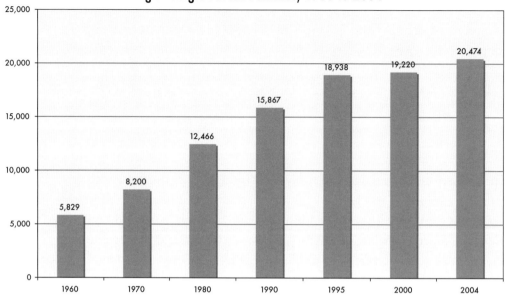

Source: U.S. Census Bureau. "Living Arrangements of Children Under 18 Years Old: 1960 to Present." Table CH-1. Released September 21, 2006. <http://www.census.gov/population/socdemo/hh-fam/ch1.pdf>

Thirty-six percent of children with single biological mothers are below the poverty line.

Single-Parent Families by Race and Ethnicity

In 2004, 22 percent of white children, 56 percent of black children, and 31 percent of Hispanic children lived in single-parent families. Both the percentages of black children and Hispanic children increased slightly since 2000.

Source: U.S. Census Bureau. "Living Arrangements of White Children Under 18 Years Old: 1960 to Present," Table CH-2, "Living Arrangements of Black Children Under 18 Years Old: 1960 to Present," Table CH-3, "Living Arrangements of Hispanic Children Under 18 Years Old: 1960 to Present," Table CH-4. Published June 29, 2005. < http://www.census.gov/population/www/socdemo/hh-fam.html>

In 2004, 27 percent of white families, 63 percent of black families, and 35 percent of Hispanic families were headed by a single parent.

Source: U.S. Census Bureau. "All Parent/Child Situations, by Type, Race, and Hispanic Origin of Householder or Reference Person: 1970 to Present." Table FM-2. Published June 29, 2005. < http://www.census.gov/population/socdemo/hh-fam/fm2.pdf>

A study of health records for Puerto Rican infants and their mothers in the U.S. mainland found that only 19% of recent migrants from Puerto Rico were living absent the infant's father, compared with 28% of earlier migrants, and 38% of mainland-born mothers.

Source: Landale, Nancy, et al. "Does Americanization Have Adverse Effects on Health? Stress, Health Habits, and Infant Health Outcomes Among Puerto Ricans." *Social Forces, 78* (2000): 613-641.

Single Parenthood and Poverty

Thirty-six percent of children with single biological mothers are below the poverty line. This is roughly three times higher than the number of children with married parents. Only 15 percent of children with single biological fathers are below the poverty line.

Source: Kreider, Rose M. and Jason Fields. *Living Arrangements of Children: 2001.* Current Population Studies, P70-104. Table 2. Washington, D.C.: US Census Bureau, 2005.

In a study of more than 16,000 single and married households, about 83 percent of single parent families and 33 percent of husband-wife families were in the lower income group. More single-parent families were in the bottom range of the lower income group with an average yearly income of $17,000, compared to $25,400 for married households. Although their incomes differed, their total expenditures on a child were only 5% different between single parent and two-parent households. Hence, single parents as a group spent a larger percentage of their income on their children compared to two parent households. This difference was true even for the higher income group.

Source: Lino, Mark. "Expenditures on Children by Families, 2003." *Family Economics and Nutrition Review, 16* (2004): 31-38.

Those in uninsured, single-mother households experienced above average levels of hardship. This included food and medical insufficiencies.

Source: Beverly, Sondra G. "Material hardship in the United States: Evidence from the Survey of Income and Program Participation." *Social Work Research, 25* (September 2001): 143-151.

In 2003, the median family incomes of married-couple, single-father, and single-mother families were $62,405, $41,959, and $29,307, respectively.

Source: DeNavas-Welt, Carmen, Bernadette D. Proctor, and Robert J. Mills. *Income, Poverty, and Health Insurance in the United States: 2003.* Current Population Studies, P60-226. Table 1. Washington, D.C.: US Census Bureau, 2004.

In 1997, 65 percent of poor children lived in households that did not include their biological fathers, compared to 25 percent of children who were not poor.

Source: *Kids Count Data Book 2000.* Baltimore, MD: The Annie E. Casey Foundation, 2000: 12.

By the age of six, 68% of children in nonmarried households have experienced at least one year of poverty versus 12% of children in married households; by age 17, the percentages rise to 81% versus 22%, respectively.

Source: Rank, Mark R., and Thomas A. Hirschl. "The Economic Risk of Childhood in America: Estimating the Probability of Poverty Across the Formative Years." *Journal of Marriage and the Family, 61* (November 1999): 1058-1067.

One-quarter of children living in single-mother homes in which the mother works are still poor.
Source: Wertheimer, Richard F. "Working Poor Families with Children." Figure 2. Washington, D.C.: *Child Trends*, February 1999.

Among children living in single-mother families, 60 percent of children born out of wedlock are poor, compared with 37 percent of children born within marriage.
Source: Halpern, Ariel. "Poverty among Children Born Outside of Marriage: Preliminary Findings from the National Survey of America's Families." Washington, D.C.: The Urban Institute, December 1999.

Only about 10% of mother-father families live below the poverty line, whereas 47% of single-mother and 22% of single-father families live below the poverty line.
Source: Bianchi, S.M. "The Changing Demographic and Socioeconomic Characteristics of Single-Parent Families." *Marriage & Family Review, 20* (1995): 71-97.

Effects of Single Parenthood on Mothers

A Swedish study found even after controlling for differences in socioeconomic status and medical and psychiatric history, single mothers were 2.2 times more likely to commit suicide, 3 times more likely to die a violent death, and 2.4 times more likely to experience alcohol-related deaths compared to married and cohabiting mothers.
Source: Weitoft, Gunilla., Bengt Haglund, and Mans. Rosen. "Mortality Among Lone Mothers in Sweden: A Population Study." *Lancet, 355* (2000): 1215-1219.

In a qualitative study of single mothers in the rural Northeast, single mothers faced tremendous obstacles in their everyday lives of cooking, cleaning and caring for their children despite having higher incomes and living in a state with a generous means-tested program. They had to make special arrangements for things such as yard work and car repair and very few had time to follow personal pursuits.
Source: Nelson, Margaret K.. "How Men Matter: Housework and Self-Provisioning Among Rural and Single-Mother and Married-Couple Families in Vermont, US." *Feminist Economics, 10* (July 2004): 9-36.

A study of 2,921 mothers revealed that single mothers were twice as likely as married mothers to experience a bout of depression in the prior year. Single mothers also reported higher levels of stress, fewer contacts with family and friends, less involvement with church or social groups and less overall social support.
Source: Cairney, John and Michael Boyle et al. "Stress, Social Support and Depression in Single and Married Mothers." *Social Psychiatry and Psychiatric Epidemiology, 38* (August 2003): 442-449.

Parenting and Single-Parent Families

Single parents were more likely to be concerned that their child is acting "too grown-up, too fast" (49%), compared to married parents (32%). Single parents were also more likely than married parents to worry about insulating their child from drugs and alcohol (73% vs. 52%), paying the bills (51% vs. 31%), and getting health insurance and medical care for their child (49% vs. 30%).

Half of single parents (50%) agree with the statement "There's so much stress in my life that being a parent can be overwhelming" compared to 34% of married parents.
Source: Farkas, Steve, Jean Johnson, and Ann Duffett. *A Lot Easier Said Than Done: Parents Talk About Raising Children in Today's America*. New York, NY: Public Agenda, 2002: 32.

In an analysis of data collected from 90,000 students participating in the National Longitudinal Study of Adolescent Health, it was found that supervision of adolescents was significantly lower for both single-father and single-mother homes than for intact families.
Source: Cookston, Jeffrey T. "Parental Supervision and Family Structure: Effects on Adolescent Problem Behaviors." *Journal of Divorce & Remarriage 31* (1999): 107-127.

Fathers are four times more likely to be the primary caregiver in two-parent households than in single mother households.
Source: *Child Trends,* "Charting Parenthood: A Statistical Portrait of Fathers and Mothers in America." Ed. Tamara Halle. Washington DC, 2004.

In a large study of male adolescents and their primary caretakers (n=1517), single-parent families and families with teenage mothers displayed significantly worse interactions (such as poor supervision, poor communication, and physical punishment) over time than did families consisting of two biological parents present in the household.
Source: Loeber, Rolf, et al. "Stability of Family Interaction from Ages 6 to 18." *Journal of Abnormal Child Psychology, 28* (2000): 353-369.

In a 1999 nationally representative survey of over 42,000 households, it was found that children living in single-parent households were significantly more likely than children in two-parent homes to be living with a highly aggravated parent (16% versus 7%) and/or a parent in poor mental health (27% versus 11%).
Source: Vandivere, Sharon, Kristin Moore, and Martha Zaslow. "Children's Family Environment." Table 1. *Assessing the New Federalism: Snapshots of America's Families II*. Washington, D.C.: Urban Institute, 2000.

Mobility and Single-Parent Families
Single mothers have a 26% chance of switching living arrangements at least once during a 32-month period.
Source: London, Rebecca A. "The dynamics of single mothers' living arrangements." *Population Research and Policy Review, 19* (February 2000): 73-96.

Children living in single-parent families are nearly three times as likely to have moved in the past year compared to children living in two-parent, married households (43.2% versus 14.2%).
Source: U.S. Census Bureau. "Geographical Mobility." *Current Population Reports*, Series P20, Nos. 463, 473, 481, 485, 497 and 510. Washington, D.C.: U.S. Census Bureau.

Out-of-Wedlock Childbearing

"The real source of the [welfare] problem is the inordinate number of out-of-wedlock births in this country."
FORMER PRESIDENT BILL CLINTON, 1995

"And baby makes three! Remember that? Man and woman wed in holy matrimony followed by baby? Forget it. We don't do that anymore. Today, having a baby is like swinging through McDonald's for a burger. One baby all the way, hold the dad."
KATHLEEN PARKER, SYNDICATED COLUMNIST FOR THE ORLANDO SENTINEL, MARCH 29, 1998.

Attitudes About Out-Of-Wedlock Childbearing

According to a 2003 Gallup Poll, 51% percent of U.S. adults thought out-of-wedlock pregnancy was morally acceptable, compared to 46% who disagreed. In 2002, the split stood at 45% for and 50% against.
Source: Gallup Poll. "Data Bite." *Christian Century*, 9 August 2003: 12.

According to the University of Michigan Survey Research Center, 54% of female high school seniors say they believe that having a child outside of marriage is a worthwhile lifestyle, up from 33% in 1980. Forty-percent of female twentysomethings would consider having a baby on their own if they reached their mid-30s and they hadn't found the right man to marry.
Source: Conlin, Michelle and Jessi Hempel. "UnMarried America." *Business Week 20* October 2003: 110.

Young adults are more likely to believe that a single parent can raise a child on their own. In the 18-34 group of a poll of 1,031 adults, 82 percent approved of a single motherhood and 81 percent approved of single fatherhood. However, only 69 percent agreed that single men are equally competent at raising children as single women.
Source: Fetto, John. "Does Father Really Know Best?" *American Demographics* June 2002: 10-11.

85% of Americans say that "the number of children being born to single parents" is either a "serious" or "critical" social problem.
Source: Gallup, George. "Report on Status of Fatherhood In the United States." *Emerging Trends 20* (September 1998): 3-5. Published by the Princeton Religion Research Center, Princeton, NJ.

Ninety-three percent of unwed mothers reported that they wanted the father to be involved in raising their child. All of the cohabiting fathers and 96 percent of non-resident fathers said they intended to stay involved with their child.
Source: Norland, Christina. "Father Involvement, Maternal Health Behavior and Infant Health." *Fragile Families Research Brief No.5.* Princeton, NJ and New York, NY: Bendheim-Thomas Center for Research on Child Wellbeing and Social Indicators Survey Center, 2001:1-2.

...54% of female high school seniors say they believe that having a child outside of marriage is a worthwhile lifestyle...

85% of Americans say that "the number of children being born to single parents" is either a "serious" or "critical" social problem.

According to a nationally representative survey of adults ages 20-29, a clear majority (62%) agreed that, while it may not be ideal, it's okay for an adult woman to have a child on her own if she has not found the right man to marry.
Source: Whitehead, Barbara Dafoe, and David Popenoe. "The State of Our Unions 2001: The Social Health of Marriage in America." Piscataway, NJ: The National Marriage Project, 2001.

In a nationally representative survey of 1,709 adults, 64 percent of respondents replied that it was "generally acceptable" for someone to have a child without being married.
Source: Washington Post/Kaiser/Harvard Racial Attitudes Survey. Telephone survey conducted by the Washington Post, the Henry J. Kaiser Family Foundation, and Harvard University, March 8-April 22, 2001. Fieldwork was conducted by ICR of Media, Pa.

Women who are single and college-educated are three times more likely to be previously childless by the age of thirty-four. They also carry more independent views about marriage and having lower quality partners which increases the odds of later out-of-wedlock pregnancy.
Source: Usdansky, Margaret L. and Sara McLanahan. "Looking for Murphy Brown: Are College-Educated, Single Mothers Unique?" *Working Paper* # 03-05-FF. Princeton, NJ: Center for Research on Child Wellbeing, June 2003: 20-22.

Fifty-four percent of teenagers today agree with the statement, "Having a baby without being married is a worthwhile lifestyle or not affecting anyone else," compared with only 37 percent in 1976.
Source: Bachman, J.G., L. D. Johnston and P. M. O'Malley. *Monitoring the Future: Questionnaire Responses from the Nation's High School Seniors, 1996.* Ann Arbor, MI: Survey Research Center at the University of Michigan, 2001, and earlier editions. Cited in Popenoe, David, and Barbara Dafoe Whitehead. *The State of Our Unions 2001: The Social Health of Marriage in America.* Figure 18. Piscataway, NJ: The National Marriage Project, 2001.

A study of 51 out-of-wedlock mothers indicated the following:
• One-third were romantically and steadily involved with the father of their child at birth.
• Two-thirds were indifferent or skeptical about marriage.
• One-half stated that there was "no-chance" they would marry their last child's father and 84% overall felt there was less than a 50-50 chance they would marry the father of their child.
• Over 90% indicated that they have a high desire for father involvement and 98% ranked "showing love and affection" as the most important fatherhood trait.
Source: DeJong, Fred J., Mark C. Eastburg, and Rachel Venema. *What Do Welfare Clients Have to Say About Marriage and Family Formation.* FIA Family Formation Study. Grand Rapids, MI: Calvin College Printing Services, 2003.

Among African Americans, over 70 percent say that it would be unacceptable for a daughter to have a child out of wedlock.
Source: Offner, Paul. "Reducing Non-Marital Births." *Welfare Reform and Beyond Policy Brief No. 5.* Washington, D.C.: The Brookings Institution, August 2001.

Among African Americans, over 70 percent say that it would be unacceptable for a daughter to have a child out of wedlock.

The Facts About Out-of-Wedlock Births

Non-marital childbearing has increased over the last 30 years, rising from 6 percent of all births in 1960 to one-third of all births in 2000.

Source: Center for Research on Child Wellbeing. "In-Hospital Paternity Establishment and Father Involvement in Fragile Families." *Fragile Families Research Brief. Number 30.* Princeton, NJ: Center for Research on Child Wellbeing, 2005.

One out of every three children born in 2003 (35.2 percent) was born to unmarried parents. In total, 1.42 million children were born out of wedlock in 2003, the highest number ever reported.

Source: Hamilton, Brady E., Joyce A, Martin, and Paul D. Sutton. *Births: Preliminary Data for 2003.* Vol. 53, No. 9. Hyattsville, MD: National Center for Health Statistics, 2004.

Although the number of teen births to unmarried mothers decreased for the fifth straight year, the proportion of teen births to teen mothers increased in 2003. This occurred because the total births to teens decreased while the number of births to unmarried teens stayed constant.

Source: Hamilton, Brady E., Joyce A, Martin, and Paul D. Sutton. *Births: Preliminary Data for 2003.* Vol. 53, No. 9. Hyattsville, MD: National Center for Health Statistics, 2004.

Eighty-two percent of all teen births occurred outside of marriage and 35% of births to all women occurred outside of marriage. In both the 20-24 and 15-44 age groups, nonmarital births have remained steady since 1994.

Source: *Child Trends.* Facts at a Glance. Publication #2005-02. Washington, DC: Child Trends, 2005: 2.

The birth rate for unmarried teens has decreased by a fifth since 1994, but the birth rate for unmarried women ages 20 and older has continued to increase over the same period.

Source: *America's Children in Brief: Key National Indicators of Well-Being.* Washington, DC: Federal Interagency Forum on Child and Family Statistics, 2004: 5.

Although 65% of new mothers said they were in steady, committed and exclusive relationships with their baby's father, only 40% described their relationship that way 2 to 5 months after birth.

Source: Mincy, Ron, et al. *Fragile Families in Focus: Executive Summary.* Baton Rouge, LA: TANF Executive Office of Oversight and Evaluation, 2004: 5.

For new parents, 71% of the mothers and 51% of the fathers had at least one child from an outside relationship.

Source: Mincy, Ron, et al. *Fragile Families in Focus: Executive Summary.* Chart V. Baton Rouge, LA: TANF Executive Office of Oversight and Evaluation, 2004: 11.

Unmarried parents are generally younger than married parents. Mothers average seven years younger with a median age of 22 while fathers average six years younger with a median age of 25. Forty-three percent of unmarried mothers have children with at least two men, while only 15% of married mothers have children with different fathers.

Source: Parke, Mary. *Who Are "Fragile Families" and What Do We Know About Them?* Center for Law and Social Policy Brief No. 4. Washington, D.C.: Center for Law and Social Policy, 2004: 3.

One out of every three children born in 2003 (35.2 percent) was born to unmarried parents.

Forty-three percent of unmarried mothers have children with at least two men, while only 15% of married mothers have children with different fathers.

From 1990-1994, 40.5 percent of all births to first-time mothers were out of wedlock.
Source: Bachu, Amara. *Trends in Premarital Childbearing: 1930-1994.* Current Population Reports, P23-197. Table 1. Washington, D.C.: U.S. Census Bureau, 1999.

The proportion of single mothers who have never been married continues to rise, from 33 percent in 1990 to 43 percent in 2000. A majority of single mothers with children under six years old have never been married.
Source: Fields, Jason, and Lynn M. Casper. "America's Families and Living Arrangements: March 2000." Current Population Reports, P20-537. Table 4. Washington, D.C.: U.S. Census Bureau, 2001; and earlier reports.

From 1990-1994, 53 percent of first births among women ages 15 to 29 were conceived out of wedlock, up threefold from 18 percent between 1930-1934.
Source: Bachu, Amara. *Trends in Premarital Childbearing: 1930-1994.* Current Population Reports, P23-197. Table 1. Washington, D.C.: U.S. Census Bureau, 1999.

Excluding miscarriages, 78% of pregnancies among never-married women concluding in 1994 were unintended, compared to 63% of pregnancies among formerly married women and 31% among married women.
Source: Henshaw, Stanley K. "Unintended Pregnancy in the United States." *Family Planning Perspectives, 30* (January/February 1998): 24-29.

Preliminary survey data from the Fragile Families and Child Wellbeing Study, a longitudinal study of 2,670 unmarried couples with children, suggests that most unwed fathers are highly involved shortly after the child's birth:

- 50% of unmarried parents were living together at the time of the child's birth, and another 33% were romantically involved but living apart.
- 80% of the fathers were involved in helping the baby's mother during the pregnancy, either financially or in other ways (such as transportation).
- 73% of mothers reported that the chances that they will marry the baby's father are "fifty-fifty" or greater; 88% of fathers reported that the odds of marrying the mother of their child are "fifty-fifty" or greater.
- 64% of the mothers and 75% of the fathers agreed with the statement, "it is better for children if their parents are married."
- 90% of unmarried mothers rated "husband having a steady job" and "emotional maturity" as very important qualities for a successful marriage.
- 37% of the mothers and 34% of the fathers lack a high school degree, and less than a third had any education beyond high school.
- 30% of the fathers were unemployed in the week before their child was born.

* Compared to a nearly perfect response rate from mothers, only 75 percent of fathers responded to the survey, resulting in a selection effect that most likely inflates the above percentages for fathers.
Source: McLanahan, Sara, Irwin Garfinkel, Nancy E. Reichman, Julien Teitler, Marcia Carlson, and Christian Norland Audigier. *The Fragile Families and Child Wellbeing Study Baseline Report.* The Center for Research on Child Wellbeing (Princeton University) and the Social Indicators Survey Center (Columbia University), August 2001.

Women aged 20 and older with less than a high school diploma are at least three times as likely to have a baby out of wedlock, when compared to a woman who has attended some college.

Source: U.S. Department of Health and Human Services. Public Health Service. Center for Disease Control and Prevention. National Center for Health Statistics. *Report to Congress on Out-of-Wedlock Childbearing.* Hyattsville, MD (Sept. 1995): 6.

Out-of-Wedlock Childbearing by Race and Ethnicity

Almost 75% of white mothers who have a child in large urban areas are married to their child's biological father throughout the first year. In contrast, less than one-quarter of black mothers and about one-half of Hispanic mothers are married over the same time period. Approximately 8% of white mothers separate from their child's biological father within the first year, compared to 30% of black mothers and 16% of Hispanic mothers.

Source: Osborne, Cynthia. *The Relationship Between Family Structure and Mothering Behavior Within Race and Ethnic Groups.* Working Paper #04-06-FF. Princeton, NJ: Center for Research on Child Wellbeing, 2004: 16-17.

> **In 2003, 23.5 percent of births to white mothers, 68.5 percent of births to black mothers, and 45.0 percent of births to Hispanic mothers were out of wedlock.**

In 2003, 23.5 percent of births to white mothers, 68.5 percent of births to black mothers, and 45.0 percent of births to Hispanic mothers were out of wedlock.

Source: Hamilton, Brady E., Joyce A, Martin, and Paul D. Sutton. Births: Preliminary Data for 2003. Vol. 53, No. 9. Hyattsville, MD: National Center for Health Statistics, 2004.

During the 1990s, the percentage of out-of-wedlock births grew fastest among white women, increasing from 20.4% in 1990 to 27.1% in 2000. By 2003, the number had dropped to 23.5%.

Source: Ventura, Stephanie J., and Christine A. Bachrach. *Nonmarital Childbearing in the United States: 1940-99.* National Vital Statistics Reports, Vol. 48, No. 16. Table A. Hyattsville, Maryland: National Center for Health Statistics, 2000; see also Martin, Joyce A., Brady E. Hamilton, and Stephanie J. Ventura. *Births: Preliminary Data for 2000.* National Vital Statistics Reports, Vol. 49, No. 5. Table C. Hyattsville, Maryland: National Center for Health Statistics, 2001; Hamilton, Brady E., Joyce A, Martin, and Paul D. Sutton. *Births: Preliminary Data for 2003.* Vol. 53, No. 9. Hyattsville, MD: National Center for Health Statistics, 2004.

In 2002, there were 66.2 births per 1,000 unmarried African-American women, down from the peak of 90.7 per 1,000 unmarried African-American women in 1989.

Source: Martin, Joyce A. *Births: Final Data for 2002.* National Vital Health Statistics, Vol. 52, No. 10. Table 17. Hyattsville, MD: National Center for Health Statistics, 2003.

Out-of-Wedlock Births to Teenagers

Boys born to teen mothers are 2.51 times more likely to father a child between ages 14 and 26.

Source: Jafee, Sara et al. "Predicting Early Fatherhood and Whether Young Fathers Live with Their Children: Prospective Findings and Policy Reconsiderations." *Journal of Child Psychology & Psychiatry, 42* (September 2001): 803-815.

> **In 2002, 80 percent of births to teenage mothers were out of wedlock, up from 68 percent in 1990 and 48 percent in 1980.**

In 2002, 80 percent of births to teenage mothers were out of wedlock, up from 68 percent in 1990 and 48 percent in 1980.

Source: Martin, Joyce A. Births: Final Data for 2002. National Vital Health Statistics, Vol. 52, No. 10. Table 17. Hyattsville, MD: National Center for Health Statistics, 2003.

Each year, almost 1 million teenage women—10% of all women aged 15-19 and 19% of those who have had sexual intercourse—become pregnant.
Source: Alan Guttmacher Institute. Teenage Pregnancy: Overall Trends and State-by-State Information. New York: AGI, 1999, Table 1; see also Henshaw, S.K. U.S. Teenage Pregnancy Statistics with Comparative Statistics for Women Aged 20- 24. New York: AGI, 1999, p. 5.

78% of teen pregnancies are unplanned, accounting for about 1/4 of all accidental pregnancies annually.
Source: Henshaw, S.K. "Unintended Pregnancy in the United States." *Family Planning Perspectives, 30* (1998): 24-29, 46, Table 1.

Teen mothers account for only 28% of all out-of-wedlock births, down from 50% in 1970.
Source: Ventura, Stephanie J., and Christine A. Bachrach. *Nonmarital Childbearing in the United States: 1940-99*. National Vital Statistics Reports, Vol. 48, No. 16. Table 2. Hyattsville, Maryland: National Center for Health Statistics, 2000.

The fathers of babies born to teenage mothers are likely to be older than the women: About 1 in 5 infants born to unmarried minors are fathered by men 5 or more years older than the mother.
Source: Lindberg, L.D., et al. "Age Differences between Minors who Give Birth and their Adult Partners." *Family Planning Perspectives, 29* (1997): 61-66.

> Teen mothers account for only 28% of all out-of-wedlock births, down from 50% in 1970.

Percent of Teen Births that Were Non-Marital, 1960 to 2003

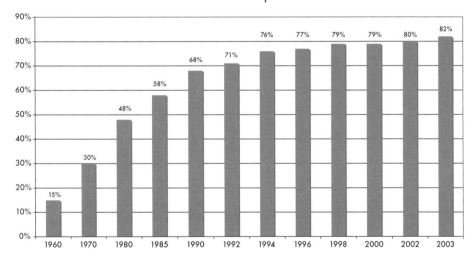

Source: Ventura, Stephanie J., and Christine A. Bachrach. Nonmarital Childbearing in the United States: 1940-99. Table 4. National Vital Statistics Reports, Vol. 48, No. 16. Hyattsville, Maryland: National Center for Health Statistics, 2000; Martin, Joyce A., et al. Births: . Final Data for 2000. Vol. 50, No. 5. Hyattsville, Maryland: National Center for Health Statistics, 2002; Hamilton, Brady E., Joyce A. Martin , Paul D. Sutton . Births: Preliminary data for 2003. National Vital Statistics Reports. Vol. 53, No. 9. Hyattsville, MD: National Center for Health Statistics. 2004.

Number of Out-of-Wedlock Births, 1940 to 2003

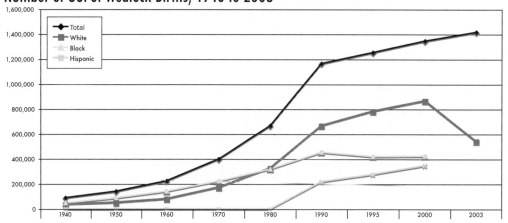

Percentage of Out-of-Wedlock Births, 1940 to 2003

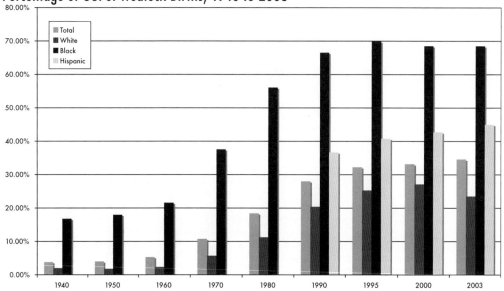

Out-of-Wedlock Births, Data Table, 1940 to 2003

	Total	White	Black	Hispanic
1940	89,500	40,300	49,200	-
	3.80%	2.00%	16.80%	-
1950	141,600	53,500	88,100	-
	4.00%	1.80%	18.00%	-
1960	224,300	82,500	141,800	-
	5.30%	2.30%	21.60%	-
1970	398,700	175,100	223,600	-
	10.70%	5.70%	37.60%	-
1980	666,700	329,000	318,800	-
	18.40%	11.20%	56.10%	-
1990	1,165,000	669,700	455,300	218,500
	28.00%	20.40%	66.50%	36.70%
1995	1,254,000	785,000	421,500	277,600
	32.20%	25.30%	69.90%	40.80%
2000	1,346,000	868,000	425,000	347,000
	33.20%	27.10%	53.30%	42.70%
2003	1,415,804	545,000	-	-
	34.60%	23.50%	68.50%	45.00%

Note: Numbers for Black births prior to 1970 actually refer to all non-white births.
Source: Ventura, Stephanie J., and Christine A. Bachrach. Nonmarital Childbearing in the United States: 1940-99. National Vital Statistics Reports, Vol. 48, No. 16. Table A. Hyattsville, Maryland: National Center for Health Statistics, 2000; see also Martin, Joyce A., Brady E. Hamilton, and Stephanie J. Ventura. Births: Preliminary Data for 2000. National Vital Statistics Reports, Vol. 49, No. 5. Hyattsville, Maryland: National Center for Health Statistics, 2001; Hamilton, Brady E., Joyce A, Martin, and Paul D. Sutton. Births: Preliminary Data for 2003. Vol. 53, No. 9. Hyattsville, MD: National Center for Health Statistics, 2004.

Unmarried... With Children

Eighty-three percent of unwed mothers reported being romantically involved with the father at the time of the child's birth. They are either cohabiting or seeing each other frequently each week. Seventy-three percent of unmarried mothers and 88 percent of the fathers of their children believed that they had a 50-50 chance of marrying each other.

Source: McLanahan, Sara, Irwin Garfinkel, Nancy E. Reichman, Julien Teitler, Marcia Carlson, and Christina Norland Audigier. *Fragile Families and Child Wellbeing Baseline Report: The National Report.* Princeton, NJ: Center for Research on Child Wellbeing, 2001: 8.

Between 1965 and 1994, the percentage of first births conceived outside of marriage that led to marriage prior to the birth fell from 54.4% to 23.3%.

Source: Bachu, Amara. *Trends in Premarital Childbearing: 1930-1994.* Current Population Reports, P23-197. Table 1. Washington, D.C.: U.S. Census Bureau, 1999.

At least one-half of the rise in the percentage of births occurring outside of marriage is due to the decline in the probability that a non-marital pregnancy will lead to marriage.

Source: Akerlof, G.A., J.L. Yellen, and M.L. Katz. "An Analysis of Out-Of-Wedlock Childbearing in the United States." *Quarterly Journal of Economics, 111* (1996): 277-317.

Almost one-third of non-marital births are to women who have been previously married.

Source: Brown, Susan L. "Fertility Following Marital Dissolution: The Role of Cohabitation." *Journal of Family Issues, 21* (May 2000): 501-524.

Among formerly married women, about 30 percent of births out of wedlock are planned.

Source: Department of Health and Human Services. *Report to Congress on Out-of-Wedlock Childbearing.* Washington, D.C.: GPO, 1995.

In a study of 1,180 formerly married women from the 1987-1988 National Survey of Families and Households, women who had no children at the time of their marital dissolution were nearly seven times more likely than women with three or more children to have a post-marital, out-of-wedlock birth. The odds of having a post-marital, out-of-wedlock birth was more than 4.5 times higher for women who were younger than 25 years old when their marriage dissolved compared to women who were age 30 or older at the time of marital dissolution.

Source: Brown, Susan L. "Fertility Following Marital Dissolution: The Role of Cohabitation." *Journal of Family Issues, 21* (May 2000): 501-524.

Births to Unmarried Women, by Race, 1960 to 2003

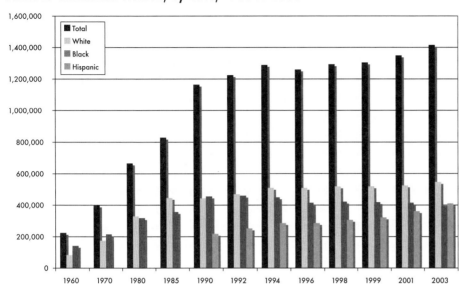

Births to Unmarried Women, by Race, Data Table, 1960 to 2003

	Total	White	Black	Hispanic
1960	224,300	82,500	141,800	-
		37%	63%	
1970	398,700	175,100	215,100	-
		44%	54%	
1980	665,700	329,000	318,800	-
		49%	48%	
1985	828,200	445,600	356,200	-
		54%	43%	
1990	1,165,000	443,000	455,300	218,500
		38%	39%	19%
1992	1,225,000	468,700	459,000	251,700
		38%	37%	21%
1994	1,290,000	508,000	448,300	286,500
		39%	35%	22%
1996	1,260,000	508,200	415,200	285,500
		40%	33%	23%
1998	1,294,000	517,200	421,400	305,400
		40%	33%	24%
1999	1,305,000	517,800	417,300	320,900
		40%	32%	25%
2001	1,349,200	524,300	414,500	361,700
		39%	31%	27%
2003	1,415,800	545,400	394,800	410,500
		39%	28%	29%

Note: Numbers for Black births prior to 1970 actually refer to all non-white births.
Source: Ventura, Stephanie J., and Christine A. Bachrach. Nonmarital Childbearing in the United States: 1940-99. National Vital Statistics Reports, Vol. 48, No. 16. Table A. Hyattsville, Maryland: National Center for Health Statistics, 2000; see also Martin, Joyce A., Brady E. Hamilton, and Stephanie J. Ventura. Births: Preliminary Data for 2000. National Vital Statistics Reports, Vol. 49, No. 5. Hyattsville, Maryland: National Center for Health Statistics, 2001; Hamilton, Brady E., Joyce A, Martin, and Paul D. Sutton. Births: Preliminary Data for 2003. Vol. 53, No. 9. Hyattsville, MD: National Center for Health Statistics, 2004.

Birth Rates for Unmarried Women, 1980-2002

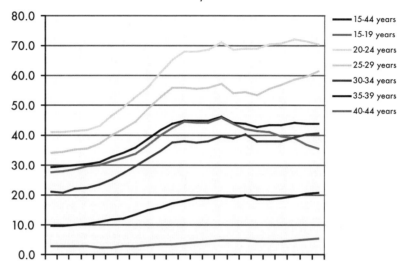

Birth Rates for Unmarried Women, Data Table, 1980-2002

	All Ages	15-19 Years	20-24 Years	25-29 Years	30-34 Years	35-39 Years	40-44 Years
1980	29.4	27.6	40.9	34	21.1	9.7	2.6
1981	29.5	27.9	41.1	34.5	20.8	9.8	2.6
1982	30.0	28.7	41.5	35.1	21.9	10.0	2.7
1983	30.3	29.5	41.8	35.5	22.4	10.2	2.6
1984	31.0	30.0	43.0	37.1	23.3	10.9	2.5
1985	32.8	31.4	46.5	39.9	25.2	11.6	2.5
1986	34.2	32.3	49.3	42.2	27.2	12.2	2.7
1987	36.0	33.8	52.6	44.5	29.6	13.5	2.9
1988	38.5	36.4	56.0	48.5	32.0	15.0	3.2
1989	41.6	40.1	61.2	52.8	34.9	16.0	3.4
1990	43.8	42.5	65.1	56	37.6	17.3	3.6
1991	45.0	44.6	67.8	56	37.9	17.9	3.8
1992	44.9	44.2	67.9	55.6	37.6	18.8	4.1
1993	44.8	44.0	68.5	55.9	38.0	18.9	4.4
1994	46.2	45.8	70.9	57.4	39.6	19.7	4.7
1995	44.3	43.8	68.7	54.3	38.9	19.3	4.7
1996	43.8	42.2	68.9	54.5	40.2	19.9	4.8
1997	42.9	41.4	68.9	53.4	37.9	18.7	4.6
1998	43.3	40.9	70.4	55.4	38.1	18.7	4.6
1999	43.3	39.7	70.8	56.9	38.1	19.0	4.6
2000	44.1	39.0	72.2	58.5	39.3	19.7	5.0
2001	43.8	37.0	71.3	59.5	40.4	20.4	5.3
2002	43.7	35.4	70.5	61.5	40.8	20.8	5.4

Source: Ventura, Stephanie J., and Christine A. Bachrach. Nonmarital Childbearing in the United States: 1940-99. Table 2. National Vital Statistics Reports, Vol. 48, No. 16. Hyattsville, Maryland: National Center for Health Statistics, 2000; Martin, Joyce A., et al. Births: Final data for 2001. Table 16. National Vital Statistics Reports, Vol. 51, No. 2. Hyattsville, Maryland: National Center for Health Statistics. 2002.Hamilton, Brady E., Joyce A. Martin , Paul D. Sutton . Births: Preliminary data for 2003. National Vital Statistics Reports. Vol. 53, No. 9. Table A. Hyattsville, MD: National Center for Health Statistics. 2004.

Cohabitation and Out-of-Wedlock Births

Approximately 40 percent of non-marital births occur to cohabiting women.

Source: Musick, K., and Larry Bumpass. *How Do Prior Experiences in the Family Affect Transitions to Adulthood?* Paper presented at the National symposium on Transitions to Adulthood in a Changing Economy: No Work, No Family, No Future? University Park, PA, October 1997.

Paternity Establishment

In-hospital paternity establishment was connected to a 16% greater chance of financial contributions from the father. Fathers who establish paternity in the hospital were also more likely to be supportive of the mother and were 15% more likely to have seen the child in the last month when compared to fathers who did not establish paternity.

Source: Mincy, Ronald, Irwin Garfinkel, and Lenna Nepomnyaschy. "In-Hospital Paternity Establishment and Father Involvement in Fragile Families." *Journal of Marriage and Family, 67* (August 2005): 611-625.

In 1996, there were 9.3 million children under age 18 who were born outside marriage and who did not have legally identified fathers, up from 3.8 million in 1978.

Source: Barton, Paul E. *Welfare Indicators of Dependency.* Princeton, NJ: Educational Testing Service, 1998: 25.

In 1999, 1.5 million paternities were acknowledged or established, up from 1.45 million in 1998, 1.3 million in 1997, 516,000 in 1992, and 110,000 in 1978.

Source: U.S. Department of Health and Human Services, Administration for Children and Families, Office of Child Support Enforcement. *Child Support Enforcement: Twenty-Third Annual Report to Congress, 1999.*

In 1999, 614,000 paternities were established through in-hospital acknowledgement programs.

Source: U.S. Department of Health and Human Services, Administration for Children and Families, Office of Child Support Enforcement. *Child Support Enforcement: Twenty-Third Annual Report to Congress, 1999.*

A 1994 study found that paternity is established in only about one-third of nonmarital births.

Source: Adams, C., F. Landsbergen, and D. Hecht. "Organizational Impediments to Paternity Establishment and Child Support." *Social Science Review 72* (1994): 109-126. "Responsible Fathering: an Overview and Conceptual Framework." Ed. William Doherty et al. *U.S. Department of Health and Human Services. Rept., October 1996.*

Consequences of Out-of-Wedlock Childbearing
Out-of-Wedlock Childbearing and Father Absence

In an analysis of data from the National Survey of Families and Households, the most important determinant of whether the father lived with his children was marital status at the time of the child's birth. Fully 80% of men who were married to the child's mother at the child's birth were living with all of their biological children, compared to only 22.6% of men who were not in a co-residential union relationship with the child's mother at the time of the child's birth.

Source: Clarke, L., E.C. Cooksey, and G. Verropoulou. "Fathers and Absent Fathers: Sociodemographic Similarities in Britain and the United States." *Demography, 35* (1998): 217-228.

Approximately 40 percent of non-marital births occur to cohabiting women.

Romantic involvement at the time of a child's birth significantly predicts future involvement for fathers. Only 43% of non-romantically attached fathers had seen their child in the previous month before the survey. The quality of the parents' relationship, strong fathering attitudes, and supportiveness were also connected to father involvement.

Source: Carlson, Marcia, Sara McLanahan, and Jeanne Brooks-Gunn. *Unmarried But Not Absent: Fathers' Involvement with Children After a Non-marital Birth.* Paper presented at the National Poverty Center's "Marriage and Family Formation Among Low Income Couples: What Do We Know From Research?" Georgetown University. Washington, DC. 4 September 2003.

Out-of-Wedlock Childbearing and Poverty

Children with unmarried parents are three times more likely to be living below the poverty line. A child with a biological mother and her unmarried partner have the highest odds of being below the poverty line. Thirty-eight percent of children in this living arrangement are poor.

Source: Kreider, Rose M. and Jason Fields. *Living Arrangements of Children: 2001.* Current Population Studies, P70-104. Table 2. Washington, D.C.: US Census Bureau, 2005.

During the year before their babies were born, 43% of unmarried mothers received welfare or food stamps, 21% received some type of housing subsidy, and 9% received another type of government transfer (unemployment insurance etc.). For women who have another child, the proportion who receive welfare or food stamps rises to 54%.

Source: McLanahan, Sara. *The Fragile Families and Child Wellbeing Study: Baseline National Report.* Princeton, NJ: Center for Research on Child Wellbeing, 2003: 13.

Twenty-three percent of unmarried mothers in large U.S. cities reported cigarette use during their pregnancy. Seventy-one percent were on Medicare.

Source: McLanahan, Sara. *The Fragile Families and Child Wellbeing Study: Baseline National Report.* Table 7. Princeton, NJ: Center for Research on Child Wellbeing, 2003: 16.

Consequences of Out-of-Wedlock Childbearing for Child Well-Being

At the time of pregnancy, 51% of adolescent mothers listed their child's biological father as part of their social network. Three years later, the percent dropped to 27%, behind best friends (44%) and new male partners (36%). However, more support from fathers during the perinatal period and less support from a new male partner at 3 years postpartum predicted relationship continuity between adolescent mothers and their child's biological father at the three year mark. But father absence and/or father strain was correlated with negative psychological adjustment for their child.

Source: Gee, Christina B. and Jean E. Rhodes. "Adolescent Mothers' Relationship With Their Children's Biological Fathers: Social Support, Social Strain, and Relationship Continuity." *Journal of Family Psychology, 17* (September 2003): 370-383.

Babies born to married mothers are less likely to have a low birthweight. In 2002, 7 percent of births to married mothers were low birthweight, compared to 10 percent of births to unmarried mothers. This relationship held for each race and ethnicity group as well. Six percent of infants born to married, White, non-His-

Children with unmarried parents are three times more likely to be living below the poverty line.

panic mothers were low birthweight, compared to 9% of infants in the unmarried mothers group. Similar figures were found for Black mothers (12% vs. 14%) and Hispanic mothers (6% vs. 7%).

Source: Federal Interagency Forum on Child and Family Statistics. *America's Children: Key National Indicators of Well-Being 2005.* Washington, D.C.: U.S. Government Printing Office, 2005: 66.

A Tennessee study analyzing outcomes of over one million children ages one to four found that children born to unmarried parents faced an elevated risk of death by injury compared to children born to two married parents, even after taking into account differences in income, education levels, race and age.

Source: Scholer, Seth J., Edward F. Mitchel, Jr., and Wayne A. Ray. "Predictors of Injury Mortality in Early Childhood." *Pediatrics,* *100* (1997): 342-347.

A study of 673 mothers that assessed the levels of parental monitoring of their children found that unmarried mothers were twice as likely to be in the lowest level of parental monitoring compared to married mothers.

Source: Chilcoat, Howard D., Naomi Breslau, and James C. Anthony. "Potential Barriers to Parent Monitoring: Social Disadvantage, Marital Status, and Maternal Psychiatric Disorder." *Journal of the American Academy of Child and Adolescent Psychiatry, 35* (1996): 1673-1682.

Out-of-Wedlock Childbearing Begets More Out-of-Wedlock Childbearing

Expectant mothers who were raised by single mothers were more likely to have a history of childhood maltreatment, less likely to live with the father of the baby, and less likely to expect support from him.

Source: Zelenko, Marina, Lynne Huffman, James Lock, Quinn Kennedy and Hans Steiner. "Poor Adolescent Expectant Mothers: Can We Assess Their Potential for Child Abuse?" *Journal of Adolescent Health* (October 2001): 271-278.

Daughters of adolescent moms are 83% more likely to become teen mothers themselves. Daughters of teen moms, whether or not they become teen moms themselves, are 50% more likely to bear children out of wedlock than daughters of older moms.

Source: Maynard, Rebecca A. (Ed.). *Kids Having Kids: Economic Costs and Social Consequences of Teen Pregnancy.* Washington, D.C.: The Urban Institute Press, 1997.

Out-of-Wedlock Childbearing Connects to Violence

A study of the 19-year period from 1973 to 1992 found that as a country's out-of-wedlock pregnancies increased, the country's murder rates increased as well. Out-of-wedlock pregnancies accounted for an 80% variance.

This data was consistent from United Nations sources across 45 countries that also connected out-of-wedlock pregnancy and murder rates.

Source: Mackey, Wade and Nancy S. Coney. "The Enigma of Father Presence in Relationship to Sons' Violence and Daughters' Mating Strategies" Empiricism in Search of a Theory." *Journal of Men's Studies, 8* (April 2000): 349.

Babies born to married mothers are less likely to have a low birthweight.

Daughters of adolescent moms are 83% more likely to become teen mothers themselves.

Divorce

"Children of divorce are real, complex people who are deeply shaped by a new kind of fractured family life — one whose current prevalence is unprecedented in human history. These children are not nostalgic for "tidy," "perfect," "idyllic" families. They grieve the real losses that follow from their parents' divorce. They don't need new words to describe what they've been through. Ordinary words will serve quite well — provided that people are willing to listen to them."

ELIZABETH MARQUARDT IN "THE BAD DIVORCE" FROM FIRST THINGS, FEBRUARY 2005.

"[Children of divorce] enter future relationships with an expectation of failure. So when problems occur, which will happen, they see this as failure and leave too soon rather than trying to work things out."

ROBERT BILLINGHAM, ASSOCIATE PROFESSOR OF HUMAN DEVELOPMENT AND FAMILIES STUDIES AT INDIANA UNIVERSITY, QUOTED IN USA TODAY MAGAZINE, SEPTEMBER 2003.

> Ninety-four percent of the 1,503 respondents of a telephone survey felt that divorce was a serious national problem.

"[Divorce] has reduced the levels of parental time and money invested in children. In sum, it has changed the very nature of American childhood. Just as no patient would have designed today's system of health care, so no child would have chosen today's culture of divorce... Those who are concerned about what the downsizing of corporations is doing to workers should also be concerned about what the downsizing of families through divorce is doing to parents and children."

BARBARA DAFOE WHITEHEAD, THE DIVORCE CULTURE, ALFRED A. KNOPF, NEW YORK, 1997.

"I grew up with my stepmother. My parents were nowhere to be found. There's no getting around that. It definitely makes you go, 'What is love?' They say they love me; love me means don't live with me. I don't understand."

BILLY CORGAN, FORMER LEAD SINGER, SMASHING PUMPKINS , ZWAN.

"Children do not dismiss their fathers just because there has been a divorce.... The poignancy of their reactions is astounding, especially among the six-, seven-, and eight-year-olds. They cry for their daddies — be they good, bad, or indifferent daddies. I have been deeply struck by the distress children of every age suffer at losing their fathers."

JUDITH WALLERSTEIN AND SANDRA BLAKESLEE, FROM SECOND CHANCES: MEN, WOMEN, AND CHILDREN A DECADE AFTER DIVORCE. NEW YORK: HOUGHTON MIFFLIN, 1996: 234.

Attitudes About Divorce

Ninety-four percent of the 1,503 respondents of a telephone survey felt that divorce was a serious national problem.

Source: National Fatherhood Initiative. *With This Ring…: A National Survey on Marriage in America.* Gaithersburg, MD, 2005: 4.

According to a national survey of 2,000 adults, 55% agreed that "Parents who break up too easily instead of trying to stay together for the sake of the kids" were "very common."
Source: Farkas, Steve, and Jean Johnson. "Kids These Days: What Americans Really Think About the Next Generation." New York: Public Agenda, 1997: 39.

According to a poll by Roper Starch Worldwide, 32% of Americans would prefer to leave a spouse and disrupt their family for someone they love, while 29% would remain in a long stable marriage with someone they don't love. The question stumped 39% of those surveyed.
Source: Poll by Roper Starch Worldwide. "New Nationwide Survey on 'American Dream' at Millennium Reveals Surprising Ambivalence About Work and Technology." New York, January 4, 2000.

In a nationally representative survey of adults ages 20-29, 88 percent agreed that the divorce rate is too high and that the United States would be better off if we could have fewer divorces.
Source: Whitehead, Barbara Dafoe, and David Popenoe. "The State of Our Unions 2001: The Social Health of Marriage in America." Piscataway, NJ: The National Marriage Project, 2001.

In a 1997 Time/CNN poll, 59% of respondents said the government should not make it harder for couples to get a divorce, while 61% said it should be harder for married couples with young children to get a divorce.
Source: Time/CNN poll, as cited in "There is No No-Fault Divorce." The Wichita Eagle, Wichita, KS, August 13, 1998.

Over the last three decades, only a quarter to a third of Americans have favored liberalizing divorce laws, while on average 52% have advocated tougher laws and 21% keeping laws unchanged. This opposition to easier divorce probably contributed to the leveling-off of the divorce rate in the early 1980s, but has not led to a general tightening of divorce laws or a notable drop in the divorce rate.
Source: Smith, Tom W. "The Emerging 21st Century Family." GSS Social Change Report No. 42. Chicago, IL: University of Chicago, National Opinion Research Center, 1999: 5-6.

In a 1999 poll by the Center for Gender Equality, 44% of women think divorce should be harder to get.
Source: Center for Gender Equality, 1999, as cited in Leo, John, "Reversal in the Sex Revolution." The Washington Times, February 27, 1999.

According to a 1995 USA Today poll, 76 percent of children think divorce should be harder to obtain. Three out of four children think most couples do not try hard enough to save their marriages.
Source: As cited in Hill, John R., and Nick Stinnett. Breaking Up is Hard on You: The High Co$t of Divorce. Birmingham, AL: The Alabama Family Alliance, 1998: 4.

...44% of women think divorce should be harder to get.

...76 percent of children think divorce should be harder to obtain.

In a national survey conducted by the Pew Research Center for the People and the Press, 53% of those polled believed that increasing acceptance of divorce had been a change for the worse compared to only 30% who felt it was a change for the better.
Source: "Best and Worst of the Century," *The Washington Post,* July 11, 1999.

The Facts About Divorce

Divorces are very costly to the public. A single divorce can cost state and federal governments about $30,000, when such things as increased food stamps and public housing usage, increased bankruptcies and juvenile delinquency are included. The 1.4 million divorces in 2002 cost taxpayers more than $30 billion.
Source: Schramm, David. "The Costly Consequences of Divorce in Utah: The Impact on Couples, Community, and Government." Unpublished manuscript. Logan, UT: Utah State University, 2003 as cited in *The National Marriage Project. The State of Our Unions 2005: The Social Health of Marriage in America.* Piscataway, NJ: The National Marriage Project, 2005: 17.

Number of Divorces, by Year, 1960 to 2003

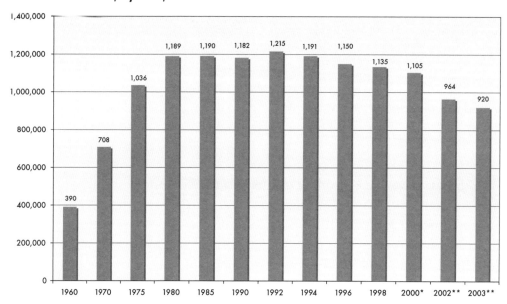

Numbers are in thousands.
*Data does not include California, Colorado, Indiana, and Louisiana.
**Data does not include California, Hawaii, Indiana, Louisiana, or Oklahoma.
Source: U.S. Census Bureau. Vital Statistics of the United States. Statistical Abstract of the United States 2000. Table 144. Washington, D.C.: GPO, 2001; National Center for Health Statistics. Births, Marriages, Deaths and Divorces: Provisional Data for 2001. Table 1. National Vital Statistics Reports, Vol. 50, No. 14. Hyattsville, MD: National Center for Health Statistics, 2002. Munson ML, Sutton PD. Births, marriages, divorces, and deaths: Provisional data for 2003. National Vital Statistics Reports, Vol. 52 No. 22. Hyattsville, Maryland: National Center for Health Statistics. 2004.

Despite the rise in cohabitation, the National Center of Health Statistics still predicts that half of first-time marriages will end in divorce.
Source: Roberts, Sam. "Till Death Do Us Part, Or Whatever." *The New York Times,* 27 June 2004: 4.14.

After 5 years, 20 percent of all first marriages have disrupted due to separation or divorce. The percentage of marital disruption increases to 33 percent, 43 percent, and 50 percent after 10 years, 15 years, and 20 years, respectively.
Source: Bramlett, Matthew D., and William D. Mosher. *First Marriage Dissolution, Divorce, and Remarriage: United States.* Advance Data from Vital and Health Statistics, No. 323. Hyattsville, MD: National Center for Health Statistics, 2001

In 2002, of the 19.7 million children in the U.S. living with only one parent, approximately 50 percent are living with a divorced or separated parent.
Source: U.S. Census Bureau, *Children's Living Arrangements and Characteristics: March 2002*, P20-547. Table C3. Washington, DC: GPO, 2003.

If the flattening out of divorce rates during the late 1990s persists into the future, not much more than 40 percent of today's first marriages would end in divorce, down from earlier projections of 50 percent.
Source: Popenoe, David, and Barbara Dafoe Whitehead. *The State of Our Unions 2000: The Social Health of Marriage in America.* New Brunswick, NJ: The National Marriage Project, 2000: 27.

In 2002, 21.6 million adults identified themselves as divorced, representing 9.6% of the population, up from 4.3 million in 1970 or 2% of the total population.
Source: U.S. Census Bureau, *America's Families and Living Arrangements: 2003*, P20-553. Table C3. Washington, DC: GPO, 2003.

The proportion of ever-married adults who have been divorced doubled from 17% in 1972 to 34% in 1998.
Source: Smith, Tom W. "The Emerging 21st Century Family." *General Social Survey Social Change Report, No. 42*, National Opinion Research Center, University of Chicago, November 24, 1999.

According to a nationwide survey of 4,000 adults, 11 percent of the adult population is currently divorced, and 25 percent of all adults have experienced at least one divorce during their lifetime.
Source: Barna Research Group, Ltd. (Ventura, California). "Christians Are More Likely to Divorce Than Are Non-Christians." December 21, 1999.

The median age of divorce for husbands has been between 32 and 36 years since 1970.
Source: U.S. Census Bureau. Current Population Reports, P20-514. *Statistical Abstract of the United States 1999*. Table 72. Washington, D.C.: U.S. Census Bureau, 2000.

In 1984, a child living with only one parent was almost twice as likely to be living with a divorced parent as with a never-married parent. By 1994, the child was just as likely to be living with a divorced parent as with a never-married parent.
Source: Saluter, Arlene F. *Marital Status and Living Arrangements, March 1994*. Washington, D.C.: GPO, 1995.

Roughly 66 percent of the increase in single parenthood among whites since 1960 has been the result of divorce.
Source: Garfinkel, Irwin and Sara S. McLanahan. *Single Mothers and Their Children: A New American Dilemma.* Washington, D.C.: Urban Institute, 1989. 52-54; see also Saluter, Arlene F. Marital Status and Living Arrangements: March 1994. U.S. Bureau of the Census. Current Pop. Rept., p20-484. Washington D.C.: GPO, 1996.

In 2002, of the 19.7 million children in the U.S. living with only one parent, approximately 50 percent are living with a divorced or separated parent.

Using data from the National Center for Health Statistics, researchers determined "no-fault divorce laws had a significant positive effect on the divorce rate across the 50 states."

Source: Nakonezny, Paul A., Robert D. Shull and Joseph Lee Rodgers. "The Effects of No-Fault Divorce Law on the Divorce Rate Across the 50 States and Its Relation to Income, Education, and Religiosity." *Journal of Marriage and the Family, 57* (1995): 477-488.

Due to such factors such as household costs and transportation, the cost of contact with a child in Australia is much more expensive after a separation. For contact with one child for 20 percent of the year, costs of contact represent about 40 percent of the costs for that same child in an intact couple household with a medium income and more than half of the costs for that child in a low income household.

Source: Henman, Paul and Kyle Mitchell. "Estimating the Cost of Contact for Non-resident Parents: A Budget Standards Approach." *Journal of Social Policy, 30* (July 2001): 495-520.

Predictors of Divorce

Data from the National Survey of Families and Households indicates that parental divorce increased the likelihood of choosing a spouse from a divorced family by 58%. Moreover, marriages in which either spouse comes from a divorced family are twice as likely to fail as marriages in which neither spouse came from a divorce family. Marriages in which both spouses come from divorced families are more than three times more likely to fail.

Source: Wolfinger, Nicholas H. "Family structure homogamy: The effects of parental divorce on partner selection and marital stability." *Social Science Research, 32* (March 2003): 80-97.

> **Virtually no studies demonstrated that financial problems are the number one cause of divorce.**

Virtually no studies demonstrated that financial problems are the number one cause of divorce.

Source: Andersen, Jan D. "Financial Problems and Divorce: Do Demographic Characteristics Strengthen the Relationship?" *Journal of Divorce & Remarriage* (2005): 149-161.

Sixty-five percent of ex-husbands and 78 percent of ex-wives listed lack of commitment as their main reason for divorce. Sixty-two percent of both divorced men and women wished they had worked harder at their marriage.

Source: National Fatherhood Initiative. *With This Ring…: A National Survey on Marriage in America.* Gaithersburg, MD: National Fatherhood Initiative, 2005: 4.

A study of 17,346 family members over 140 years and nine generations showed that children from divorced homes are significantly more likely to get divorced than children from non-divorced homes.

Source: Kunz, Jenifer. "The Intergenerational Transmission of Divorce: A Nine Generation Study." *Journal of Divorce & Remarriage* (2000):169-175.

A grandparents' divorce can have adverse affects on their children and grandchildren. A study of 691 grandparents found that grandchildren whose grandparents divorced had lower levels of education, higher levels of marital discord, and lower quality relationships with their parents.

Source: Amato, Paul R. and Jacob Cheadle. "The Long Reach of Divorce: Divorce and Child Well-Being Across Three Generations." *Journal of Marriage and Family, 67* (February 2005): 191-215.

Data from a national, longitudinal study revealed that parents attitudes towards divorce are positively related to their children's attitudes towards divorce. This held true even controlling for parents' marital status. Separation was also positively associated with attitudes towards divorce.
Source: Kapinus, Carolyn. "The Effect of Relationship Experiences and Parents' Attitudes on Young Adults' Views of Divorce." *Journal of Divorce & Remarriage, 39* (2003): 143-157.

Adolescent boys who felt close to their custodial or noncustodial fathers in 11th grade were less likely to divorce than those without a close relationship. A close relationship with a noncustodial father, however, is not a replacement for a custodial father. Children with close relationships with noncustodial fathers were still more likely to divorce than children with close custodial relationships.
Source: Risch, Sharon C., Kathleen M. Jodl and Jaquelynne S. Eccles. "Role of the Father-Adolescent Relationships in Shaping Adolescents' Attitudes Toward Divorce." *Journal of Marriage and Family, 66* (February 2004): 46-58.

In terms of predicting divorce as it relates to time spent at work, wives' are better indicators than husbands are. Married women who expect that their marriages will fail are more likely to increase the amount of time worked per week and per year. Men's economic behavior does not change despite high expectations for marriage dissolution.

Wives' and not husbands' anticipation of divorce was associated with a lower likelihood of child bearing among couples who stayed together.
Source: South, Scott J., Sunita Bose, and Katherine Trent. "Anticipating Divorce: Spousal Agreement, Predictive Accuracy, and Effects on Labor." Supply and Fertility." *Journal of Divorce & Remarriage, 30* (2004): 1-22.

Divorce is highest among those who marry very young (younger than age 21), get married because of a pregnancy, are of lower socioeconomic status, and are non-religious.
Source: Kposowa, Augustine J. "The Impact of Race on Divorce in the United States." *Journal of Comparative Family Studies, 29* (Autumn 1998): 529-548.

Approximately 57,000 extra divorces per year in the U.S. occurred in the first 3 years after the implementation of no-fault divorce laws.
Source: Rodgers, Joseph Lee, Paul A. Nakonezny, and Robert D. Shull. "The Effect of No-Fault Divorce Legislation on Divorce Rates: A Response to a Reconsideration." *Journal of Marriage and the Family, 59* (1997): 1026-1030.

In an analysis of divorce rate trends in the U.S., it was found that states with high levels of joint physical custody awards (over 30%) in 1989 and 1990 evidenced significantly greater declines in divorce rates in 1991 through 1995. Overall, divorce rates declined nearly four times faster in high joint custody states during this time period compared to states where the awarding of joint physical custody was rare.
Source: Kuhn, Richard, and John Guidubaldi. "Child Custody Policies and Divorce Rates in the United States." Paper presented at the 11th National Conference of the Children's Rights Council. Washington, D.C., 1997.

In a study of 130 divorced women, it was found that regardless of a woman's socioeconomic status, incompatibility and lack of emotional support were the most frequently cited determinants of divorce.

Source: Dolan, Mary A., and Charles D. Hoffman. "Determinants of Divorce Among Women: A Reexamination of Critical Influences." *Journal of Divorce and Remarriage, 28* (1998): 97-106.

Using data from the Panel Study of Income Dynamics for 1968 to 1985, it was found that when a wife has no earnings, low earnings by her husband increases the risk of divorce. However, when the wife has earnings, low earnings by the husband has no effect on the marriage. Overall, either very low or very high earnings by wives, but not the middle range of earnings, increases the risk of divorce.

Source: Ono, Hiromi. "Husbands' and Wives' Resources and Marital Dissolution." *Journal of Marriage and the Family, 60* (August 1998): 674-689.

> ...the person who anticipates gaining custody of the children is the one most likely to file for divorce.

In a longitudinal study of 2,621 men and women in their childbearing years, drawn from the National Survey of Families and Households, men with traditional attitudes toward marriage and family life had a higher divorce rate than men with egalitarian attitudes (25 percent versus 16 percent). For women the opposite was true. Women with traditional attitudes toward marriage and family life were less likely to divorce compared to women with more egalitarian attitudes.

Source: Kaufman, Gayle. "Do Gender Attitudes Matter? Family Formation and Dissolution Among Traditional and Egalitarian Men and Women." *Journal of Family Issues, 21* (January 2000): 128-144.

In a longitudinal study of 1,184 couples tracked from 1980 to 1992, a woman's income was positively associated with divorce, whereas frequency of church attendance and the birth of a new child were negatively associated with divorce.

Source: Knoester, Chris, and Alan Booth. "Barriers to Divorce: When Are They Effective? When Are They Not?" *Journal of Family Issues, 21* (January 2000): 78-99.

Who Files for Divorce

According to an analysis of 46,000 divorce cases from the four U.S. states that keep such statistics, women are twice as likely to file for divorce as are men. More women than men obtain desertion-based divorces, but adultery cases are evenly split between men and women. Furthermore, the person who anticipates gaining custody of the children is the one most likely to file for divorce.

Source: Brinig, Margaret, and Douglas Allen. "These Boots Are Made for Walking: Why Most Divorce Filers Are Women." *American Law and Economics Review, 2* (Spring 2000): 126-169.

Using a sample of 16,243 ever-married women from the June 1985 marriage and fertility supplement to the U.S. Bureau of the Census's Current Population Survey, it was found that 47% of African-American women were expected to end their marriages within 15 years, compared to 17% of whites. That is, African-American women were nearly 1.8 times as likely to divorce as their white counterparts.

Source: Kposowa, Augustine J. "The Impact of Race on Divorce in the United States." *Journal of Comparative Family Studies, 29* (Autumn 1998): 529-548.

Divorce and Subsequent Remarriage

Seventy-five percent of divorced women remarry within 10 years.
Source: Bramlett, Matthew D., and William D. Mosher. *First Marriage Dissolution, Divorce, and Remarriage: United States.* Advance Data from Vital and Health Statistics, No. 323. Hyattsville, MD: National Center for Health Statistics, 2001.

Five years after divorce, 58% of white women, 32% of African-American women, and 44% of Hispanic women, are remarried.
Source: Bramlett, Matthew D., and William D. Mosher. *First Marriage Dissolution, Divorce, and Remarriage: United States.* Advance Data from Vital and Health Statistics, No. 323. Hyattsville, MD: National Center for Health Statistics, 2001.

Remarriages have a higher probability of disruption than first marriages. After 10 years, 39% of remarriages resulted in either separation or divorce.
Source: Bramlett, Matthew D., and William D. Mosher. *First Marriage Dissolution, Divorce, and Remarriage: United States.* Advance Data from Vital and Health Statistics, No. 323. Hyattsville, MD: National Center for Health Statistics, 2001.

The Consequences of Divorce
Divorce Is the Problem

Not only did children who grew up with a lone parent experience greater emotional and behavioral problems, children who moved from a two-parent household to a single-parent household during researchers' study of the National Longitudinal Survey of Children and Youth experienced similar problems. Family breakup, hence, can exert an almost immediate effect on children. Reconstituting the family after a divorce through remarriage may not necessarily help. Children in stepfamilies also demonstrated more emotional and behavioral problems than children in two-parent households. Researchers suggested that these children may still carry baggage from their previous experience as a child in a lone-parent family.
Source: Ram, Bali and Feng Hou. "Changes in Family Structure and Child Outcomes: Roles of Economic and Familial Resources." *Policy Studies Journal, 31* (2003): 309-330.

In a study of 18,000 children, it was found that children whose parents divorced when they were age 7-22 were 11% more likely to suffer "a wide variety of adult emotional disorders, such as depression, anxiety, phobias, and obsessions," with the likelihood of such problems doubling as the children entered adulthood. By the time these children had reached age 33, the children of divorce were 25% more likely to have emotional problems than children whose parents stayed married. Statistical analyses show that the harm divorce causes is not due to the income, race, or social status of the parents, but to the "divorce itself."
Source: Cherlin, Andrew J., P. Lindsay Chase-Lansdale, and Christine McRae. "Effects of Parental Divorce on Mental Health Throughout the Life Course." *American Sociological Review 63* (April 1998): 239-249.

A study of 5,530 boys and girls showed that the higher adolescents' satisfaction with their relationship with the parent of the same sex prior to residential separation the greater the increase in juvenile delinquency in two years later.
Source: Videon, Tami M. "The Effects of Parent-Adolescent Relationships and Parental Separation on Adolescent Well-Being." *Journal of Marriage and Family, 64* (May 2002): 489-503.

Remarriages have a higher probability of disruption than first marriages.

Death and divorce have different economic impacts on Canadian families. The average annual income of men from intact families is $20,769, compared to bereaved and divorced families at $19,790 and $17,721, respectively. For women, those from intact, bereaved, and divorced backgrounds earn on average $16,148, $15,363, and $14,185. Men from divorced families earn about 12% less than those from intact families. Women earn 9% less. Moreover, both women and men are more likely to rely on public assistance than those from intact families.
Source: Corak, Miles. "Death and Divorce: The Long-Term Consequences of Parental Loss on Adolescents." *Journal of Labor Economics, 19* (July 2001): 682-715.

A literature review of research on residential mobility found that transitions reduce children's academic functioning, and may negatively affect other aspects of child well-being. These effects were particularly marked for children of single parents.
Source: Scanlon, Edward and Kevin Devine. "Residential Mobility and Youth Well-Being: Research, Policy, and Practice Issues." *Journal of Sociology and Social Welfare, 28* (March 2001): 119-138.

The younger a child is at the time of his or her parents' separation, the lower their adolescent attachment to the parents tends to be, the less maternal or paternal care the child perceives as an adolescent, and the more maternal or paternal overprotection the child perceives as an adolescent.
Source: Woodward, Lianne, David M. Fergusson, and Jay Belsky. "Timing of Parental Separation and Attachment to Parents in Adolescence: Results of a Prospective Study from Birth to Age 16." *Journal of Marriage and Family, 62* (February 2000): 162-174.

A study of family drawings of 180 children showed that children from intact, biological families were more likely to draw their parents together than children from step- and single-parent families.
Source: Dunn, Judy, Thomas G. O'Connor, and Irit Levy. "Out of the Picture: A Study of Family Drawings by Children From Step-, Single-Parent, and Non-Step Families." *Journal of Clinical Child and Adolescent Psychology, 31* (2002): 505-512.

A 15-year study on a nationally representative sample of families found that divorce was associated with improved outcomes for about 30% of the children who experienced divorce. However, fully 70% of children who experienced divorce had worse outcomes on a number of measures than if their parents had stayed married.
Source: Amato, Paul R. and Alan Booth. *A Generation at Risk: Growing Up in an Era of Family Upheaval.* Cambridge: Harvard University Press, 1997.

In a longitudinal study of adolescents living in intact, divorced and to-be-divorced families, no support was found for the hypothesis that the negative effects of divorce already exist prior to the divorce. Rather, divorce and its accompanying disruption of family processes were associated with adolescent adjustment difficulties.
Source: Forehand, Rex, Lisa Armistead, and Corrine David. "Is Adolescent Adjustment Following Parental Divorce a Function of Predivorce Adjustment?" *Journal of Abnormal Child Psychology, 25* (1997): 157-164.

In a study of 400 Iowa families, it was found that "...the negative effects of divorce are greater and more consistent than those of marital discord. This suggests that family structure differences in child adjustment are not simply a continuation of problems fostered by parental conflict prior to divorce." The authors conclude, "Children undoubtedly perceive persistent parental discord as frustrating and annoying, but in most cases its effect on the child's emotional and behavioral functioning is probably less than that of divorce."
Source: Ronald L. Simons and Associates. *Understanding the Differences between Divorced and Intact Families: Stress Interaction and Child Outcomes.* Thousand Oaks, CA: Sage Publications, Inc., 1996.

"Using a 12-year longitudinal study of adults growing up in conflict-ridden, two-parent families, it was found that children have higher levels of well-being if their parents stay together than if they divorce."
Source: Amato, Paul R., Laura S. Loomis and Alan Booth. "Parental Divorce, Marital Conflict, and Offspring Well-Being During Early Adulthood." *Social Forces 73.3* (March 1995): 895-915.

An analysis of a nationally representative sample of over 2,000 married people found that even after controlling for the parents' marital quality, children whose parents divorced were 76 percent more likely to divorce themselves.
Source: Amato, Paul R., and Alan Booth. *A Generation At Risk: Growing Up in an Era of Family Upheaval.* Cambridge, MA: Harvard University Press, 1997: 115.

Economic Consequences of Divorce
Divorce places a significant and disproportionate financial strain on women and children. Using data drawn from the 1986-1991 panels of the Survey of Income and Program Participation, it was found that 16-18 months after a couple's separation, 42.5 percent of custodial mothers not yet receiving child support lived in poverty, while 35.4 percent of those receiving child support lived in poverty. Among the non-custodial fathers, only 10.6 percent lived in poverty, regardless if they were or were not yet paying child support.
Source: Bartfield, Judi. "Child Support and Postdivorce Economic Well-Being of Fathers, Mothers, and Children." *Demography, 37* (May 2000): 203-213.

In 1994 constant dollars, median family income is about $26,600 for divorced women, compared with $53,200 for continuously married women. When women who have remarried or entered into a cohabiting union are excluded, median family income for lone, divorced women falls to $21,000.
Source: Smock, Pamela J., Wendy D. Manning, and Sanjiv Gupta. "The Effect of Marriage and Divorce on Women's Economic Well-Being." *American Sociological Review, 64* (1999): 794-812.

A longitudinal study of the effects of divorce among African Americans found that women suffered an economic loss of 25% and men suffered a 7% economic loss.
Source: Pollock, Gene E. and Atlee L. Stroup. "Economic Consequences of Marital Dissolution for Blacks." *Journal of Divorce and Remarriage, 26.1/2* (1997): 49-62.

Consequences of Divorce for Child Well-Being
A study of a pool of 35,284 people over twenty-five years of age indicated that children from single-mother homes produced by divorce were significantly less likely than those from two-biological-parent families to complete high school, attend college, or graduate from college. They held jobs of lower average status and they measured lower on general psychological well-being scales. By contrast, children from widowed single-mother homes were not significantly different from children from two-biological-parent homes.
Source: Bilbarz, Timothy J. and Greg Gottainer. "Family Structure and Children's Success: A Comparison of Widowed and Divorced Single-Mother Families." *Journal of Marriage and Family, 62* (May 2000): 533-548.

...children whose parents divorced were 76 percent more likely to divorce themselves.

A study of 238 divorced mothers and their sons showed that family structure transitions had a negative effect on the boys' academic achievement. The more transitions the child experienced, the more poorly he did in school.
Source: Martinez, Jr., Charles R. and Marion S. Forgatch. "Adjusting to Change: Linking family Structure Transitions With Parenting and Boys' Adjustment." *Journal of Family Psychology, 16* (June 2002): 107-117.

A 2002 study discovered that children with divorced parents are more likely than children with married parents to have behavior problems such as aggression and acting out. Researchers postulated that the children's behaviors are response to divorced parents' poor parenting, which stemmed from the economic and psychological stresses of single parenthood.
Source: Hilton, Jeanne M. and Stephen Desrochers. "Children's Behavior Problems in Single Parent and Married Parent Families: Development of a Predictive Model." *Journal of Divorce and Remarriage, 37* (2002): 13-36.

> ...children with divorced parents are more likely than children with married parents to have behavior problems such as aggression and acting out.

A study of 1,014 adults found that those whose parents divorce by age seven were twice as likely to suffer from major depression than those raised in intact families. This held even for children whose parents remarried.
Source: Gilman, Stephen E. and Ichiro Kawachi, et al. "Family Disruption in Childhood and Risk of Adult Depression." *American Journal of Psychiatry, 160* (May 2003): 939-946.

A study of 304 men and women showed that individuals from non-divorced families were closer to their siblings, communicated more often with their siblings, and had better rapport with their siblings compared to those from divorced families. Marital satisfaction was a predictor of sibling communication, closeness, and support.
Source: Milevsky, Avidan. "Perceived Parental Marital Satisfaction and Divorce: Effects on Sibling Relations in Emerging Adults." *Journal of Divorce & Remarriage, 41* (2004): 115-128.

A study of 2,636 Dutch parent-child couples revealed that the average emotional adjustment was lowest overall in postdivorce families, followed by two-parent families with low marital quality. Compared to the total influence of two-parent families with a high marital quality, all other family arrangements experienced a negative influence on adolescent emotional adjustment.
Source: Vanderwalk, Inge and Ed Spruijt, et al. "Marital Status, Marital Process, and Parental Resources in Predicting Adolescents' Emotional Adjustment." *Journal of Family Issues, 25* (April 2004): 291-317.

Boys from homes broken by divorce and death were more likely to be violent or delinquent. Adolescent from homes broken by desertion had the highest rate of maltreatment. This relationship held even after holding for socioeconomic status.
Source: Heck, Cary and Anthony Walsh. "The Effects of Maltreatment and Family Structure on Minor and Serious Delinquency." *International Journal of Offender Therapy and Comparative Criminology, 44* (April 2000): 178-193.

Children from both biological and adoptive two-parent households that experienced divorce experienced higher rates of behavioral and substance abuse problems when compared to children from married families. Internalizing behaviors after divorce were more common for adoptive children while biological children experienced lower social adjustment and achievement scores.
Source: O'Connor, Thomas G., Avshalom Caspi, John C. DeFries, and Robert Plomin. "Are Associations Between Parental Divorce and Children's Adjustment Genetically Mediated? An Adoption Study." *Development Psychology, 36* (July 2000): 429-437.

Although college students from divorced families may not drink more compared to students from intact families, they are more likely to experience negative outcomes from drinking. Students from divorced families in a study of 1,200 were more likely to drive after having several drinks, drive when they know they've had too much, and drink while driving. They also reported getting occasional lower grades from drinking too much.
Source: Billingham, Robert E., William Wilson, and William C. Gross. "Parental Divorce and Consequences of Drinking Among College Students." *College Student Journal, 33* (September 1999): 322-327.

Children whose parents had recently divorced are more likely to report cocaine use compared to children whose parents had been divorced four years or more. They were also more likely to be under the influence of cocaine while at school.
Source: Jeynes, William H. "The Effects of Recent Parental Divorce on Their Children's Consumption of Marijuana and Cocaine." *Journal of Divorce & Remarriage, 35* (2001): 43-65.

Two-hundred sixty-four college students were asked about their sibling relationships. Those who had experienced parental divorce during later childhood or adolescence experienced significantly fewer positive feelings toward the sibling in adulthood and recalled fewer positive feelings, beliefs, and behaviors toward the sibling in adulthood when compared to those who experienced divorce earlier in childhood or came from married households.
Source: Riggio, Heidi R. "Relations Between Parental Divorce and the Quality of Adult Sibling Relationships." *Journal of Divorce & Remarriage 36* (2001): 67-82.

According to a study of 1,237 children from the Netherlands, those who had experienced divorce had more sex partners than those from intact families. Boys from divorced homes also showed more tendencies towards delinquent behaviors after divorce when compared to girls and boys from intact families.
Source: Spruijt, Ed and Vincent Duindam. "Problem Behavior of Boys and Young Men after Parental Divorce in the Netherlands." *Journal of Divorce & Remarriage, 43* (2005): 141-155.

Lower levels of involvement with their children in postdivorce fathers are connected with the levels of conflict with the ex-spouse, greater geographic distance from the child, and a lack of clarity regarding his role as a nonresident father.
Source: Leite, Randall W. and Patrick McKenry. "Aspects of Father Status and Postdivorce Father Involvement with Children." *Journal of Family Issues, 33* (July 2002): 601-623.

In a sample of ethnically diverse 11- to 14-year-olds of divorced and married parents, it was found that children of divorce had significantly more substance-using friends and were less likely to use effective coping and social skills.
Source: Neher, Linda, and Jerome L. Short. "Risk and Protective Factors for Children's Substance Use and Antisocial Behavior Following Parental Divorce." American Journal of Orthopsychiatry 68 (January 1998): 154-161; see also Short, Jerome L. "Predictors of Substance Use and Mental Health of Children of Divorce: A Prospective Analysis." *Journal of Divorce and Remarriage, 29* (1998): 147-166.

In a study of 300 adolescents, those from broken homes were more likely to show a higher level of distrust of other people than their peers from intact families.
Source: Guiliani, Christina, Raffaella Iafrate, and Rosa Rosnati. "Peer-Group and Romantic Relationships in Adolescents from Intact and Separated Families." *Contemporary Family Therapy, 20* (1998): 93-106.

> ...adolescents... from broken homes were more likely to show a higher level of distrust of other people than their peers from intact families.

In a prospective longitudinal study of 398 adoptive and biological families, it was found that children who experienced their biological parents' separation by the age of 12 exhibited higher rates of behavioral problems and substance abuse and lower levels of achievement in social adjustment compared with children whose parents' marriages remained intact. Adoptive children whose adoptive parents divorced exhibited higher levels of behavioral problems and substance abuse compared to adoptees whose parents did not divorce.

Source: O'Connor, Thomas G., Avshalom Caspi, John C. DeFries, and Robert Plomin. "Are Associations Between Parental Divorce and Children's Adjustment Genetically Mediated? An Adoption Study." *Developmental Psychology, 36* (2000): 429-437.

In a study of 120 students at the University of Sydney, consisting of 40 males and 40 females with married parents and 20 males and 20 females with divorced parents, those who had experienced parental divorce evidenced more externalizing behavior problems even two years after the divorce.

Source: Dixon, Caitlan, Margaret A. Chalres, and Alan A. Craddock. "The Impact of Experiences of Parental Divorce Conflict on Young Australian Adult Men and Women." *Journal of Family Studies, 4* (April 1998): 21-34.

A 23-year, seven-wave study of 867 families in the Detroit area found that compared to children who lived with both parents, children whose parents divorced were more likely to:
- endorse premarital sex
- approve of cohabitation
- express negative attitudes towards marriages

Source: Axinn, William G. and Arland Thornton. "The Influence of Parents' Marital Dissolutions on Children's Attitudes Toward Family Formation." *Demography, 33* (1996): 66-81.

A longitudinal analysis of childhood mortality rates found that female divorce rates within a county are positively associated with higher mortality rates for children.

Source: Singh, Gopal K. and Stella M. Yu. "U.S. Childhood Mortality, 1950 through 1993: Trends and Socioeconomic Differentials." *American Journal of Public Health, 86* (1996): 505-512.

"Divorce in childhood was significantly related to higher emotional problems, lower school performance, and poorer family economic standing at age 16."

Source: Chase-Lansdale, P. Lindsay, Andrew J. Cherlin, and Kathleen E. Kiernan. "The Long-Term Effects of Parental Divorce on the Mental Health of Young Adults: A Developmental Perspective." *Child Development, 66* (1995): 1614-1634.

After evaluating a sample of 12,537 young people, researchers concluded that "parental divorce increases the likelihood that young men and women will have a child out of wedlock."

Source: Cherlin, Andrew J., Kathleen E. Kirenan and P. Lindsay Chase-Lansdale. "Parental Divorce in Childhood and Demographic Outcomes in Young Adulthood." *Demography, 32* (1995): 299-316.

Impact of Divorce on Boys

An analysis of a sample of 497 sixteen-year-old boys from the Montreal Longitudinal-Experimental Study found that divorce increased the risk of theft and fighting, regardless of the degree of financial hardship.

Source: Pagani, Linda, Bernard Boulerice, Frank Vitaro, and Richard E. Tremblay. "Effects of Poverty on Academic Failure and Delinquency in Boys: A Change and Process Model Approach." *Journal of Child Psychology & Psychiatry & Allied Disciplines, 40* (1999): 1209-1219.

Impact of Divorce on Girls

Daughters who have experienced divorce develop pro-divorce attitudes even when controlling for her parents' attitudes.
Source: Kapinus, Carolyn A. "The Effect of Parents' Attitudes Toward Divorce on Offspring's Attitudes: Gender and Parental Divorce as Mediating Factors." *Journal of Family Issues, 25* (January 2004): 112-135.

In a study of the effects of divorce on 77 girls (ages 6-9 years) over a four-year period, it was found that those girls who experienced parental separation between birth and two years of age evidenced more pervasive and long-lasting disruptive behavior than girls who had experienced parental separation between the ages of three and five years.
Source: Japel, Christa, Richard E. Tremblay, Frank Vitaro, and Bernard Boulerice. "Early Parental Separation and the Psychosocial Development of Daughters 6-9 Years Old." *American Journal of Orthopsychiatry, 69* (January 1999): 49-60.

Using data collected from three generations from a large sample of largely working-class and middle-class families residing in Southern California, it was found that parental divorce increased the likelihood that a daughter's first marriage would end in divorce by 114 percent.
Source: Feng, Du, et al. "Intergenerational Transmission of Marital Quality and Marital Instability." *Journal of Marriage and the Family, 61* (1999): 451-463.

Using a sample of more than 1,000 college students, women with divorced parents were less likely to have a secure attachment style, more likely to have an avoidant attachment style, and were less idealistic in their romantic beliefs.
Source: Sprecher, Susan, Rodney Cate, and Lauren Levin. "Parental Divorce and Young Adults' Beliefs About Love." *Journal of Divorce and Remarriage, 28* (1998): 107-120.

In a longitudinal study of 10,353 teenagers and young women in Great Britain, young women whose parents divorced were more than three times as likely to have an out-of-wedlock birth compared to young women whose parents stayed married.
Source: Cherlin, Andrew J., Kathleen E. Kiernan, and P. Lindsay Chase-Lansdale. "Parental Divorce in Childhood and Demographic Outcomes in Young Adulthood." *Demography 32* (1995): 299-318.

Comparison of the Impact of Divorce on Boys and Girls

Following divorce, fathers are more likely to be primary custodian of their sons than their daughters.
Source: Saluter, Arlene. Marital Status and Living Arrangements: March 1994. *Current Population Reports, P20-484*. Washington, D.C.: GPO, 1995.

In a study of gender and age differences in children's adjustment to parental divorce, it was found that girls adjusted better than boys, older children adjusted better than younger children, and children in father-headed families adjusted better than those in mother-headed families.
Source: Howell, Susan H., Pedro R. Portes, and Joseph H. Brown. "Gender and Age Differences in Child Adjustment to Parental Separation." *Journal of Divorce and Remarriage, 27* (1997): 141-158.

> ...parental divorce increased the likelihood that a daughter's first marriage would end in divorce by 114 percent.

A study of 71 college students found that daughters from divorced homes had more relationship problems and higher levels of depression than sons whose parents had divorced.
Source: McCabe, Kristen M. "Sex Differences in the Long-Term Effects of Divorce in Children: Depression and Heterosexual Relationship Difficulties in the Young Adult Years." *Journal of Divorce and Remarriage, 27* (1997):123-134.

Consequences of Divorce Into Adulthood

In a longitudinal study of 2,500 children of divorce, twenty years after the divorce less than one-third of boys and one-quarter of girls reported having close relationships with their fathers. In contrast, seventy percent of youths from the comparison group of intact families reported feeling close to their fathers.
Source: Hetherington, E. Mavis, and John Kelly. *For Better or For Worse: Divorce Reconsidered.* New York: W.W. Norton and Company, 2002: 231.

College students who experienced divorce reported significantly more current life stress, family conflict, and avoidant coping as well as less supportive parenting (before divorce), family cohesion and friend support. They also reported higher levels of current antisocial behavior, anxiety, and depression than their peers.
Source: Short, Jerome L. "The Effects of Parental Divorce During Childhood on College Students." *Journal of Divorce & Marriage, 38* (2002): 143-155.

A study of 40,000 Taiwanese residents found that insomnia was associated with divorce.
Source: "Why the Sleepless Nights?" *The New York Times* 31 May 2005: D6.

In a representative national sample of 2,592 adults, adult children of divorce had lower levels of education, occupational status, and income; higher levels of economic hardships; were more likely to marry young, divorce, and remarry several times; were more likely to find themselves in unhappy relationships; and were less trustful of people in general. These associations held after controlling for sex, minority status, age, parental death, and parental education.
Source: Ross, Catherine E., and John Mirowsky. "Parental Divorce, Life-Course Disruption, and Adult Depression." *Journal of Marriage and the Family, 61* (November 1999): 1034-1045.

In a 25-year follow-up study of adults who had experienced parental divorce when they were 2 1/2 through 6 years of age, it was found that although the majority graduated from high school, one-third never pursued post-secondary school education despite the fact that two-thirds had fathers who were well-paid professionals or successful businessmen.
Source: Wallerstein, Judith S., and Julia Lewis. "The Long-Term Impact of Divorce on Children: A First Report From a 25-Year Study." *Family and Conciliation Courts Review, 36* (1998): 368-383.

Compared with children raised in single-mother families produced by the death of the father, children raised in single-mother homes produced by divorce have significantly lower levels of education, occupational status, and happiness in adulthood.
Source: Biblarz, Timothy J., and Greg Gottainer. "Family Structure and Children's Success: A Comparison of Widowed and Divorced Single-Mother Families." *Journal of Marriage and the Family, 62* (May 2000): 533-548.

In a study of 7,743 young adults in 39 countries, individuals whose parents remained married reported higher levels of life satisfaction than those whose parents were divorced.
Source: Gohm, Carol L., et al. "Culture, Parental Conflict, Parental Marital Status, and the Subjective Well-Being of Young Adults." *Journal of Marriage and the Family, 60* (1998): 319-334.

...twenty years after the divorce less than one-third of boys and one-quarter of girls reported having close relationships with their fathers.

In a study of 93 engaged couples, couples in which the woman's parents had divorced showed more negative communication during conflict discussions than did couples in which neither partner's parents had divorced.
Source: Sanders, Matthew, W. Kim Halford, and Brett Behrens. "Parental Divorce and Premarital Couple Communication." *Journal of Family Psychology, 13* (1999): 60-74.

Using data from both waves of the National Survey of Families and Households (n=10,008), it was found that children who experience parental family structure transitions such as divorce and remarriage are not only more likely to divorce later in life, but to end multiple marriages. This pattern holds even after controlling for socioeconomic characteristics of both respondents and their families of origin.
Source: Wolfinger, Nicholas H. "Beyond the Intergenerational Transmission of Divorce: Do People Replicate the Patterns of Marital Instability They Grew Up With?" *Journal of Family Issues, 20* (November 2000): 1061-1086.

Using data from Britain's National Child Development Study, it was found that as children of divorce entered into adulthood, the mental health gap separating them from children of intact marriage widened significantly, with children of divorce suffering an increasingly disproportionate share of emotional problems.
Source: Cherlin, Andrew J., P. Lindsay Chase-Landsdale, and Christine McRae. "Effects of Parental Divorce on Mental Health Through the Life Course." *American Sociological Review, 63* (April 1998): 239-249.

In a study of 150 college students, those whose parents had divorced were significantly more likely to say they would divorce for arguing, "no love," and "no magic"— attitudes that predict the likelihood of divorce in the future.
Source: Mulder, Carole, and Marjorie Lindner Gannoe. "Attitudes Toward Divorce Based on Gender, Parental Divorce, and Parental Relationships." *Journal of Divorce and Remarriage, 31* (1999): 179-188.

In a study of young Caucasian adults from divorced (n = 119) and married (n = 123) families, it was found that young adults from married families reported more secure romantic attachments than those from divorced families.
Source: Summers, Pete, Rex Forehand, Lisa Armistead, and Lynne Tannenbaum. "Parental Divorce During Early Adolescence in Caucasian Families: The Role of Family Process Variables in Predicting the Long-Term Consequences for Early Adult Psychosocial Adjustment." *Journal of Consulting & Clinical Psychology, 66* (1998): 327-336.

In a study of 464 adults in romantic relationships, women from divorced families reported less trust and satisfaction and more ambivalence and conflict in their relationships than women from intact families.
Source: Jacquet, Susan E., and Catherine A. Surra. "Parental Divorce and Premarital Couples: Commitment and Other Relationships Characteristics." *Journal of Marriage and the Family, 63* (August 2001): 627-638.

Children of divorce are less likely as adults to offer their needy, elderly parents co-residence with them.
Source: Goldscheider, Frances K., and Leora Lawton. "Family Experiences and the Erosion of Support for Intergenerational Coresidence." *Journal of Marriage and the Family, 60* (August 1998): 623-632.

A study of 418 white, young adults found that young women whose parents had divorced in the past three years were more depressed, more likely to have reported that others said they needed psychological help, and more likely to see themselves as needing psychological help than their peers who lived with both married parents.
Source: Cooney, Teresa M. and Jane Kurz. "Mental Health Outcomes Following Recent Parental Divorce: The Case of Young Adult Offspring." *Journal of Family Issues, 17.4* (July 1996): 495-513.

A longitudinal study of over 1,500 California adults found that those whose parents had divorced died an average of four years sooner than their counterparts whose parents remained married.
Source: Tucker, Joan et al. "Parental Divorce: Effects on Individual Behavior and Longevity." *Journal of Personality and Social Psychology, 73* (1997): 381-191.

A study of 287 undergraduate students found that daughters whose parents had divorced have lower self esteem and less secure attachment styles than women whose parents had remained married.
Source: Evans, Julie J. and Bernard L. Bloom. "Effects of Parental Divorce among College Undergraduates." *Journal of Divorce and Remarriage, 26.1/2* (1997): 69-88.

A study using a nationally representative sample of over 3,700 women found that divorce or family disruption in childhood is significantly related to subsequent out-of-wedlock births. The impact remained significant even when income levels were taken into account.
Source: Wu, Lawrence L. "Effects of Family Instability, Income, and Income Instability on the Risk of a Premarital Birth." *American Sociological Review, 61* (1996): 386-406.

An analysis of a national sample of 1,387 married individuals found that for wives whose parents had divorced, the odds that she would divorce increased by 59%. When the parents of both spouses had divorced, the odds of divorce increased by 189%.
Source: Amato, Paul R. "Explaining the Intergenerational Transmission of Divorce." *Journal of Marriage and the Family, 58* (August 1996): 628-640.

Impact of Divorce on Parenting
Parents have the greatest effect on their children's thoughts on divorce during the late teen years.
Source: Kapinus, Carolyn A. "The Effect of Parents' Attitudes Toward Divorce on Offspring's Attitudes: Gender and Parental Divorce as Mediating Factors." *Journal of Family Issues 25* (January 2004): 112-135.

Divorce affects fathers' and mothers' time with their children differently. In a study of 1,463 men and women, fathers who divorced experienced a decline in weekly contact with their child when compared to stably-married fathers. Although divorced mothers were more likely than stably-married mothers to report an increase in contact with their adult child, they also experienced a slightly higher risk of little or no contact with an adult child.
Source: Shapiro, Adam. "Later-Life Divorce and Parent-Adult Contact and Proximity: A Longitudinal Analysis." *Journal of Family Issues, 24* (March 2003): 264-285.

A study of 112 college students found that those whose parents had divorced had more negative expectations about parenthood than their peers whose parents had remained married.
Source: Langhinrichsen-Rohling, Jennifer, and Collen Dostal. "Retrospective Reports of Family-of-Origin Divorce and Abuse and College Students: Pre-parenthood Cognitions." *Journal of Family Violence, 11* (1996): 331-348.

In a longitudinal study of 1,265 children, children whose parents separated exhibited lower attachment to parents during their adolescence and had more negative perceptions of maternal and paternal care and protection during childhood. These findings persisted after controlling for the confounding effects of family social background, marital conflict, parenting, child behavior, and remarriage.
Source: Woodward, Lianne, David M. Ferguson, and Jay Belsky. "Timing of Parental Separation and Attachment to Parents in Adolescence: Results of a Prospective Study from Birth to Age 16." *Journal of Marriage and the Family 62* (February 2000): 162-174.

...daughters whose parents had divorced have lower self esteem and less secure attachment styles than women whose parents had remained married.

Divorce and non-custody damage father-child relationships less when children are older at the time of divorce.
Source: Amato, P.R., and A. Booth. *A Generation at Risk: Growing Up in an Era of Family Upheaval.* Cambridge, MA: Harvard University Press, 1997.

Using data from a twelve-year longitudinal study of over 2,000 people who were married at the beginning of the study, it was found that after a divorce, lower levels of affection were found between fathers and children, whereas the level of affection between mothers and children remained nearly the same.
Source: Amato, Paul R. and Alan Booth. "A Prospective Study of Divorce and Parent-Child Relationships." *Journal of Marriage and the Family, 58* (May 1996): 356-365.

In a study of over 500 families, divorced, non-residential fathers were less likely to help their children solve problems, to discuss standards of conduct, or to enforce discipline compared with fathers in nuclear families. This reduced involvement in parenting was associated with an increased probability that a boy would display conduct problems.
Source: Simons, Ronald L., et al. "Explaining the Higher Incidence of Adjustment Problems Among Children of Divorce Compared with Those in Two-Parent Families." *Journal of Marriage and the Family, 61* (November 1999): 1020-1033.

Impact of Divorce on the Health of Adults
A study of 8,652 people age 51 to 61 indicated that the longer one spends in a divorced or widowed state, the higher the increase in likelihood of heart and lung disease, cancer, high blood pressure, diabetes, stroke, and lower mobility. People who were married at the time of the study had 20% fewer chronic conditions.
Source: Shellenbarger, Sue. "Another Argument for Marriage: How Divorce Can Put Your Health at Risk." *Wall Street Journal* 16 June 2005: D1; Jayson, Sharon. "Relationships can affect your health years later." *USATODAY.com.* 26 June 2005. Accessed 29 June 2005. <http://www.usatoday.com/news/health/2005-06-26-relationships_x.htm>

Compared with married individuals, divorcees exhibit lower levels of psychological well-being, more health problems and greater risk of mortality, more social isolation, less satisfying sex lives, more negative life events, greater levels of depression and alcohol use, and lower levels of happiness and self-acceptance.
Source: Bramlett, Matthew D., and William D. Mosher. First Marriage Dissolution, Divorce, and Remarriage: United States. Advance Data from Vital and Health Statistics, No. 323. Hyattsville, MD: National Center for Health Statistics, 2001; see also Amato, Paul R. "The Consequences of Divorce for Adults and Children." *Journal of Marriage and the Family, 62.4* (2000): 1269-87.

Using a sample of 844 fathers from the National Survey of Families and Households, it was found that although both custodial and non-custodial divorced dads were more depressed than their married counterparts, divorced fathers with co-resident children were the least happy of all three groups.
Source: Shapiro, Adam, and James D. Lambert. "Longitudinal Effects of Divorce on the Quality of the Father-Child Relationship and on Fathers' Psychological Well-Being." *Journal of Marriage and the Family, 61* (May 1999): 397-408.

Men, compared to women, have poorer adjustments to divorce, lower levels of overall satisfaction, greater morbidity, and lower satisfaction with divorce settlements in regard to custody, visitation, and property settlements.
Source: Kramer, L., and C.A. Washo. "Evaluation of a Court-Mandated Prevention Program for Divorcing Parents: The Children's First Program." Family Relations 42 (1993); 179-186; see also Shapiro, A.D. "Explaining Psychological Distress in a Sample of Remarried and Divorced Persons." Journal of Family Issues 17 (1996): 186-203; and Sheets, V.L., and S.L. Braver. "Gender Differences in Satisfaction with Divorce Settlements." *Family Relations, 45* (1996): 336-342.

> Men, compared to women, have poorer adjustments to divorce, lower levels of overall satisfaction, greater morbidity, and lower satisfaction with divorce settlements in regard to custody, visitation, and property settlements.

A study of 500 married and divorced women found that divorced women had higher levels of stressful events and depression than their married counterparts. This difference was observed immediately following divorce and three years later.

Source: Lorenz, Frederick O. et al. "Married and Recently Divorced Mothers' Stressful Events and Distress: Tracing Change Across Time." *Journal of Marriage and the Family, 59* (1997): 219-232.

Impact of Divorce on Transitions

Children who experienced at least one residential transition averaged 1.86 changes in their living arrangements. Among women who experienced at least one transition, over 60% experienced two transitions and about 30% experienced three transitions.

Source: Teachman, Jay D. "The Childhood Living Arrangements of Children and the Characteristics of Their Marriages." *Journal of Family Issues, 25* (January 2004): 86-111.

Child Custody
Custody Arrangements

In the spring of 2002, 13.4 million parents had custody of 21.5 million children under 21 years of age whose other parent lived elsewhere. Of this total, 5 of every 6 custodial parents were mothers (84.4 percent) and 1 in 6 were fathers (15.6 percent).

Source: Grall, Timothy. *Child Support for Custodial Mothers and Fathers: 2001. Current Population Reports, P60-225.* U.S. Census Bureau. Washington, DC: GPO, 2003.

Mothers become the primary residential parent for 85-90% of all children following divorce, whereas fathers become the primary residential parent for 10-15% of children. This ratio has remained fairly stable throughout the last several decades.

Source: Saluter, Arlene. *Marital Status and Living Arrangements: March 1994. Current Population Reports, P20-484.* U.S. Census Bureau. Washington, D.C.: GPO, 1995.

On average, noncustodial fathers are better off financially than custodial mothers. Whereas 30 percent of custodial families are poor and one quarter of custodial mothers do not work, only 15 percent of noncustodial fathers are poor and 90 percent work.

Source: Wheaton, Laura, and Elaine Sorensen. "Reducing Welfare Costs and Dependency: How Much Bang for the Child Support Buck?" *The Georgetown Public Policy Review, 4* (Fall 1998): 23-37.

Fathers are increasingly likely to ask for and gain shared custody of their children.

Source: Cancian, M., and D.R. Meyer. "Who Gets Custody?" *Demography, 35* (1998): 147-157.

Mothers with joint custody report lower levels of child-rearing stress and better co-parental relations than those with sole custody.

Source: Ardittin, Joyce A., and Debra Madden-Derdich. "Joint and Sole Custody Mothers: Implications for Research and Practice." *Families in Society 78* (Jan/Feb 1997): 36-45.

Families with joint custody had more frequent father-child visitation, more rapid maternal repartnering, and fewer child adjustment problems (net of predivorce selection factors).

Source: Gunnoe, Majorie Lindner and Sanford L. Braver. "The Effects of Joint Legal Custody on Mothers, Fathers, and Children Controlling for Factors That Predispose a Sole Maternal versus Joint Legal Award." *Law and Human Behavior, 25* (2001): 25-43.

About 63% of custodial mothers and 38.6% of fathers had child support awards.

Source: Grall, Timothy. *Child Support for Custodial Mothers and Fathers: 2001. Current Population Reports, P60-225.* U.S. Census Bureau. Washington, DC: GPO, 2003.

Mothers with joint custody report lower levels of child-rearing stress and better co-parental relations than those with sole custody.

About 63% of custodial mothers and 38.6% of fathers had child support awards.

Visitation Arrangements

In 2001, 85.3% of the 6.9 million custodial parents due child support payments in 2001 had arrangements for joint child custody or visitation privileges with non-custodial parents, and approximately three-fourths of these parents received some support payments. Of the custodial parents due child support but who did not have joint custody or visitation agreements, about half received any payments.

Source: Grall, Timothy. *Child Support for Custodial Mothers and Fathers: 2001. Current Population Reports, P60-225*. U.S. Census Bureau. Washington, DC: GPO, 2003.

A study of non-resident fathers participating in a voluntary automatic electronic fund transfer program found the majority of the fathers reported experiencing serious problems with respect to issues related to visitation. No support was found for the assumption that the primary reason for access denial is non-payment of child support.

Source: Fields, Lynda Fox, Beverly W. Mussetter, and Gerald T. Powers. "Children Denied Two Parents: An Analysis of Access Denial." *Journal of Divorce & Remarriage, 28* (1997): 49-62.

Using a sample of 1,172 cases of mother-headed households with non-resident fathers from the first wave of the National Survey of Families and Households (NSFH), a national probability sample of adults in households in the U.S., it was found that the percentage of mothers who were satisfied (85%) with the fathers' involvement was greatest in families in which fathers visited the most.

Source: King, Valarie, and Holly E. Heard. "Nonresident Father Visitation, Parental Conflict, and Mother's Satisfaction: What's Best for Child Well-Being?" *Journal of Marriage and the Family, 61* (May 1999): 385-396.

Effects of Custody Mediation

Although mediation may increase the number of changes in a child's living arrangements due to increased cooperation and flexibility, fathers remain much more satisfied if they mediated rather than went through litigated custody. At the 12-year follow-up, even in contested cases, mediation helps both parents remain involved in their child's life post-divorce without increasing interparental conflict.

Source: Emery, Robert E., Lisa Laumann-Billings, Mary C. Waldron, David A. Sbarra and Peter Dillon. "Child Custody, Mediation and Litigation: Custody, Contact, and Coparenting 12 Years After Initial Dispute Resolution." *Journal of Counseling and Clinical Psychology, 69* (April 2001): 323-332.

Fathers are more likely to stay involved with their children following divorce if they participate in custody mediation instead of custody litigation.

Source: Dillon, P., and R.E. Emery. "Divorce Mediation and Resolution of Child Custody Disputes: Long Term Effects." *American Journal of Orthopsychiatry, 66* (1996): 131-140.

Research involving randomized trials of mediation versus litigation of child custody disputes has found that mediation results in a larger percentage of custody dispute settlements, higher levels of satisfaction, higher rates of compliance with divorce settlements, and greater encouragement of co-parenting cooperation.

Source: Emery, Robert E. "Hanging the Rules for Determining Child Custody in Divorce Cases." Clinical Psychology: Science and Practice 6 (Fall 1999): 323-327; see also Emery, Robert E. Renegotiating Family Relationships: Divorce, Child Custody, and Mediation. New York: Guilford Press, 1994; Emery, Robert E., S. Matthews, and K. Kitzmann. "Child Custody Mediation and Litigation: Parents' Satisfaction and Functioning a Year after Settlement." *Journal of Consulting and Clinical Psychology, 62* (1994): 124-129.

Association Between Custody Arrangements and Frequency of Visitation

There is a positive association between joint legal custody and both child support payments and visiting between divorced fathers and children.

Source: Arditti, J.A. "Differences Between Fathers With Joint Custody and Noncustodial Fathers." *American Journal of Orthopsychiatry, 62* (1992): 186-195; see also Pearson, J.P., and N. Thoennes. "Supporting Children After Divorce: The Influence of Custody on Support Levels and Payments." *Family Law Quarterly, 22* (1988): 319-339.

An analysis of data from the National Survey of Families and Households found that even after controlling for socioeconomic status and the quality of family relationships before separation, fathers with joint legal custody see their children more frequently, have more overnight visits, and pay more child support than fathers in situations where the mothers have sole legal custody.

Source: Seltzer, Judith. "Fathers' by Law: Effects of Joint Legal Custody on Nonresident Fathers' Involvement with Children." *Demography, 35* (May 1998): 135-146.

In a study of 2,100 college students who had experienced divorce as an adolescent, families with joint custody agreements were less likely to move. Of the 40% of families with joint legal custody, only half reported any moves. For the 38% of families with sole maternal custody, 75% had experienced moves. Moreover, children enjoyed more financial support if they did not have to move. They received over $1,800 more per year if they did not relocate with their mother. Young people also worried more when it was the father who moved in contrast to those in the never-moved group.

Source: Braver, Sanford L., Ira M. Ellman, and William V. Fabricius. "Relocation of Children After Divorce and Children's Best Interests: New Evidence and Legal Considerations." *Journal of Family Psychology, 17* (June 2003): 206-219.

Frequency of Visitation and Child Well-Being

Using a sample of 1,172 cases of mother-headed households with non-resident fathers from the first wave of the National Survey of Families and Households, frequent father-child contact was not related to child well-being.

Source: King, Valarie, and Holly E. Heard. "Nonresident Father Visitation, Parental Conflict, and Mother's Satisfaction: What's Best for Child Well-Being?" *Journal of Marriage and the Family, 61* (May 1999): 385-396.

A 25-year follow-up of adults who had experienced parental divorce when they were 2.5 through 6 years of age found that no child who saw his or her father under a rigidly enforced court order or unmodified parental agreement had a good relationship with him after reaching adulthood.

Source: Wallerstein, Judith S., and Julia Lewis. "The Long-Term Impact of Divorce on Children: A First Report From a 25-Year Study." *Family and Conciliation Courts Review, 36* (1998): 368-383.

Comparison of Different Custody Arrangements on Child Well-Being

In an analysis of youths living in single-mother and single-father households using the 1990 wave of the National Education Longitudinal Study and among adults reared by single parents using data from the General Social Surveys, 1972-1994, no difference was found between those living with their single mothers versus those living with their single fathers.

Source: Downey, Douglas B., James W. Ainsworth-Darnell, and Mikaela J. Dufur. "Sex of Parent and Children's Well-Being in Single Parent Households." *Journal of Marriage and the Family, 60* (November 1998): 878-893.

There is a positive association between joint legal custody and both child support payments and visiting between divorced fathers and children.

Child Support

"To me, that's the easy way out: give [the kids] some money and then run off. The money doesn't comfort them at night. They can't say, "Hey, Dollar Bill, I had a nightmare last night" and expect the Dollar Bill to rock them and hold them. Money is there because it is a necessity. But if you give a child love and attention, money is the last thing they are going to look for."

ISAIAH, AGE 40, AS QUOTED IN: ROY, KEVIN. "LOW-INCOME SINGLE FATHERS IN AN AFRICAN-AMERICAN COMMUNITY AND THE REQUIREMENTS OF WELFARE REFORM." JOURNAL OF FAMILY ISSUES 20 (JULY 1999): 432-457.

Child Support Awards

In 2001, 59.1% of custodial parents had child support agreements in place. Parents without awards most often explained that they didn't get an award because they didn't feel they needed one or because the other parent couldn't afford to pay. Award rates were 63% for mothers and 3.6% for fathers.

Source: Grall, Timothy. *Child Support for Custodial Mothers and Fathers: 2001*. Current Population Reports, P60-225. U.S. Census Bureau. Washington, DC: GPO, 2003.

If a custodial parent has a low income (between $12,500 and $17,000) and the noncustodial parent has an income of $25,000, neither parent can cover their expenditures and the children will suffer. Only when the custodial parent has an income above $25,000 and receives income from her ex who has an income of at least $25,000, that she is able to cover her expenses for two persons (mother and child).

The noncustodial parent who is paying regular child support always is in the red. If he is able to increase his income to $35,000, he is still in the red and cannot cover his expenses unless his spends at a lower income category. (The average income for a single householder with no children is $36,000 a year.) If his income remains at $25,000, then he would need to spend at the next income level of $17,000 a year.

Source: Folse, Kimberly and Hugo Varela-Alvarez. "Long-run economic consequences of child support enforcement for the middle class." *The Journal of Socio-Economics 31* (2002): 273-286.; DeNavas-Walt, Carmen and Robert Cleveland. *Money Income in the United States, 2001*. Current Population Reports, P60-218. Table 1. Washington, DC: U.S. Census Bureau, 2002: 4.

Amount of Child Support Paid

In 2001, $21.9 billion (62.6 percent) of the $34.9 billion in child support owed was actually paid.

Source: Grall, Timothy. *Child Support for Custodial Mothers and Fathers: 2001*. Current Population Reports, P60-225. U.S. Census Bureau. Washington, DC: GPO, 2003.

$20.1 billion in child support was collected in Fiscal Year 2002, compared to $15.8 billion in 1999, $14.3 billion in 1998, and $13.4 billion in 1997.

Source: *Child Support Enforcement FY 2002 Preliminary Data Report*. Table 13. U.S. Department of Health and Human Services, Administration for Children and Families, Office of Child Support Enforcement: Washington, DC, 2003.

In 2001, 59.1% of custodial parents had child support agreements in place.

In 2001, $21.9 billion (62.6 percent) of the $34.9 billion in child support owed was actually paid.

The federal government collected $1.1 billion in delinquent child support by intercepting income tax refunds of non-paying parents for Fiscal Year 1998, a 70% increase since 1992. Collections from tax refunds were made on behalf of nearly 1.3 million families, including 869,000 families with children receiving TANF and 428,000 non-TANF families.

Source: *Child Support Enforcement FY 1999 Preliminary Data Report.* Table 3. U.S. Department of Health and Human Services, Administration for Children and Families, Office of Child Support Enforcement: Washington, D.C., 2000.

Proportion of Child Support Paid

Only 52 percent of children with a parent living elsewhere receive any financial assistance from their nonresident parent.

Source: Sorensen, Elaine, and Chava Zibman. "To What Extent Do Children Benefit from Child Support?" Washington, D.C.: *The Urban Institute,* January 2000.

In 2001, just 44.8 percent of custodial parents due child support received all of the payments they were due, up from only 41 percent in 1997. Over the same period, the proportion of custodial parents receiving at least a portion of the amount owed decreased slightly from 75 percent to 74 percent.

Source: Grall, Timothy. *Child Support for Custodial Mothers and Fathers: 2001.* Current Population Reports, P60-225. U.S. Census Bureau. Washington, DC: GPO, 2003.

Of the 7.1 million mothers due child support payments in 2001:
- 45.4% received the full payment
- 74.7% received partial payment
- 22.1% never received payment

Of the 674,000 fathers due child support payments in 1997:
- 39.0% received the full payment
- 67.4% received partial payment
- 28.7 never received payment.

Source: Grall, Timothy. *Child Support for Custodial Mothers and Fathers: 2001.* Current Population Reports, P60-225. U.S. Census Bureau. Washington, DC: GPO, 2003.

According to an analysis of more than 20 years of household survey data collected by the U.S. Census Bureau, in 1976 only 4 percent of never married mothers received child support; by 1997, the percent of never married mothers who received child support had increased to 18 percent. In 2001, the number stood at 31.2%.

Source: Sorensen, Elaine J. *Testimony before the Subcommittee on Human Resources of the House Committee on Ways and Means, U.S. House of Representatives.* September 23, 1999.; Source: Grall, Timothy. *Child Support for Custodial Mothers and Fathers: 2001.* Current Population Reports, P60-225. U.S. Census Bureau. Washington, DC: GPO, 2003.

Association Between Payment of Child Support and Custody Arrangement/Visitation

In 2001, 77 percent of noncustodial parents who had either joint custody or visitation rights paid some or all of the child support they owed, compared to only 55.8 percent of noncustodial parents without either joint custody or visitation rights.

Source: Grall, Timothy. *Child Support for Custodial Mothers and Fathers: 2001.* Current Population Reports, P60-225. U.S. Census Bureau. Washington, DC: GPO, 2003.

Only 52 percent of children with a parent living elsewhere receive any financial assistance from their nonresident parent.

In a study of 135 African-American unwed mothers in Baltimore, only 27% of the fathers who did not provide financial assistance to their children saw their children regularly (once a month or more), compared to 84% of the fathers who did provide financial assistance.
Source: Coley, Rebekah Levine, and P. Lindsay Chase-Lindsdale. "Stability and Change in Paternal Involvement Among Urban African American Fathers." *Journal of Family Psychology, 13* (1999): 416-435.

In a study using a nationally representative sample of 164 divorced families, it was found that fathers with joint legal custody see their children more frequently, have more overnight visits, and pay more child support than fathers in families in which the mother has sole legal custody.
Source: Seltzer, Judith A. "Father by Law: Effects of Joint Legal Custody on Nonresidential Fathers' Involvement with Children." *Conference on Father Involvement.* National Institute of Child and Human Development. Bethesda, Maryland. 10-11 Oct. 1996.

Other Predictors of Child Support Payment

Using data from two waves of the National Survey of Families and Households, it was found that non-resident fathers who live farther away from their children pay less child support than fathers who live closer.
Source: Manning, Wendy D., and Pamela J. Smock. "'Swapping' Families: Serial Parenting and Economic Support for Children." *Journal of Marriage and the Family, 62* (February 2000): 111-122.

According to data from the Panel Survey of Income Dynamics, states' that adopted unilateral divorce laws caused to large downward trend in child support payments between 1968 and 1997. On average, when a state allows unilateral divorce laws, real child support payments decrease by $300 for ever-married women. Inflation was also culpable for the decline.
Source: Case, Anne C., I-Fen Lin, and Sara S. McLanahan. "Explaining Trends in Child Support: Economic, Demographic, and Policy Effects." *Demography, 40* (February 2003): 171-189.

In a study of five-year compliance patterns among Wisconsin child support cases, it was found that never-married fathers were significantly less likely to pay child support, and the amount they paid declined more rapidly over time, compared with divorced fathers.
Source: Meyer, Daniel R., and Judi Bartfeld. "Patterns of Child Support Compliance in Wisconsin." *Journal of Marriage and the Family, 60* (May 1998): 309-318.

In a study of 133 non-resident fathers, it was found that fathers "swap" families when they form new ones: child support payments to non-residential children dropped when new biological children appeared in the father's home.
Source: Manning, Wendy D., and Pamela J. Smock. "'Swapping' Families: Serial Parenting and Economic Support for Children." *Journal of Marriage and the Family, 62* (February 2000): 111-122.

In Maryland, child support payments increased 9% over a three-month period once a driver's license suspension program for non-child-support-paying parents had been implemented.
Source: Child Support. The Children's Foundation. Washington, D.C. (June 1997).

...never-married fathers were significantly less likely to pay child support.

Impact of Child Support on Poverty

In 2001, 23.4 percent of custodial parents with awards who did not receive any child support due them were poor, compared to 33.3 percent in 1993. Despite the decrease, the rate for custodial parent families was still four times higher than the rate for married-couples (6.1%) in 2001.
Source: Grall, Timothy. Child Support for Custodial Mothers and Fathers: 2001. Current Population Reports, P60-225. U.S. Census Bureau. Washington, DC: GPO, 2003.

In 2001, the poverty rate of custodial mothers was two times higher than the poverty rate for custodial fathers, with 25.0 percent of custodial mothers living in poverty. This number, however, was down from 36.8% in 1993.
Source: Grall, Timothy. Child Support for Custodial Mothers and Fathers: 2001. Current Population Reports, P60-225. U.S. Census Bureau. Washington, DC: GPO, 2003.

For mothers and fathers who received child support payments in 1997, child support payments accounted for 16% of custodial mothers' total income and 8% of custodial fathers' income.
Source: Grall, Timothy. Child Support for Custodial Mothers and Fathers: 1997. Current Population Reports, P60-212. U.S. Census Bureau. Washington, D.C.: GPO, 2000.

Child support collections reduced the combined cost of AFDC, Food Stamps, and Medicaid by 2 percent in 1989. If all custodial mothers had child support orders that were fully paid, child support collections could reduce costs by another 8 percent.
Source: Harper, Cynthia, and Sara McLanahan. "Father Absence and Youth Incarceration." Paper presented at the annual meeting of the American Sociological Association. San Francisco, CA, 1998.

Impact of Child Support on Mothers and Fathers

Fathers neither lessen nor increase their work effort in response to the amount of child support they are required to pay. On the other hand, receiving child support results in women reducing their work effort and being employed fewer hours per week, enabling them to spend more time at home with their children.
Source: Klawitter, M. "Child Support Awards and the Earnings of Divorced Non-Custodial Fathers." *Social Service Review, 68* (September 1994): 351-368; see also Klawitter, M. "Who Gains, Who Loses From Changing U.S. Child Support Policies?" *Policy Sciences 27* (1994): 197-219; and Freeman, Richard B., and Jane Waldfogel. "Does Child Support Enforcement Policy Affect Male Labor Supply?" In Irwin Garfinkel, Sara S. McLanahan, Daniel R. Meyer, and Judith A. Seltzer (Eds.), *Fathers Under Fire: The Revolution in Child Support Enforcement*. New York: Russell Sage Foundation, 1998: 94-127.

Aggressive child support enforcement reduces the likelihood of remarriage, especially for low-income men. Once fathers remarry, however, child support enforcement is unlikely to prevent them from having children in subsequent marriages.
Source: Bloom, David E., Cecilia Conrad, and Cynthia Miller. "Child Support and Fathers' Remarriage and Fertility." In Irwin Garfinkel, Sara S. McLanahan, Daniel R. Meyer, and Judith A. Seltzer (Eds.), *Fathers Under Fire: The Revolution in Child Support Enforcement*. New York: Russell Sage Foundation, 1998: 128-156.

Stronger child support enforcement reduces the likelihood that a non-resident father will father a child out-of-wedlock.
Source: Case, Anne. "The Effects of Stronger Child Support Enforcement on Nonmarital Fertility." In Irwin Garfinkel, Sara S. McLanahan, Daniel R. Meyer, and Judith A. Seltzer (Eds.), *Fathers Under Fire: The Revolution in Child Support Enforcement*. New York: Russell Sage Foundation, 1998: 191-215.

When child support payments increase beyond $2,000 per year, the incidence of serious parental conflict rises.
Source: Seltzer, Judith A., Sara S. McLanahan, and Thomas L. Hanson. "Will Child Support Enforcement Increase Father-Child Contact and Parental Conflict after Separation?" In Irwin Garfinkel, Sara S. McLanahan, Daniel R. Meyer, and Judith A. Seltzer (Eds.), *Fathers Under Fire: The Revolution in Child Support Enforcement*. New York: Russell Sage Foundation, 1998: 31-60.

In 2001, the poverty rate of custodial mothers was two times higher than the poverty rate for custodial fathers.

Stronger child support enforcement reduces the likelihood that a non-resident father will father a child out-of-wedlock.

Impact of Child Support on Child Well-Being

In a study of 7,346 children from the National Longitudinal Survey of Youth, nonresident father visitation was not related to any of the measures of child well-being, but child support payments were associated with better outcomes in terms of scholastic competence and achievement.
Source: King, Valerie. "Variation in the Consequences of Nonresident Father Involvement for Children's Well-being." *Journal of Marriage and the Family, 56* (1999): 963-972.

In a review of 12 studies published since 1990 that examined associations between fathers' payment of child support and child outcomes, 9 studies reported a positive and significant relationship between the amount of child support paid by nonresident fathers and child well-being, including school grades and behavior problems at school, reading and math scores, and years of educational attainment.
Source: Marsiglio, William, Paul Amato, Randal D. Day, and Michael E. Lamb. "Scholarship on Fatherhood in the 1990s and Beyond: Past Impressions, Future Prospects." *Journal of Marriage and the Family, 62* (2000): 1173-1191.

In a longitudinal study of 6,403 males who were 14 to 22 years old at the time of initial contact, it was found that receipt of child support did not reduce the risk of future incarceration for boys growing up in divorced, unmarried, or stepfamilies.
Source: Harper, Cynthia, and Sara McLanahan. "Father Absence and Youth Incarceration." Paper presented at the annual meeting of the American Sociological Association. San Francisco, CA, 1998.

Using data from the 1996 National Household Education Survey (n = 20,702), children whose non-resident fathers paid child support were more likely to get A's and less likely to have ever repeated a grade, been suspended, or expelled than students whose nonresident fathers paid no child support.
Source: Nord, Christine Winquist, and Jerry West. *Fathers' and Mothers' Involvement in Their Children's Schools by Family Type and Resident Status.* NCES 2001-032. Washington, D.C.: U.S. Department of Education, National Center for Education Statistics, 2001.

The beneficial effects of child support are greater when the child support agreement is reached cooperatively rather than by court order.
Source: Argys, L.M., H.E. Peters, J. Brooks-Gunn, and J.R. Smith. *Contributions of Absent Fathers to Child Well-Being: The Impact of Child Support Dollars and Father-Child Contact.* Paper presented at the NICHD Conference on Father Involvement. Bethesda, MD, 1996.

A study of the effects of child support payments found that receipt of child support positively affects children's cognitive ability and behavior.
Source: Argys, L.M., H.E. Peters, J. Brooks-Gunn, and J.R. Smith. *Contributions of Absent Fathers to Child Well-Being: The Impact of Child Support Dollars and Father-Child Contact.* Paper presented at the NICHD Conference on Father Involvement. Bethesda, MD, 1996.

A study using a national sample of 637 women who had received welfare found that women who received child support were less likely to return to welfare after they had left the rolls. In contrast, women who had left welfare and did not receive any child support payments were 31% more likely to return to welfare than those who had received child support payments.
Source: Meyer, Daniel R. and Maria Cancian. Wisconsin Department of Workforce Development. Rept., December 1996.

...receipt of child support positively affects children's cognitive ability and behavior.

Stepfamilies

"Suddenly it was like—bang, zoom!—there were eight kids around. I remember we had to draw a picture of our house and family and I ran out of places to put people, I put them on the roof. When [my dad and step-mom] split up, I never saw those people again."

TOM HANKS, ACTOR, REFLECTING ON HIS FATHER'S REMARRIAGE TO A WOMAN WITH FIVE CHILDREN, AS CITED IN BARBARA DAFOE WHITEHEAD, *THE DIVORCE CULTURE*, ALFRED KNOPF, NEW YORK, 1997.

"[A stepfamily is like] a trolley car that rolls along the tracks, with people getting on and off."

WILLIAM R. BEER, "STRANGERS IN THE HOUSE: THE WORLD OF STEPSIBLINGS AND HALF-STEPSIBLINGS," 1989.

"No kid is aching to get a stepparent, so expect a long and sometimes arduous period. Don't take it personally. The child is mournful or angry over the absence of the biological parent and may not necessarily dislike [the stepparent]; she just doesn't like the arrangement."

YLONDA GAULT CAVINESS IN *ESSENCE*, DECEMBER 2002.

The Facts About Stepfamilies

In 2001, of the 72.5 million children living in the United States:
- 14.6% lived in blended families (10.6 million)
- 7% lived with at least one stepparent (5.1 million)
- 11% lived with at least one stepsibling or half-sibling (8.1 million)

Source: Kreider, Rose M. and Jason Fields. *Living Arrangements of Children: 2001*. Current Population Studies, P70-104. Table 6. Washington, D.C.: US Census Bureau, 2005.

About four-fifths of the children living with a stepparent in 2001 lived with their biological mother and a stepfather.

Source: Kreider, Rose M. and Jason Fields. *Living Arrangements of Children: 2001*. Current Population Studies, P70-104. Table 6. Washington, D.C.: US Census Bureau, 2005.

From 1980 to 1990, the number of stepfamilies in the U.S. increased by 36 percent to 5.3 million.

Source: "Stepparent Families and the Payment of Child Support." U.S. Department of Health and Human Services, Office of Child Support Enforcement. *Child Support Report, 22* (February 2000): 3.

According to a 1997 Gallup Youth Survey, 11 percent of American teens live with a stepfather.

Source: Gallup, George. "Report on Status of Fatherhood In the United States." *Emerging Trends, 20* (September 1998): 3-5. Published by the Princeton Religion Research Center, Princeton, NJ.

A recent estimate indicates that about 40% of all women and 30% of all children will spend some time in a stepfamily, when accounting for both remarriages and cohabitation.

Source: Bumpass, Larry L., R. Kelly Raley, and James A. Sweet. "The Changing Character of Stepfamilies: Implications of Cohabitation and Nonmarital Childbearing." *Demography, 32* (August 1995): 425-437.

...about 40% of all women and 30% of all children will spend some time in a stepfamily...

Stability of Stepfamilies

An analysis of 8,177 ever-married men and women revealed that couples who raise stepchildren face a risk of divorce over 4 times greater than couples without stepchildren.

Source: Hall, David R.and John Z. Zhao. "Cohabitation and Divorce in Canada: Testing the Selectivity Hypothesis." *Journal of Marriage and the Family, 57* (1995): 421-427.

A study using a nationally representative sample of 9,463 adults indicated that more than half of all stepfamilies were disrupted after ten years.

Source: Bumpass, Larry L., R. Kelly Raley, and James A. Sweet. "The Changing Character of Stepfamilies: Implications of Cohabitation and Nonmarital Childbearing." *Demography, 32* (August 1995): 425-437.

Research has found that "second marriages run a greater risk of dissolution than first marriages, and the risk is even higher when children are involved."

Source: Bray, James H. "Children's Development in Early Remarriage." *Impact of Divorce, Single Parenting, and Stepparenting on Children.* Eds. E.M. Hetherington and J.D. Arasteh. Hillsdale, New Jersey: 279-298.

Stepfamily Relationships

In a study of 86 stepfamilies and 65 intact, biological families, stepfamilies had less favorable overall conditions of contact and evidenced less cooperation than biological families.

Source: Banker, Brenda S., and Samuel L. Gaertner. "Achieving Stepfamily Harmony: An Intergroup-Relations Approach." *Journal of Family Psychology, 12* (1998): 310-325.

Differences Between Stepfather and Stepmother Families

Stepmother families have been found to be more problematic than stepfather families.

Source: Fine, M.Q., P. Voyandoff, and B.W. Donnelly. "Relations Between Parental Control and Warmth and Child Well-Being in Stepfamilies." Journal of Family Psychology 7 (1993): 222-232; see also Furstenberg, FF., Jr. "The New Extended Family: The Experience of Parents and Children After Remarriage." In K. Pasley and M. Ihinger-Tallman (Eds.) *Remarriage and Stepparenting: Current Research and Theory.* New York: Guilford Press, 1987: 42-61.

In a study of 86 stepfamilies and 65 intact, biological families, members of stepfather families were found to have more favorable overall conditions of family contact and evidenced more cooperation within the family than stepmother families.

Source: Banker, Brenda S., and Samuel L. Gaertner. "Achieving Stepfamily Harmony: An Intergroup-Relations Approach." *Journal of Family Psychology, 12* (1998): 310-325.

Stepfather Well-Being

In a study of pre- and post-partum depression in men, it was found that men living in step-families and partners of single mothers experienced more than twice the rates of depressive symptoms before and after the birth than men in intact, married households.

Source: Deater-Deckard, Kirby, Kevin Pickering, Judith F. Dunn, and Jean Golding. "Family Structure and Depressive Symptoms in Men Preceding and Following the Birth of a Child." *American Journal of Psychiatry, 155* (June 1998): 818-823.

..."second marriages run a greater risk of dissolution than first marriages, and the risk is even higher when children are involved."

Stepparent-Stepchild Relationships

Stepparent-child relationships have been characterized as more detached, more conflicted, more negative, less warm, and less involved than parent-child relationships in first marriages.

Source: Bray, J.H., and S.H. Berger. "Developmental Issues in Stepfamilies Research Project: Family Relationships and Parent-Child Interactions." *Journal of Family Psychology, 7* (1993): 76-90; see also Hetherington, E.M., and W.G. Clingempeel. "Coping with Marital Transitions: A Family Systems Perspective." *Monographs of the Society for Research in Child Development, 57* (Serial No. 227, 1992); Anderson, J.Z., and G.D. White. "An Empirical Investigation of Interaction and Relationship Patterns in Functional and Dysfunctional Nuclear Families and Stepfamilies." *Family Process 25* (1986): 407-422; Sauer, L.E., and M.A. Fine. "Parent-Child Relationships in Stepparent Families." *Journal of Family Psychology, 1* (1988): 434-451; and White, Lynn. "Contagion in Family Affection: Mothers, Fathers, and Young Adult Children." *Journal of Marriage and the Family, 61* (May 1999): 284-294.

Remarriage does not confer upon stepparents any legal relationship with their stepchildren.

Source: "Stepparent Families and the Payment of Child Support." U.S. Department of Health and Human Services, Office of Child Support Enforcement. *Child Support Report, 22* (February 2000): 3.

Using data from the National Survey of Families and Households (NSFH), 31 percent of step-fathers said it was difficult to get relatives to treat stepchildren the same as biological children.

Source: Marsiglio, W. "Stepfathers with Minor Children Living at Home: Parenting Perceptions and Relationship Quality." *Journal of Family Issues, 13* (1995): 214.

A study of 39 stepfathers found that those who frequently showed both warmth and control parenting behaviors reported having better adjusted to their stepparenting role than the stepfathers who did not engage in these behaviors.

Source: Fine, Mark A., Lawrence H. Ganong, and Marilyn Coleman. "The Relation Between Role Constructions and Adjustments Among Stepfathers." *Journal of Family Issues, 18.5,* (September 1997): 503-525.

In a study using a national probability sample of 1,250 fathers of school-aged children it was found that stepfathers spent less time with children than fathers in family structures where there are two biological parents.

Source: Cooksey, Elizabeth C. and Michelle M. Fondell. "Spending Time with His Kids: Effects of Family Structure on Fathers' and Children's Lives." *Journal of Marriage and the Family, 58* (August 1996): 693-707.

A Gallup Youth Survey indicated that less than 1% of teens felt that their stepparent best understood them, compared to 31% who said their biological mothers best understood them and 14% who said it was their biological father who best understood them.

Source: "Youthviews." *Gallup Youth Survey, 4* (June 1997).

Adjustment of Boys and Girls in Stepfamilies

Of adolescents with residential fathers, 81% percent agreed or strongly agreed that they think highly of their father. Almost two-thirds (61 percent) agreed or strongly agreed that they wanted to be like their father. More than three-quarters (76 percent) reported that they enjoy time spent with their father.

Children from biological and stepparent families, however, feel differently from each other. In mid-adolescence, 82% of teens living with biological parents thought highly of their fathers, compared to 67% of teens from stepparent families. Sixty-three percent of teens with biological fathers agreed with "I want to be like my [father figure]," compared to only 39% of children with stepfathers. For the statement, "I enjoy spending time with my [father figure]," the proportions were 78 percent and 59 percent, respectively.

Source: Moore, Kristin A., et al. *Parent-Teen Relationships and Interactions: Far More Positive Than Not.* Child Trends Research Brief. Publication # 2004.25. Washington, DC: Child Trends, 2004.

A study using a national sample of 482 adolescents showed that when a stepfather enters the home, children exhibit more behavioral problems compared to their peers who live with both biological parents, and the impact is stronger for boys than for girls.

Source: Mott, Frank L., Lori Kowaleski-Jones, and Elizabeth G. Menaghen. "Paternal Absence and Child Behavior: Does a Child's Gender Make a Difference?" *Journal of Marriage and the Family, 59* (February 1997): 103-118.

Consequences of Stepfamilies for Child Well-Being
Stepfamilies Compared to Single-Parent Families

Studies find that remarriage by a single mother "does not resolve the negative consequences for her child(ren) that are associated with growing up in a single-parent family."

Source: U.S. Department of Health and Human Services. Public Health Service. Center for Disease Control and Prevention. National Center for Health Statistics. *Report to Congress on Out-of-Wedlock Childbearing.* Hyattsville, MD (Sept. 1995): 13.

Educational Problems

Children raised by step-, adoptive-, or foster mothers obtain one year less schooling, on average, than her other birth children.

Source: Case, Anne, I-Fen Lin, and Sara McLanahan. "Educational attainment of siblings in stepfamilies." *Evolution and Human Behavior, 22* (July 2001): 269-289.

Emotional and Behavioral Problems

Using a sample of 994 two-parent married households, it was found that families with a stepfather were marked by less father and mother involvement and that children living with a stepfather generally had more behavior problems than those living with two biological parents. However, when stepfathers were highly involved with their stepchildren, the children exhibited fewer behavior problems.

Source: Amato, Paul R., and Fernando Rivera. "Paternal Involvement and Children's Behavior Problems." *Journal of Marriage and the Family, 61*(1999): 375-384.

Number of Children in Various Family Arrangements, 2004

	Total	White	Black	Hispanic*
Total	73,205	55,902	11,424	13,752
Living with Two Parents	49,603	41,550	3,972	8,886
Living with One Parent	20,474	12,518	6,415	4,220
Living with Single Mother	17,072	10,050	5,758	3,489
Living with Single Father	3,402	2,468	657	731
Living with Neither Parent	3,129	1,834	1,037	646
Living with Grandparents	1,504	826	586	246
Living with Other Relatives	796	449	265	235
Living in Other Arrangement	829	560	186	166

*Persons of Hispanic origin may be of any race.
Source: U.S. Census Bureau. "Household Relationship and Living Arrangements of Children Under 18 Years, by Age, Sex, Race, Hispanic Origin: 2004; All Races, White only, Black only, and Hispanic only." Table C2. Internet Release Date June 29, 2005. <http://www.census.gov/population/socdemo/hh-fam/cps2004/tabC2-all.csv>

In a longitudinal study of 6,403 males who were 14 to 22 years old at the time of initial contact, it was found that after controlling for family background variables such as mother's education level, race, family income, and number of siblings, as well as neighborhood variables such as unemployment rates and median income, boys who grew up in stepparent families were almost three times as likely to end up in prison compared to those reared in intact, two-parent households.
Source: Harper, Cynthia, and Sara McLanahan. "Father Absence and Youth Incarceration." Paper presented at the annual meeting of the American Sociological Association, San Francisco, CA, 1998.

In a study of 427 French-Canadian boys participating in a longitudinal study from kindergarten onwards, it was found that boys who experienced remarriage between the ages of 12 and 15 were at greater risk for delinquency, and especially theft and fighting, than those who did not.
Source: Pagani, Linda, Richard E. Tremblay, Frank Vitaro, Margaret Kerr, et al. "The Impact of Family Transition on the Development of Delinquency in Adolescent Boys: A 9-Year Longitudinal Study." *Journal of Child Psychology & Psychiatry & Allied Disciplines, 39* (May 1998): 489-499.

A study of 648 children living in New York found that those children living within a stepfamily had a higher risk of developing disruptive disorders compared to children who lived with two biological parents. Girls living within stepfamilies were at a higher risk of suffering from depression and anxiety disorders compared to girls who lived with both biological parents.
Source: Kasen, Stephanie, et al. "A Multiple-Risk Interaction Model: Effects of Temperament and Divorce on Psychiatric Disorders in Children." *Journal of Abnormal Child Psychology, 24* (1996): 121-150.

In a survey of 272 high school students, family cohesion and marital status were the strongest protective factors against suicidal behavior, with students in intact families as the least likely to be suicidal and those in remarried families as the most likely to be suicidal. Thirty-eight percent of teens in stepfamilies reported suicidal behavior, compared to 20 percent among teens from single-parent homes, and just 9 percent among teens from intact families.
Source: Rubenstein, Judith L., et al. "Suicidal Behavior in Adolescents: Stress and Protection in Different Family Contexts." *American Journal of Orthopsychiatry 68* (1998): 274-284.

A Canadian study examining the ages at which young children leave home found that children living in stepfamilies left home earlier than their peers who lived with both biological parents.
Source: Zhao, John, Fernando Rajulton, and Zenaida R. Ravanera. "Leaving Parental Homes in Canada: Effects of Family Structure, Gender, and Culture." *Canadian Journal of Sociology/ Revue canadienne de sociologie, 20* (Winter 1995): 31-50.

Child Abuse

In a longitudinal study of 644 families in upstate New York, children living in stepfather families were three times more likely to be abused than children in non-stepfather households.
Source: Brown, Jocelyn, et al. "A Longitudinal Analysis of Risk Factors for Child Maltreatment: Findings of a 17-Year Prospective Study of Officially Recorded and Self-Reported Child Abuse and Neglect." *Child Abuse & Neglect, 22* (1998): 1065-1078.

Cohabitation

"Premarital cohabitation tends to be associated with lower marital quality and to increase the risk of divorce. Given wide variation in data, samples, measures of marital instability, and independent variables, the degree of consensus about this central finding is impressive."

PAMELA J. SMOCK. "COHABITATION IN THE UNITED STATES: AN APPRAISAL OF RESEARCH THEMES, FINDINGS, AND IMPLICATIONS." *ANNUAL REVIEW OF SOCIOLOGY 26* (2000): 1-20.

"In marriage, the goal is taking care of the other person, in sickness and in health, for richer or poorer. Contrast this with cohabitation, where the goal is not so much to determine whether I am up to the task of taking care of your needs, but whether you are up to the task of taking care of mine. The 'trial' in a trial marriage is not a test of oneself, but a test of the other. When cohabitors assert that they are testing their compatibility for each other, what they really mean is that they are testing how well the other person fulfills their needs."

WADE HORN, PH.D., "FATHERLY ADVICE" COLUMNIST, *THE WASHINGTON TIMES*, MARCH 31, 1998.

Attitudes About Cohabitation

Only 19% of high school seniors expressed negative views on cohabitation. Eighty two percent said cohabiting couples are "experimenting with a worthwhile alternative lifestyle" or "doing their own thing and not affecting anybody else."
Source: Bachman, Jerald G., et al. "Monitoring the Future: Questionnaire Responses from the Nation's High School Seniors." The University of Michigan. Ann Arbor, MI: Survey Research Center at the Institute for Social Research, 2002.

Sixty-two percent of men and women age 20-29 agree that living together with someone before marriage is a good way to avoid an eventual divorce.
Source: Whitehead, Barbara Dafoe, and David Popenoe. "The State of Our Unions 2001: The Social Health of Marriage in America." Piscataway, NJ: The National Marriage Project, 2001.

Poor, Unmarried Parents' Beliefs About Marriage

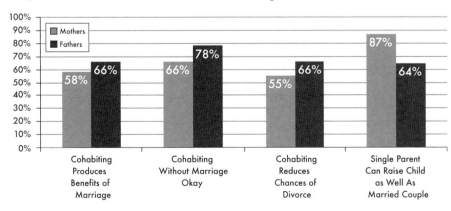

Source: Mincy, Ron, et al. Fragile Families in Focus: Executive Summary. Chart VIII. Baton Rouge, LA: TANF Executive Office of Oversight and Evaluation, 2004: 12.

Nearly 60% of high school seniors agreed that "it is usually a good idea for a couple to live together before getting married in order to find out whether they really get along."
Source: Bachman, J.G., L. D. Johnston and P. M. O'Malley. *Monitoring the Future: Questionnaire Responses from the Nation's High School Seniors, 1995.* Ann Arbor, MI: Survey Research Center at the University of Michigan, 1997.

Forty-three percent of men and women in their twenties reported that they would only marry someone if he or she agreed to live together with them first, in order to find out whether they really get along.
Source: Whitehead, Barbara Dafoe, and David Popenoe. "The State of Our Unions 2001: The Social Health of Marriage in America." Piscataway, NJ: The National Marriage Project, 2001.

The Facts About Cohabitation

In 2003, 4.6 million unwed couples lived together down from 5.5 million in 2000. Only 523,000 couples lived together outside of marriage in 1970.
Source: Fields, Jason. 2003. *America's Families and Living Arrangements, 2003.* Current Population Reports, P20-553. Table 8. U.S. Census Bureau, Washington, DC.; U.S. Census Bureau. Profiles of General Demographic Characteristics: 2000. 2000 Census of Population and Housing. Table DP-1. Washington, DC: GPO, 2001; see also U.S. Census Bureau. *Marital Status and Living Arrangements: March 1998* (Update). Current Population Reports, P20-514. Washington, DC: GPO, 1998; Whitehead, Barbara Dafoe, and David Popenoe. *The State of Our Unions 2001: The Social Health of Marriage in America.* Figure 7. Piscataway, NJ: The National Marriage Project, 2001.

40% of all cohabitations among men and women involve parents with children.
Source: *Child Trends,* "Charting Parenthood: A Statistical Portrait of Fathers and Mothers in America." Ed. Tamara Halle. Washington DC, 2004.

Among unmarried women ages 25 to 39, about half have lived with an unmarried partner at some time in the past, and about one-quarter are currently living with a partner. Nearly half of the cohabiting unions among couples in this age group include children.
Source: Bumpass, Larry, and Hsien-Hen Lu. "Trends in Cohabitation and Implications for Children's Family Contexts in the U.S." *Population Studies, 54* (March 2000): 29-41.

Over half (56%) of all first marriages are now preceded by cohabitation, compared to only 11% of marriages in 1970.
Source: Bumpass, Larry, and Hsien-Hen Lu. "Trends in Cohabitation and Implications for Children's Family Contexts in the U.S." CDE Working Paper No. 98-15. Center for Demography Ecology, University of Wisconsin-Madison, 1999.

Length of Cohabitations

Most cohabitations are short-lived. They typically last for about a year and then are transformed into marriages or dissolve.
Source: Waite, Linda J. "Cohabitation: A Communitarian Perspective." In M.K. Whyte (Ed.), *Strengthening American Marriages: A Communitarian Perspective.* Lanham, MD: Rowman and Littlefield, 2000: 11-30.

Only one in six cohabitations lasts at least three years, and only one in ten lasts five years or more. In contrast, 80 percent of couples who marry for the first time are still married five years later.
Source: Bumpass, Larry, and Hsien-Hen Lu. "Trends in Cohabitation and Implications for Children's Family Contexts in the U.S." CDE Working Paper No. 98-15. Center for Demography Ecology, University of Wisconsin-Madison, 1999; see also Abma, Joyce C., et. al. "Fertility, Family Planning and Women's Health: New Data From the 1995 National Survey of Family Growth." National Center for Health Statistics. *Vital Health Statistics, 23* (19), 1995: Table 36.

A British study of 9,114 new parents found that even after controlling for maternal age, education, economic hardship, previous relationship history, depression, and relationship quality, married biological parents were three times more likely to still be living together two years later compared to cohabiting biological parents.
Source: O'Connor, Thomas G., et al. "Frequency and Predictors of Relationship Dissolution in a Community Sample in England." *Journal of Family Psychology, 13* (1999): 436-449.

Over half (56%) of all first marriages are now preceded by cohabitation, compared to only 11% of marriages in 1970.

Most cohabitations are short-lived. They typically last for about a year and then are transformed into marriages or dissolve.

Although a committed relationship had lasted through pregnancy, about a third of poor, unmarried couples that lived together at pregnancy were no longer cohabiting 2 to 5 months after the child's birth.
Source: Mincy, Ron, et al. *Fragile Families in Focus: Executive Summary.* Baton Rouge, LA: TANF Executive Office of Oversight and Evaluation, 2004: 5.

About 38 percent of Fragile Families lived together before the pregnancy, but only 20% continued to do so after the birth. Of those that left cohabitation, 45% devolved in a "visiting" relationship where the father and mother were romantically attached and the father occasionally visited the child. Forty-one percent only had interaction with the child.
Source: Mincy, Ron, et al. *Fragile Families in Focus: Executive Summary.* Baton Rouge, LA: TANF Executive Office of Oversight and Evaluation, 2004: 9.

Cohabitation and Marriage

A qualitative study of 25 couples asked couples who were cohabiting their reasons for living together. "Cohabitation is a trial marriage" was rarely listed as a primary reason for the living arrangement.
Source: Sassler, Sharon. "The Process of Entering into Cohabiting Unions." *Journal of Marriage and Family, 66* (May 2004): 491-505.

A 25 year study of 1,119 adults showed that cohabitors had less marital happiness and more marital conflict compared to noncohabitors. They were more likely to be divorced at the follow-up; cohabitation increased the odds of divorce by 151%.
Source: Kamp Dush, Claire M., Catherine L. Cohan, and Paul R. Amato. "The Relationship Between Cohabitation and Marital Quality and Stability: Change Across Cohorts?" *Journal of Marriage and Family, 65* (August 2003): 539-549.

In the last decade, the proportion of cohabiting couples who went on to eventually marry decreased from 57% to 44%.
Source: Bumpass, Larry, and Hsien-Hen Lu. "Trends in Cohabitation and Implications for Children's Family Contexts in the U.S." CDE Working Paper No. 98-15. Center for Demography Ecology, University of Wisconsin-Madison, 1999.

Good economic circumstances increase the likelihood of marriage among cohabiting individuals.
Source: Pamela J. Smock. "Cohabitation in the United States: An Appraisal of Research Themes, Findings, and Implications." *Annual Review of Sociology, 26* (2000): 1-20; see also Clarkberg, ME. "The Price of Partnering: The Role of Economic Well-Being in Young Adults' First Union Experiences." *Social Forces 77* (1999): 945-68; and Smock, Pamela J., and Wendy D. Manning. "Cohabiting Partners' Economic Circumstances and Marriage." *Demography 34* (1997): 331-41.

Sixty-six percent of white women's first cohabiting partnerships result in marriage, compared with only 49 percent of first cohabiting partnerships for African American women.
Source: Bumpass, Larry, and Hsien-Hen Lu. "Trends in Cohabitation and Implications for Children's Family Contexts in the U.S." CDE Working Paper No. 98-15. Center for Demography Ecology, University of Wisconsin-Madison, 1999.

While black and white couples are about equally likely to expect to get married, blacks are substantially less likely to actually do so.
Source: Brown, S.L. "Union Transitions Among Cohabitors: The Significance of Relationship Assessments and Expectations." *Journal of Marriage and the Family, 62* (2000): 833-46.

In the last decade, the proportion of cohabiting couples who went on to eventually marry decreased from 57% to 44%.

Cohabiting couples are more likely to stay together when the two partners have similar income provision roles, whereas this factor is unimportant for married couples.

Source: Brines, J., and K. Joyner. "The Ties that Bind: Commitment and Stability in the Modern Union." *American Sociological Review, 64* (1999): 333-356.

Characteristics of Cohabitors

Cohabiting after divorce or separation doubles the likelihood of a postmarital, out-of-wed-lock pregnancy. Twenty percent of all postmarital births occur during cohabitation.

Source: Brown, Susan L. "Fertility Following Marital Dissolution: The Role of Cohabitation." *Journal of Family Issues, 21* (May 2000): 501-524.

Cohabitation as an alternative to marriage is most common among blacks, Puerto Ricans, and disadvantaged white women.

Source: Manning, Wendy D., and Pamela J. Smock. "Why Marry? Race and the Transition to Marriage among Cohabitors." *Demography 32* (November 1995): 509-520; see also Manning, Wendy D., and Nancy S. Landale. "Racial and Ethnic Differences in the Role of Cohabitation in Premarital Childbearing." *Journal of Marriage and the Family, 58* (February 1996): 63-77.

Most cohabitors do not pool financial resources and are more likely than married couples to value separate leisure activities, to maintain independent social lives, and to have addi-tional sex partners.

Source: Waite, Linda J. "Cohabitation: A Communitarian Perspective." In M.K. Whyte (Ed.) *Marriage in America: A Communitarian Perspective.* Lanham, MD: Rowman and Littlefield, 2000: 11-30.

Among women ages 19 to 44, 60 percent of high school dropouts have cohabited at some point compared to 37 percent of college graduates.

Source: Bumpass, Larry, and Hsien-Hen Lu. "Trends in Cohabitation and Implications for Children's Family Contexts in the U.S." *Population Studies, 54* (2000): 29-41.

Predictors of Cohabitation

Using data from the National Survey of Families and Households, a retrospective study of 13,017 adults interviewed in 1987-1988, it was determined that growing up in a non-married household increases the odds of cohabitation in adulthood and unmarried parenthood.

Source: Goldscheider, Frances K., and Calvin Goldscheider. "The Effects of Childhood Family Structure on Leaving and Returning Home." *Journal of Marriage and the Family, 60* (August 1998): 745-756.

The Cohabitation Experience

Very few couples cohabit as an alternative, but those who cohabit as a step towards mar-riage are not sizeable either. Researchers identify this cohabitation process of short dura-tion and high separation frequency as an "alternative to single."

Source: Heuveline, Patrick and Jeffrey M. Timberlake. "The Role of Cohabitation in Family Formation: The United States in Comparative Perspective." *Journal of Marriage and Family 66* (December 2004): 1214-1230.; Rindfuss, Ronald R. and Audrey VandenHuevel. "Cohabitation: A Precursor to Marriage or an Alternative to Being Single?" *Population and Development Review, 16* (December 1990): 703-726.

In a study of couples in the UK, married couples were more likely to use a single alloca-tive system to pool resources as opposed to cohabiting couples who were more likely to keep money partly or completely separate. Although economic and ideological factors also influenced these couples decisions, their relationship predicted their money habits the best. Similar relationships were found in Sweden and the United States as well.

Source: Vogler, Carolyn. "Cohabiting couples: rethinking money in the household at the beginning of the twenty first century." *53* (February 2005): 1-29.

Although states with stricter enforcement policies increase the bargaining power of mar-ried women, they also reduce the bargaining power of cohabiting women. Furthermore, those who were cohabiting at birth were only better off if they married the father of their

> ...60 percent of high school dropouts have cohabited at some point compared to 37 percent of college graduates.

child in the stricter states. Those who remained in cohabitation or who broke-up with the father experienced significantly greater levels of depression, worry, and hardship.

Source: Fertig, Angela, Garfinkel, Irwin, Sara S. McLanahan. *The Effect of Child Support Enforcement on Bargaining Power Among Married and Cohabiting Couples*. Working Paper #05-08-FF. Princeton, NJ: Center for Research on Child Wellbeing, 2004: 2.

Cohabiting fathers are twice as likely as married fathers to have a child from a previous relationship. They are more likely to have a lower education than their partner, more likely to have very low earnings (less than $10,000) a year, and much less likely to earn more than $25,000 a year.

Cohabiting mothers are twice as likely as married mothers to report fair or poor health at their child's birth and three times as likely to report smoking during pregnancy. They also report significantly higher levels of behavioral problems for their three year olds.

Source: Osborne, Cynthia, Sara McLanahan, and Jeanne Brooks-Gunn. *Young Children's Behavioral Problems in Married and Cohabiting Families*. Working Paper #03-09-FF. Princeton, NJ: Center for Research on Child Wellbeing, 2003: 13-15.

A study of 5,642 adults indicated that long-term cohabiting couples are the least satisfied with their relationships and with the amount of love and understanding they receive when compared to remarried and married couples. They also scored lowest on perceived levels of fairness in terms of spending money and doing household chores.

Source: Skinner, Kevin et al. "Cohabitation, Marriage, and Remarriage: A Comparison of Relationship Quality Over Time." *Journal of Family Issues, 23* (January 2002): 74-90.

Cohabiting couples report lower levels of happiness, lower levels of sexual satisfaction, and poorer relationships with their parents than their married counterparts.

Source: Waite, Linda J., and Kara Joyner. "Men's and Women's General Happiness and Sexual Satisfaction in Marriage, Cohabitation and Single Living." Unpublished manuscript, Population Research Center, University of Chicago, 1996; see also Nock, Steven L. "A Comparison of Marriages and Cohabiting Relationships." *Journal of Family Issues, 16* (January 1995): 53-76; and Amato, Paul R., and Alan Booth. *A Generation at Risk*. Cambridge, MA: Harvard University Press, 1997. Table 4-2, pg. 258.

In an analysis of 1,220 unmarried young adults sampled when they were 18, 21, or 24 years old and re-sampled 7 years later when they were 25, 28, or 31 years old, cohabiting men reported significantly more alcohol problems than both married and single men, and cohabiting women reported more alcohol problems than married women. Neither premarital levels of alcohol problems nor other demographic characteristics could explain the greater number of alcohol problems among cohabitors, suggesting that there is something about the status of cohabitation, rather than the characteristics of cohabitors, that explains their significantly higher rates of alcohol problems.

Source: Horwitz, Allan V., and Helene Raskin White. "The Relationship of Cohabitation and Mental Health: A Study of a Young Adult Cohort." *Journal of Marriage and the Family 60* (May 1998): 505-514.

A study using a nationally representative sample of more than 2,000 19- to 48-year-olds found that partners in cohabiting unions have more disagreements, fight more often, and report lower levels of happiness and fairness than their married counterparts.

Source: Brown, Susan L. and Alan Booth. "Cohabitation Versus Marriage: A Comparison of Relationship Quality." *Journal of Marriage and Family, 58* (August 1996): 668-678.

Cohabiting mothers are twice as likely as married mothers to report fair or poor health at their child's birth...

Cohabiting couples report lower levels of happiness, lower levels of sexual satisfaction, and poorer relationships with their parents than their married counterparts.

A study using a nationally representative sample of over 30,000 young adults indicated that cohabiting, non-engaged couples do not reduce drug and alcohol use, while engaged and married couples do tend to reduce drug and alcohol use.
Source: Bachman, Jerald G.et al. *Smoking, Drinking, and Drug Use in Young Adulthood: The Impacts of New Freedoms and New Responsibilities*. Mahwah, NJ: Lawrence Earlbaum and Associates, 1997.

Cohabitation and Instability

Cohabiting couples stay together an average of 26 months. They are three to four times more likely to break up than their married counterparts.
Source: Roberts, Yvonne. "Breaking Up Is Easier When You Are Poor." *Community Care, 24* January 2002: 23.

Using data from the Fragile Families Study, roughly 30% of romantically involved mothers are cohabiting part-time. Moreover, these part-time cohabitors resemble dating couples. They are less likely to get married compared to dating mothers (5 and 8%, respectively) and one-half of their relationships have dissolved in under two years. Only 17 percent of part-time mothers pooled resources compared to 15 percent of dating mothers.
Source: Knab, Jean. "Who's In and For How Much?: The Impact of Definitional Changes on the Prevalence and Outcomes of Cohabitation." Working Paper #04-05-FF. Princeton, NJ. Center for Research on Child Wellbeing, April 2005.

Length often destabilizes cohabiting relationships. Data from the National Survey of Families and Households revealed that cohabitors reported more unhappiness and less stability than married couples did. Duration serves a catalyst for problems in the relationship whereas it has no effect on married couples. Cohabitors experience a linear decline in relationship quality during the first decade.
Source: Brown, Susan L. "Relationship Quality Dynamics of Cohabiting Unions." *Journal of Family Issues, 24* (July 2003): 583-601.

For cohabitors, an increase in personal earning increases the likelihood that the union will separate due to the new-found economic independence.
Source: Wu, Zheng and Michael S. Pollard. "Economic Circumstances and the Stability of Nonmarital Cohabitation." *Journal of Family Issues 21* (April 2000): 303-328.

Cohabitors report higher levels of depression than their married peers even when taking sociodemographic factors. Cohabitors' higher relationship instability is the culprit and cohabitors' reports of instability are 25% higher than married couples. These high levels are particularly troubling for long-time cohabitors. Furthermore, children exacerbate depression in cohabitation whereas depression is unaffected by children for married couples. Longitudinal analysis indicated that the lower levels of well-being were not due to the type of people who cohabit.
Source: Brown, Susan L. "The Effect of Union Type on Psychological Well-being: Depression Among Cohabitors Versus Marrieds." *Journal of Health and Social Behavior, 41* (September 2000): 241-255.

Cohabitation and Poverty

A study of 854 men and women found that the causal mechanisms for cohabitation differ by gender. For men, economic resources quicken the route to marriage while cohabitation does not. For women, earnings potential is not connected to either marriage or cohabitation.
Source: Xie, Yu, James M. Raymo, Kimberly Goyette, and Arland Thornton. "Economic Potential and Entry Into Marriage and Cohabitation." *Demography, 40* (May 2003): 351-367.

Cohabiting couples... are three to four times more likely to break up than their married counterparts.

Compared to children living with married biological/adoptive parents, children living with cohabitors or single mothers fair very poorly in terms of child well being:

Proportion of Children Living in...

	Cohabitors (parents and partners)	Single Mothers	Married biological/ adoptive parents
Poverty	21.1%	43.5%	7.6%
Food insecurity	42.8%	53.5%	19.8%
Read to infrequently -0- to 5-year olds	23.0%	25.8%	18.0%
Behavior problems -6- to 11-year olds -12- to 17-year olds	15.7% 11.5%	9.0% 11.7%	3.5% 4.3%

Source: Acs, Gregory and Sandi Nelson. "The Kids Are Alright? Children's Well-Being and the Rise in Cohabitation." Table 1. Series B. No. B-48. Washington, DC: The Urban Institute, 2002.

One half of adult women can expect to enter cohabitation at least once between 15 and 45 years old and one third of children will experience maternal cohabitation by the age of 16. The median duration of cohabitation arrangements, however, was shortest for adults (1.17 years) and children (2.11 years).

Children who grow up with non-cohabiting single mothers are more likely to be in poverty and receive AFDC or other welfare. Only 36% of single mothers have attended or completed college compared to 53% of married parents.

Cohabiting parents are more likely to receive public assistance than married parents.
Source: Brandon, Peter D. and Larry Bumpass. "Children's Living Arrangements, Coresidence of Unmarried Fathers, and Welfare Receipt." *Journal of Family Issues, 22* (January 2001): 3-26.

Children whose mothers cohabited had the highest reliance on AFDC prior to union disruption at 21.6%, compared to 9.2% and 14.4%, respectively, for remarried and single mother groups. Children whose mothers enter a cohabiting relationship versus a remarriage are still three times more likely to be poor.

Children whose mothers moved from a single to remarried status experienced a 30% reduction in their AFDC receipt, dropping from 9.7 percent to 6.7 percent. Mothers who entered a nonmarital union still had about the same reliance on AFDC (from 24.8% to 23.1%).
Source: Morrison, Donna Ruana and Amy Ritualo. "Routes to Children's Economic Recovery After Divorce: Are Cohabitation and Remarriage Equivalent?" *American Sociological Review, 65* (August 2000): 560-580.

For all parents with children under 18, those who cohabit have a poverty rate twice as high as married couples. They also experience more material hardship as they receive less help from their families, friends, and community.
Source: Lerman, Robert I. "How Do Marriage, Cohabitation and Single Parenthood Affect Material Hardships of Families With Children?" Washington, DC: Urban Institute, 2002.

Cohabiting parents experienced poverty rates that were 7.5 to 15.4 percent higher than those of married two-parent families.
Source: Lerman, Robert I. "Impacts of Marital Status and Parental Presence on the Material Hardship of Families with Children." Washington, DC: Urban Institute and American University, 2002: 12.

Cohabitation and Domestic Violence

Long-term cohabitors hit or threw objects more often than married couples. They started with a higher level of violence and remained higher, whereas married couples had much lower levels of violence. Long-term cohabiting couples reported significantly greater satisfaction than married couples and report higher commitment, greater self-esteem, and lower depression.
Source: Stafford, Laura, Susan L. Kline, and Caroline T. Rankin. "Married individuals, cohabitors, and cohabitors who marry: A longitudinal study of relational and individual well-being." *Journal of Social and Personal Relationships, 21* (April 2004): 231-248.

Couples who cohabit before marriage have a 54% higher chance of being violent than those married couples who did not cohabit first.
Source: Brownridge, D.A. and S.S. Hall. "'Living in sin' and sinful living: toward filling a gap in the explanation of violence against women." *Aggression and Violent Behavior 5* (2000): 565-583.

Women who cohabit are less likely to support prosecution against their abusers due to a strong emotional attachment or commitment. Cohabitation reduces support for arrest by 52% and for prosecution by 62%.
Source: Bui, H.N. "Domestic violence victims' behavior in favor of prosecution: Effects of gender relations." *Women and Criminal Justice 12* (July 2001): 51-75.; Kingsnorth, Rodney F. and Randall C. Macintosh. "Domestic Violence: Predictors of Victim Support for Official Action." *Justice Quarterly, 21* (June 2004): 301-328.

Women in cohabitation arrangements are far more likely to be victims of intimate partner violence, according to researchers at SUNY Buffalo. Forty-two percent of cohabiting women have endured "severe violence" at the hands of a partner during their lives, compared to about a quarter of single and married women. Also, while one in ten married and single women reported severe violence in their current relationship (30% and 26%, respectively), twice that percentage reported such violence (20%) among cohabiting women.
Source: "Women Who Shack Up: Prey to Pushers and Brutes." *Society September/October 2004:* 5-6.

Partners who are cohabiting are less likely to agree on reports of intimate partner violence than married couples.
Source: Caetano, Raul, John Schafer, Craig Field, and Scott M. Nelson. "Agreement on Reports of Intimate Partner Violence Among White, Black, and Hispanic Couples in the United States." *Journal of Interpersonal Violence, 17* (December 2002): 1308-1322.

Women in cohabiting relationships are nine times more likely to be killed by their partner than women in marital relationships. In marriage, women's risk of murder decreases by age, whereas middle-aged cohabiting women are at the highest risk.

The study was replicated in Australia with similar results (10 times more likely).
Source: Shackelford, Todd K. "Cohabitation, Marriage, and Murder: Woman-Killing by Male Romantic Partners." *Aggressive Behavior, 27* (2001): 284-291.; Mouzos, Jenny and Todd K. Shackelford. "A Comparative, Cross-National Analysis of Partner-Killing by Women in Cohabiting and Marital Relationships in Australia and the United States." *Aggressive Behavior 30* (2004): 206-216.

Couples who cohabit before engagement are at a higher risk of physical violence and display more negative and problematic behavior than those who have made a commitment to get married and do not live together.
Source: Kline, Galena H. et al. "Timing is Everything: Pre-Engagement Cohabitation and Increased Risk for Poor Marital Outcomes." *Journal of Family Psychology, 18* (June 2004): 311-318.

Cohabiting parents experienced poverty rates that were 7.5 to 15.4 percent higher than those of married two-parent families.

Women in cohabitation arrangements are far more likely to be victims of intimate partner violence...

A study of 4,000 couples revealed that cohabiting women are at a higher risk of "intense male violence" than married women.
Source: DeMaris, Alfred, et al. "Distal and Proximal Factors in Domestic Violence: A Test of an Integrated Model." *Journal of Marriage and Family, 65* (August 2003): 652-667.

In 2002, cohabiting couples reported rates of physical aggression that were three times higher than married couples.
Source: Salari, Sonia Miner and Bret M. Baldwin. "Verbal, Physical, and Injurious Aggression Among Intimate Couples Over Time." *Journal of Family Issues, 23* (May 2002): 523-550.

In an analysis of the 1987-88 National Survey of Families and Households, 9.9 percent of cohabiting adults with no plans to marry reported an incident of domestic violence in the past year, compared to 4.7 percent of cohabiting adults with plans to marry and 3.6 percent of married couples.
Source: Waite, Linda. "Cohabitation: A Communitarian Perspective." In Martin King Whyte (Ed.), *Marriage in America*. Lanham, MD: Rowman and Littlefield, 2000: 11-30; see also Waite, Linda and Maggie Gallagher. *The Case for Marriage*. New York: Double-day, 2000, pp. 150-160.

In an analysis of the 1987-88 wave of the National Survey of Families and Households, it was found that even after controlling for education, race, age and gender, people who live together are 1.8 times more likely to report violent arguments than married couples.
Source: Waite, Linda J. "Cohabitation: A Communitarian Perspective." In M.K. Whyte (Ed.) *Marriage in America: A Communitarian Perspective*. Lanham, MD: Rowman and Littlefield, 2000: 11-30.

In a study using a nationally representative sample of 6,000 households, it was found that in the past year, 14% of cohabiting couples engaged in physical aggression toward each other, compared to only 5% of married couples. However, when demographic and social factors were controlled for, this difference was no longer statistically significant.
Source: Stets, Jan. "Cohabiting and Marital Aggression: The Role of Social Isolation." *Journal of Marriage and the Family, 53* (1991): 669-680.

Cohabitation and Faithfulness

In an analysis of more than 10,000 adults using data from the U.S. Census, the National Survey of Families and Households, and the National Health Social Life Survey, 20 percent of cohabiting women had a secondary sex partner, compared with 18 percent of dating women, and only 4 percent of married women.
Source: Forste, Renata, and Koray Tanfer. "Sexual Exclusivity Among Dating, Cohabiting, and Married Women." *Journal of Marriage and the Family, 58* (1996): 33-47.

Using data from national surveys, it was determined that cohabitors were only slightly less likely to expect sexual monogamy than married persons who had never lived together prior to marriage (94% versus 99%, respectively), yet the odds of a recent infidelity were more than twice as likely for cohabitors than for married persons.
Source: Treas, Judith, and Deirdre Giesen. "Sexual Infidelity Among Married and Cohabiting Americans." *Journal of Marriage and the Family, 62* (2000): 48-60.

In 2002, cohabiting couples reported rates of physical aggression that were three times higher than married couples.

A study using a nationally representative sample of 1,235 women ages 20 to 37 indicated that married women who had cohabited prior to marriage were 3.3 times more likely to have sex with someone other than their husband than married women who had not cohabited prior to marriage. Single women who cohabited were 1.7 times more likely to have a secondary sex partner than single women who did not live with their partners.
Source: Forste, Renata and Koray Tanfer. "Sexual Exclusivity Among Dating, Cohabiting, and Married Women." *Journal of Marriage and the Family, 58* (1996): 33-47.

Implications of Cohabitation for Children
Consequences of Cohabitation for Family Stability and Subsequent Marital Satisfaction

In a study of 1,000 former cohabitors, those who live together prior to marriage reported less satisfaction with their marriages than those who had not. Moreover, twice as many of those who cohabited before marriage reported violent interactions with their partners when compared to those who had not lived together before marriage. Males in the cohabitation group also reported lower dedication when they were married.
Source: Stanley, Scott M., Sarah W. Whitton, and Howard J. Markman. "Maybe I Do: Interpersonal Commitment and Premarital or Nonmarital Cohabitation." *Journal of Family Issues, 25* (May 2004): 496-519.

Roughly a quarter of first marriages preceded by cohabitation end by their fifth anniversary and half end by their 15th anniversary.
Source: "Findings." *Wilson Quarterly, 26* (Autumn 2002): 9-12.

Cohabiting couples who marry have poorer communication skills than those who marry without living together. Poor communication skills may contribute to the dissolution rate of couples who cohabit before marriage.
Source: Coban, Catherine L. and Stacey Kleinbaum. "Toward a Greater Understanding of the Cohabitation Effect: Premarital Cohabitation and Marital Communication." *Journal of Marriage and Family, 64* (February 2002): 180-192.

Studies of 1,425 spouses found that couples who lived together before marriage reported more disagreements, serious quarrels, and aggression. They were also twice as likely to divorce.
Source: Dush, Claire M Kamp, et al. "The Relationship Between Cohabitation and Marital Quality and Stability: Change Across Cohorts?" *Journal of Marriage and Family, 65* (August 2003): 539-549.

In a longitudinal study of cohabiting couples, it was found that, over time, cohabitors developed less positive attitudes toward marriage, grew more tolerant of divorce, and evidenced a reduced desire for children. The longer a young person cohabited, the less he or she endorsed marriage and the fewer children he or she desired.
Source: Axinn, William G., and Jennifer S. Barber. "Living Arrangements and Family Formation Attitudes in Early Adulthood." Journal of *Marriage and the Family, 59* (August 1997): 595-611.

Because a large body of recent evidence shows quite consistently that people who cohabit and then marry are much more likely to divorce than people who marry without living together, an initial conclusion might be that cohabitation changes people's attitudes in ways that make them less committed to the institution of marriage. However, people who cohabit have other characteristics that both lead them to cohabit in the first place and make them poor marriage material. Thus, in the case of divorce, selection would seem to account for the differences between marriage and cohabitation.
Source: Waite, Linda. "The Negative Effects of Cohabitation." The Responsive Community 10 (Winter 1999/2000); Lillard, Lee A., Michael J. Brien, and Linda J. Waite. "Pre-Marital Cohabitation and Subsequent Marital Dissolution — Is It Self-Selection?" *Demography, 32* (August 1995): 437-458; see also DeMaris, A., and K.V. Rao. "Premarital Cohabitation and Subsequent Martial Stability in the United States: A Reassessment." *Journal of Marriage and the Family, 54* (1992): 178-90.

> Cohabiting couples who marry have poorer communication skills than those who marry without living together.

No positive contribution of cohabitation on subsequent marriage has ever been found.
Source: Popenoe, David, and Barbara Dafoe Whitehead. *Should We Live Together? What Young Adults Need to Know about Cohabitation before Marriage*. New Brunswick, NJ: The National Marriage Project, 1999: 5.

Cohabitation and Children

In 1996, 3.3 million children lived with a parent or parents who were cohabiting, including 16 percent of children living with single fathers and 9 percent of children living with single mothers.
Source: *America's Children: Key National Indicators of Well-Being, 2001*. Table POP5.B. Washington, D.C.: Federal Interagency Forum on Child and Family Statistics, 2001.

In 2000, 41 percent of unwed cohabiting couples had children in their home, only slightly less than the proportion of married couple households with children (46 percent). For unmarried couple households in the 30-34 age group, 56 percent had children living with them.
Source: Fields, Jason. "America's Families and Living Arrangements: March 2000." *Current Population Reports*, P20-537. Washington, D.C.: U.S. Census Bureau, 2001.

Among previously-married cohabitors, the proportion of cohabitations with children present increased from 40 percent to 50 percent between 1987 and 1995.
Source: Bumpass, Larry, and Hsien-Hen Lu. "Trends in Cohabitation and Implications for Children's Family Contexts in the U.S." CDE Working Paper No. 98-15. Center for Demography Ecology, University of Wisconsin-Madison, 1999.

By one estimate, nearly half of all children today will spend some time in a cohabiting family before the age of 16.
Source: Bumpass, Larry, and Hsien-Hen Lu. "Trends in Cohabitation and Implications for Children's Family Contexts in the U.S." CDE Working Paper No. 98-15. Center for Demography Ecology, University of Wisconsin-Madison, 1999.

About 40 percent of nonmarital births (and 11 percent of births overall) occur in cohabiting unions.
Source: Bumpass, Larry, and Hsien-Hen Lu. "Trends in Cohabitation and Implications for Children's Family Contexts in the U.S." CDE Working Paper No. 98-15. Center for Demography Ecology, University of Wisconsin-Madison, 1999.

In cases in which the cohabitor's partner has children, the non-parent cohabitor has no explicit legal, financial, supervisory, or custodial rights or responsibilities regarding the children of his or her partner.
Source: Waite, Linda J. "Cohabitation: A Communitarian Perspective." In M.K. Whyte (Ed.) *Marriage in America: A Communitarian Perspective*. Lanham, MD: Rowman and Littlefield, 2000: 11-30.

By one estimate, 63% of children in cohabiting households were born not to the cohabiting couple, but to a previous union of one of the adult partners, most often the mother.
Source: Graefe, Deborah R., and Daniel T. Lichter. "Life Course Transitions of American Children: Parental Cohabitation, Marriage, and Single Motherhood." *Demography, 36* (May 1999): 205-217.

Consequences of Cohabitation for the Well-Being of Children

The birth of a child in a cohabiting relationship in the UK is correlated with long term cohabitation and the usual dissolution of the cohabitation.
Source: Ermisch, John and Marco Francesconi. "Patterns of Household and Family Formation." Ed. Richard Berthoud and Jonathan Gershuny.

No positive contribution of cohabitation on subsequent marriage has ever been found.

...nearly half of all children today will spend some time in a cohabiting family before the age of 16.

About 40 percent of nonmarital births... occur in cohabiting unions.

...cohabiting men were twice as likely as married men to move away from their children during a 30-year period.

Family Arrangements and Behavioral Problems Among Teenagers

	Proportion with Emotional and Behavioral Problems	Proportion with Low Levels of School Engagement	Proportion Suspended or Expelled from School in the Past Year
White Teenagers Living With...			
Married biological parents	3.6	18.9	7.1
Blended: mother and step- or adoptive father	10.1	23.8	9.5
Cohabitors: mother and boyfriend	10.0	39.3	23.0
Single mother	9.7	27.9	11.3
Hispanic Teenagers Living With...			
Married biological parents	2.8	17.1	9.7
Blended: mother and step- or adoptive father	8.1	34.9	23.1
Cohabitors: mother and boyfriend	37.7	66.2	42.0
Single Mother	10.8	38.3	15.2
Black Teenagers Living With...			
Married biological parents	6.1	25.7	10.4
Blended: mother and step- or adoptive father	6.1	36.1	18.9
Cohabitors: mother and boyfriend	14.9	37.1	56.4
Single Mother	11.7	32.5	30.6

Source: Nelson, Sandi, Rebecca L. Clark, and Gregory Acs. *Beyond the Two-Parent Family: How Teenagers Fare in Cohabiting Couple and Blended Families.* Table 1. Assessing the New Federalism, Series B, No. B-31. Washington, D.C.: The Urban Institute, 2001.

By age 16, three-quarters of children born to cohabiting couples will experience their parents' breakup; only one-third of children born to married parents will experience divorce or separation.
Source: Popenoe, David and Barbara Dafoe Whitehead. "Should We Live Together? What Young Adults Need to Know About Cohabitation Before Marriage." Second Edition. Piscataway, NJ: National Marriage Project, 2002: 8.

In a study of 1,409 fathers who were living with their child's mother at the time of their child's birth, cohabiting men were twice as likely as married men to move away from their children during a 30-year period.
Source: University of Michigan Institute for Social Research. "Absent Dads: How Many Live Apart From Their Children." ISR Update (Fall 2002). <http://www.isr.umich.edu/news/isrupdate-2002-11.html#absent>

Compared to teens raised by their married biological parents, teens living with their mother and her partner are 2.2 times more likely to be expelled from school and 1.9 times more likely to have a low GPA, according to a study of more than 13,000 adolescents. They were also more likely to be delinquent and have problems paying attention in class and completing homework assignments.
Source: Brown, Susan I. "Child Well-Being in Cohabiting Families." Eds. Alan Booth and Ann C. Crouter. *Just Living Together: Implications of Cohabitation on Families, Children, and Social Policy*. (New Jersey: Lawrence Erlbaum Associates, 2002) 173-187.

Adolescents whose parents were cohabiting at their time of birth are 42% more likely to be sexually active than those whose parents were married, according to a sample of 10,847 girls from the National Survey of Family Growth. Daughters in alternative living arrangements were at least 30% more likely to be sexually active than those in biological parent households. The number of living arrangements was also positively associated with sexual activity.
Source: Hogan, Dennis P., Rongjun Sun, and Gretchen T. Cornwell. "Sexual and Fertility Behaviors of American Females Aged 15-19 Years: 1985, 1990 and 1995." *American Journal of Public Health, 90* (September 2000): 1421-1425.

Teenagers in cohabiting families fare much worse than teenagers living with their biological married parents. Moreover, teens in cohabiting families fare worse, on average, than those living with single mothers: they are significantly more likely to have emotional and behavioral problems, to have low levels of school engagement, and to be suspended or expelled from school.
Source: Nelson, Sandi, Rebecca L. Clark, and Gregory Acs. *Beyond the Two-Parent Family: How Teenagers Fare in Cohabiting Couple and Blended Families*. Table 1. Assessing the New Federalism, Series B, No. B-31. Washington, D.C.: The Urban Institute, 2001.

In 1990, the poverty rate for children living in married households was 6%, 31% for children living in cohabiting households, and 45% for those living in single-mother headed households. Overall, cohabiting couples with children have only two-thirds the income of married couples with children, primarily due to the fact that male cohabitors have only about half the income of married males with children.
Source: Manning, Wendy D., and Daniel T. Lichter. "Parental Cohabitation and Children's Economic Well-Being." *Journal of Marriage and the Family, 58* (November 1996): 998-1010.

A study of 352 families indicated that children who lived with their mother and her boyfriend were more poorly adjusted psychologically and had more behavior problems than children who lived with both biological parents.
Source: Johnson, Ellen, Ruth E. K. Stein, and Mark R. Dadds. "Moderating Effects of Family Structure on the Relationship between Physical and Mental Health in Urban Children with Chronic Illness." *Journal of Pediatric Psychology, 21* (1996): 43-56.

Non-Resident Fathers
Survey Data

In a national survey of 500 Canadians, 80% agreed it was "very important" for children with divorced parents to maintain an ongoing relationship with the non-custodial parent. Two-thirds agreed that government should make it a priority to encourage and facilitate relationships between children and non-custodial parents through family law. Also, 62% agreed that the rights of fathers are neglected in divorce courts.
Source: Citizen-Compas poll, commissioned by Southam News and the Calgary-based National Foundation for Family Research and Education, November 23, 1998.

The Facts about Non-Resident Fathers

According to the 1997 National Survey of America's Families, only 34 percent of children with a non-resident parent saw that parent on a weekly basis, and 28 percent of children with a non-resident parent had no contact with their non-resident parent in the past year.
Source: Sorensen, Elaine, and Chava Zibman. "To What Extent Do Children Benefit from Child Support?" Washington, D.C.: The Urban Institute, January 2000.

According to Elaine Sorenson of the Urban Institute, an estimated one-fourth of black men aged 16 to 24 are noncustodial fathers and half of those aged 25 to 34 are non-custodial fathers.
Source: Holzer, Harry J. and Paul Offner. "The puzzle of black male unemployment." *Public Interest, 154* (Winter 2004): 74-84.

The proportion of men aged 25 to 29 living with children decreased 57% from 1965 to 1995. Over the same period, the proportion of men aged 25 to 29 living with their non-own children, however, doubled from 6% to 12%.
Source: Eggebeen, David J. "The Changing Course of Fatherhood: Men's Experiences With Children in Demographic Perspective." *Journal of Family Issues, 23* (May 2002): 486-506.

Only a third of non-resident fathers are supporting new families that include children.
Source: Meyer, Daniel E. "The Effect of Child Support on the Economic Status of Nonresident Fathers." In Irwin Garfinkel, Sara S. McLanahan, Daniel R. Meyer, and Judith A. Seltzer (Eds.), *Fathers Under Fire: The Revolution in Child Support Enforcement.* New York: Russell Sage Foundation, 1998: 67-93.

About half of all noncustodial fathers have ties to another set of kin and a quarter have three or more kids in their lives. These children include nonresident biological children of all other past/present mates, biological children and stepchildren who may reside with the father, and stepchildren who live elsewhere. Eight percent of all non-resident fathers are living with biological children they fathered prior to their current residency and another 26% live with stepchildren. About 14% of non-resident fathers are living with women who are also nonresident parents, and 42% have biological children with their current spouse or partner.
Source: Manning, Wendy D., Susan D. Stewart and Pamela J. Smock. "The Complexity of Father's Parenting Responsibilities and Involvement With Nonresident Children." *Journal of Family Issues, 24* (July 2003): 645-667.; *USA Today Magazine.* "Nonresident Fathers' Complex Parenting." May 2002: 7-8.

Twenty percent of all non-resident fathers are estimated to earn less than $6,000 a year.
Source: Garfinkel, Irwin, Sara S. McLanahan, and Thomas L. Hanson. "A Patchwork Portrait of Nonresident Fathers." In Irwin Garfinkel, Sara S. McLanahan, Daniel R. Meyer, and Judith A. Seltzer (Eds.), *Fathers Under Fire: The Revolution in Child Support Enforcement.* New York: Russell Sage Foundation, 1998: 31-60.

From the initial measurement of a sample of 298 fathers in 1992, forty percent of nonresident fathers were living with other children by 1994, showing that many were economically responsible for two households. However, the addition of children by the second measurement reduces child support to nonresidential children only when the new children are biological children. Hence, nonresident fathers may swap one set of offspring for another.
Source: Manning, Wendy and Pamela J. Smock. "'Swapping' Families: Serial Parenting and Economic Support for Children." *Journal of Marriage and Family, 62* (February 2000): 111-122.

...an estimated one-fourth of black men aged 16 to 24 are noncustodial fathers and half of those aged 25 to 34 are non-custodial fathers.

Twenty percent of all non-resident fathers are estimated to earn less than $6,000 a year.

Forty percent of nonresident fathers have incomes more than 200% below the poverty line and most of these men do not pay child support. Those who do pay have to pay a higher percentage of their income than do higher income fathers. Half of low income fathers who do not pay child support do not have a high school degree and have not held a job in the past 12 months. Nearly 20% of these men are incarcerated.

Source: Sorenson, Elaine and Laura Wheaton. *Income and Demographic Characteristics of Nonresident Fathers in 1993.* Washington, DC: The Urban Institute, 2000. Accessed 16 March 2005. <http://aspe.hhs.gov/hsp/nonresfathers00>

When compared to full-time fathers, fathers who only lived some or none of the time with their child had a lower socioeconomic status, moved more often, had more children, had more emotional problems, reported more anxiety, were dependent on marijuana and/or alcohol, spent more months disabled by a drug or alcohol problem, had more criminal convictions, were more violent to their partners, had greater financial problems, and demonstrated more antisocial behavior.

Source: Jafee, Sara et al. "Predicting Early Fatherhood and Whether Young Fathers Live with Their Children: Prospective Findings and Policy Reconsiderations." *Journal of Child Psychology & Psychiatry & Allied Disciplines, 42* (September 2001): 803-815.

Having a father in the household dramatically effects men's and women's perceptions of a father's role.

Father's Role	Respondents with father in the house	Respondents with father not in the house
Provide moral and ethical guidance	82%	71.1%
Provide emotional support to mothers/caregivers	76.9%	55.5%
Provide financial support	86.5%	59.5%
Provide support other than financial	71.9%	52.0%
Cooperate with mother/caregiver	86.1%	62.5%

Source: Andrews, Arlene Bowers, Irene Luckey, Errol Bolden, Judith Whiting-Fickling, and Katherine A. Lind. "Public Perceptions About Father Involvement: Results of a Statewide Household Survey." *Journal of Family Issues, 25* (July 2004): 603-633.

Non-Resident Fathers Tend to Disappear Over Time

A study of 1,535 children revealed that only 39.4% reported in-person, phone, or letter contact from their nonresident fathers once a month or more. Thirty one percent had such contact their fathers once or several times a year. Thirty percent reported no contact with their father at all. Only one-third of children reported having a very close relationship with their father.

Source: Stewart, Susan D. "Nonresident Parenting and Adolescent Adjustment: The Quality of Nonresident Father-Child Interaction." *Journal of Family Issues, 24* (March 2003): 217-244.

In a study of 156 nonresident mothers and 531 nonresident fathers, the mothers exhibited significantly higher levels of telephone and letter contact and extended visitation than nonresident fathers. Both nonresident mothers and fathers, however, had difficulty staying actively involved in their children's lives.

Source: Stewart, Susan D. "Nonresident Mothers' and Fathers' Social Contact with Children." *Journal of Marriage and the Family, 61* (November 1999): 894-907.

Only 32% of non-resident fathers were able to have contact with their child several times a week. Contact is higher for fathers who are still romantically involved with their child's mother.
Source: Cabrera, Natasha J., et al. "Low-Income Father's Involvement in Their Toddler's Lives: Biological Fathers From the Early Head Start Research and Evaluation Study." *Fathering, 2* (Winter 2004): 5-30.

Predictors of Frequent Contact With Non-Resident Children
Positive child-nonresident father relationships were correlated with contact between child and father and the frequency of contact between the mother and her partner. Conflict between child and father was associated with conflict between child and mother and child and stepfather. These relationships were stronger for single-parent families than for step-families.
Source: Dunn, Judy et al. "Children's perspectives on their relationships with their nonresident fathers: influences, outcomes and implications." *Journal of Child Psychology and Psychiatry* (March 2004): 553-566.

> **The quality of a father's relationship with his child's mother is a significant predictor of paternal involvement.**

For post-divorce, non-residential fathers, lower levels of involvement with their children are related to ongoing conflict with the residential mother, greater geographic distance from the children, and a lack of clarity regarding the nature of their father role. All of these factors mediate a father's satisfaction with his arrangement with his children.
Source: Leite, Randall W. and Patrick C. McKenry. "Aspects of Father Status and Postdivorce Father Involvement With Children." *Journal of Family Issues, 23* (July 2002): 601-623.

The quality of a father's relationship with his child's mother is a significant predictor of paternal involvement. The dissolution of the romantic relationship can serve as a barrier to child involvement for fathers and adolescent mothers.
Source: Gavin, Loretta A., Maureen M. Black, Sherman Minor, Yolanda Abel, Mia A. Papas and Margaret E. Bentley. "Young, Disadvantaged Fathers' Involvement With Their Involvement With Their Infants: An Ecological Perspective." *Journal of Adolescent Health* (September 2002): 266-276.

The amount that a nonresidential father contributes to his baby's mother is positively correlated with her perceptions of his competence. The more money he gives, the better she thinks of him. The less he gives, the more likely the child is a welfare recipient and the mother prevents him access. Residential fathers were generally perceived as more competent than non-residential fathers.
Source: Fagan, Jay and Marina Barnett. "The Relationship Between Maternal Gatekeeping, Paternal Competence, Mothers' Attitudes About the Father Role, and Father Involvement." *Journal of Family Issues, 24* (November 2003): 1020-1043.

> **Positive relations between teenage mothers and the nonresidential father of their child predict a greater likelihood of initiated and sustained high father involvement.**

Positive relations between teenage mothers and the nonresidential father of their child predict a greater likelihood of initiated and sustained high father involvement.
Source: Kalil, Ariel, Kathleen M. Ziol-Guest, and Rebekah Levine Coley. "Perceptions of Father Involvement Patterns in Teenage-Mother Families: Predictors and Links to Mothers' Psychological Adjustment." *Family Relations, 54* (April 2005): 197-211.

A pool of stepchildren from the NEAD study suggested that noncustodial fathers might have better contact with them if they engaged in more frequent phone calls, spend more overnight visits together, etc. Children with noncustodial mothers have less adjustment problems than those with noncustodial fathers.
Source: Gunnoe, Majorie Lindner and E. Mavis Hetherington. "Stepchildren's Perceptions of Noncustodial Mothers and Noncustodial Fathers: Differences in Socioemotional Involvement and Associations With Adolescent Adjustment Problems." *Journal of Family Psychology, 18* (December 2004): 555-563.

Geographic distance, time since separation, and remarriage of one or both parents are associated with declining father contact. Factors positively associated with father contact include higher parental socioeconomic status, older children, children born within marriage, joint custody arrangements, and a positive co-parental relationship, including the mother's attitude toward the father as a parent.
Source: King, Valarie, and Holly E. Heard. "Nonresident Father Visitation, Parental Conflict, and Mother's Satisfaction: What's Best for Child Well-Being?" *Journal of Marriage and the Family, 61* (May 1999): 385-396; see also Nord, C.W., and Nicholas Zill. "Noncustodial Parents' Participation in Their Children's Lives: Evidence from the Survey of Income and Program Participation. Vol II: Synthesis of Literature." (DHHS-100-93-0012). Washington, D.C.: U.S. Department of Health and Human Services, 1996.

Fathers are more likely to maintain regular contact with their non-resident children when there is more than one child, when at least some of the children are male, or when the children are school age or older.
Source: Cooksey, E.G., and P.H. Craig. "Parenting From a Distance: The Effects of Paternal Characteristics on Contact Between Nonresidential Fathers and Their Children." *Demography ,35* (1998): 187-200; see also Fox, G.L., and P.W. Blanton. "Noncustodial Fathers Following Divorce." *Marriage and Family Review, 20* (1995): 257-282; and Starrels, M.E. "Gender Differences in Parent-Child Relations." *Journal of Family Issues 15* (1994): 148-165.

Non-resident mothers tend to have higher frequency of contact with their children compared to non-resident fathers.
Source: Scoon-Rogers, L., and G.H. Lester. *Child Support for Custodial Mothers and Fathers: 1991.* Current Population Reports, P60-187. Washington, D.C.: U.S. Census Bureau, 1995; see also Nord, C.W., and Nicholas Zill. "Noncustodial Parents' Participation in Their Children's Lives: Evidence from the Survey of Income and Program Participation. Vol II: Synthesis of Literature." (DHHS-100-93-0012). Washington, D.C.: U.S. Department of Health and Human Services, 1996.

Non-custodial fathers who support a traditional family division of labor and who believe fatherhood is important for life satisfaction are more likely to have frequent contact with their children.
Source: Cooksey, E.G., and P.H. Craig. "Parenting From a Distance: The Effects of Paternal Characteristics on Contact Between Nonresidential Fathers and Their Children." *Demography, 35* (1998): 187-200.

What Non-Resident Fathers Do When They Are with their Children

Activities amongst nonresident fathers vary across race and ethnicities. White adolescents reported playing sports more often (24% vs. 17% for Blacks and 15% for Hispanics) while Black adolescents had a high rate of church attendance (17% vs. 11% for Whites). Hispanics had the highest percent of working on school projects (16% vs. 10% for Whites).
Source: King, Valerie, Kathleen Mullan Harris, and Holly E. Heard. "Racial and Ethnic Diversity in Nonresident Father Involvement." *Journal of Marriage and Family, 66* (February 2004): 1-21.

Using a sample of 139 non-resident mothers and 479 non-resident fathers from the 1987-1988 wave of the National Survey of Households and Families (NSHF), a national probability sample of 13,008 respondents, it was found that after controlling for sociodemographics and family characteristics, non-resident mothers and non-resident fathers engage in a similar pattern of mostly leisure activities with their children. The majority of both non-resident mothers and non-resident fathers were found to have either no contact with their child or contact based on leisure activities.
Source: Steward, Susan D. "Disneyland Dads, Disneyland Moms? How Nonresident Parents Spend Time with Absent Children." *Journal of Family Issues, 20* (July 1999): 539-556.

Impact of Non-Resident Fathers on the Well-Being of their Children

A child with a nonresident father is 54 percent more likely to be poorer than his or her father.
Source: Sorenson, Elaine and Chava Zibman. "Getting to Know Poor Fathers Who Do Not Pay Child Support." *Social Service Review, 75* (September 2001): 420-434.

For the children of non-resident fathers, negative changes in the parent-child relationship were the best predictor of a child's internalizing (depression etc.) and externalizing (violence) behaviors. Moreover, the discord and distance within the father-child relationship mediated an effect on both parental conflict and the child's problem behaviors.
Source: Pruett, Marsha Kline, Tamra Y. Williams, Glendessa Insabella and Todd D. Little. "Family and Legal Indicators of Child Adjustment to Divorce Among Families With Young Children." *Journal of Family Psychology, 17* (June 2003): 169-180.

Infants and toddlers benefit most from daily visitation from each parent at a minimum of every two to three days.
Source: Kuehnle, Kathryn and Tracy Ellis. "The Importance of Parent-Child Relationships: What Attorneys Need to Know About the Impact of Separation." *The Florida Bar Journal 76* (October 2002): 67-70; Kelly, J.B. and M.E. Lamb. "Using Child Development Research to Make Appropriate Custody and Access Decisions for Young Children." *Family and Conciliation Courts Review, 38* (2000): 297-311.

> ...boys... with nonresident fathers had lower grades than boys with resident fathers.

A study of 50 adolescent boys showed that those with nonresident fathers had lower grades than boys with resident fathers. There was also a significant positive link between father-son contact and academic performance.
Source: Jones, Kim. "Assessing Psychological and Academic Performance in Nonresident-Father and Resident-Father Adolescent Boys." *Child and Adolescent Social Work Journal, 21* (August 2004): 333-354.

In a meta-analysis of 63 studies published between 1970 and 1998 dealing with non-resident fathers and children's well-being, payment of child support, the child feeling close to the non-resident father, and authoritative parenting were found to be positively and significantly correlated with higher academic achievement and fewer behavioral and emotional problems for both boys and girls. Frequency of contact was not significantly correlated with these measures of child well-being.
Source: Amato, Paul R., and Joan G. Gilbreth. "Nonresident Fathers and Children's Well-Being: A Meta-Analysis." *Journal of Marriage and the Family, 61* (August 1999): 557-573.

> Child well-being suffered the most in families in which mothers were dissatisfied with high levels of father contact.

In an analysis of data from the National Survey of Families and Households, non-resident father visitation was not positively associated with child well-being. Child well-being suffered the most in families in which mothers were dissatisfied with high levels of father contact.
Source: King, Valarie, and Holly E. Heard. "Nonresident Father Visitation, Parental Conflict, and Mother's Satisfaction: What's Best for Child Well-Being?" *Journal of Marriage and the Family, 61* (May 1999): 385-396

When non-resident fathers maintained parenting behaviors characteristic of the residential family, such as providing emotional support to children, offering praise, and dispensing discipline when necessary, children scored higher on measures of postdivorce adjustment.
Source: Simons, R. L. (Ed.) *Understanding Differences between Divorced and Intact Families: Stress, Interaction, and Child Outcome.* Thousand Oaks, CA: Sage, 1996.

In a study of over 500 families, divorced, non-residential fathers were less likely to help their children solve problems, to discuss standards of conduct, or to enforce discipline compared with fathers in nuclear families. This reduced involvement in parenting was associated with an increased probability that a boy would display conduct problems.
Source: Simons, Ronald L., et al. "Explaining the Higher Incidence of Adjustment Problems Among Children of Divorce Compared with Those in Two-Parent Families." *Journal of Marriage and the Family, 61* (November 1999): 1020-1033.

Adolescents' feelings of closeness to their non-custodial fathers was found to be positively associated with adolescents' psychological and behavioral adjustment. Feelings of closeness to fathers, however, was only modestly correlated with the frequency of visitation.
Source: Buchanan, C.M., E.E. Maccoby, and S. M. Dornbusch. *Adolescents After Divorce*. Cambridge, MA: Harvard University Press, 1996.

In a study of non-resident father involvement, fathers' intrinsic support (reflected in trust, encouragement, and discussing problems) was found to be positively correlated with children's life satisfaction, but fathers' extrinsic support (reflected in going out to dinner, buying things, and seeing movies together) was not.
Source: Young, M.H., B.C. Miller, M.C. Norton, and E.J. Hill. "The Effect of Parental Supportive Behaviors on Life Satisfaction of Adolescent Offspring." *Journal of Marriage and the Family, 57* (1995): 813-822.

Unwed Fathers
The Facts about Unwed Fathers
Unwed Father Involvement with their Children

In a study of 135 African American unwed mothers in Baltimore, 27% of the mothers reported that the fathers were supportive during pregnancy, 44% of fathers had attended the delivery of their baby, 75% had visited their baby in the hospital, and 47% were regular caretakers of the child during the first year of life. While involvement during pregnancy and birth did not distinguish which fathers became residential fathers later on, involvement during the first year of life did.
Source: Coley, Rebekah Levine, and P. Lindsay Chase-Lindsdale. "Stability and Change in Paternal Involvement Among Urban African American Fathers." *Journal of Family Psychology, 13* (1999): 416-435.

Using data from the Child Supplement to the National Longitudinal Survey of Youth (NLYS-CS), it was found that only 33% of unwed fathers were living with their children during the first year of the child's life. Of the 40% who were visiting their children during the first year of life, less than half continued to do so two years later.
Source: McLanahan, Sara, Irwin Garfinkel, Jeanne Brooks-Gunn, and Hongxin Zhao. Unwed Fathers and Fragile Families: Paternal Involvement During Infancy. Paper presented at the Brookings Institution Roundtable on Children, January 7, 1999.

In a study of urban African American families, it was found that by the time a child was 3 years old, just one in five young single mothers said their child's father took "a lot" of responsibility for the child, compared to 88 percent of married and cohabiting mothers.
Source: Coley, Rebekah Levin, and P. Lindsay Chase-Lindsdale. "Stability and Change in Paternal Involvement Among Urban African American Fathers." *Journal of Family Psychology, 13* (September 1999): 416-435.

Predictors of Unwed Father Involvement with their Children
Fathers with jobs and education are more likely to be involved with their children after divorce or a non-marital birth.
Source: Cooksey, E.C., and P.H. Craig. "Parenting From a Distance: The Effects of Paternal Characteristics on Contact Between Non-Residential Fathers and Their Children." *Demography, 35* (1998): 187-200; see also Rangarajan, A., and P. Gleason. "Young Unwed Fathers of AFDC Children: Do They Provide Support?" *Demography, 35* (1998): 175-186.

...by the time a child was 3 years old, just one in five young single mothers said their child's father took "a lot" of responsibility for the child, compared to 88 percent of married and cohabiting mothers.

In a study of 135 African-American unwed mothers in Baltimore, employed fathers were 6 times more likely than unemployed fathers to be described as highly involved with their children during the first year of life, and fathers who were married to or cohabiting with the child's mother were 11 times more likely than non-residential fathers to be highly involved with their children during the first year of life.

Source: Coley, Rebekah Levine, and P. Lindsay Chase-Lindsdale. "Stability and Change in Paternal Involvement Among Urban African American Fathers." *Journal of Family Psychology, 13* (1999): 416-435.

Unwed Fathers and Later Marriage

Using a sample of 940 children drawn from the National Longitudinal Survey of Youth, it was found that of the unmarried mothers who later married, 50% married the child's biological father. Of the 50% of the children born out of wedlock whose mothers subsequently married someone other than the child's biological father, fewer than 30% reported having ever lived with their biological father.

Source: Cooksey, Elizabeth C. "Consequences of Young Mothers' Marital Histories for Children's Cognitive Development." *Journal of Marriage and the Family, 59* (May 1997): 245-261.

In an analysis of data from two nationally representative data sets, the National Longitudinal Survey of Young Men and the National Longitudinal Survey of Youth, it was found that having lived in a family that received welfare lowers the likelihood that an unwed father will marry the mother in the event of a nonmarital pregnancy.

Source: Zavodny, Madeline. "Do Men's Characteristics Affect Whether a Nonmarital Pregnancy Results in Marriage?" *Journal of Marriage and the Family, 61* (August 1999): 764-773.

Teen Fathers

In a study of the children of 45 teenage fathers, only 42% were living with their fathers at 18-24 months of age. Fully 40% no longer had any contact whatsoever with their fathers.

Source: Fagot, Beverly I., Katherine C. Pears, Deborah M. Capaldi, Lynn Crosby, and Craig S. Leve. "Becoming an Adolescent Father: Precursors and Parenting." *Developmental Psychology, 34* (1998): 1209-1219.

In a longitudinal study of 204 high-risk males beginning when they were 11-13 years of age, the strongest predictor of who would later become an unwed, teenage father was poor academic performance. Unwed teenage fathers, compared to those who did not go on to become fathers as teenagers, were also twice as likely to use tobacco daily, twice as likely to use marijuana, and four times as likely to use hard illegal drugs.

Source: Fagot, Beverly I., Katherine C. Pears, Deborah M. Capaldi, Lynn Crosby, and Craig S. Leve. "Becoming an Adolescent Father: Precursors and Parenting." *Developmental Psychology, 34* (1998): 1209-1219.

Less than half of all young men who have fathered children in high school finish high school. Those who do are highly unlikely to seek any higher education.

Source: *2004 Kids Count Data Book: Moving Youth From Risk to Opportunity.* Baltimore, MD: The Annie E. Casey Foundation, 2004: 11.

Men who become fathers as adolescents will finish an average of 11.3 years of school by the age of 27, compared with nearly 13 years by their counterparts who delay fathering until age 21 or older.

Source: Maynard, Rebecca A. (Ed.). *Kids Having Kids: Economic Costs and Social Consequences of Teen Pregnancy.* Washington, D.C.: The Urban Institute Press, 1997.

Teen fathers are more likely to engage in delinquent behaviors, to use alcohol routinely, deal drugs, and quit school.

Source: *When Teens Have Sex: Issues and Trends.* Baltimore, MD: The Annie E. Casey Foundation, 1998: 13.

Less than half of all young men who have fathered children in high school finish high school. Those who do are highly unlikely to seek any higher education.

Teen fathers are more likely to engage in delinquent behaviors, to use alcohol routinely, deal drugs, and quit school.

In a study of 615 boys in urban Rochester, NY, the majority of those who eventually became teen fathers were sexually active by age 16, frequently used illicit drugs, and were involved in gangs and violent behavior. Chronic drug use alone more than doubled the probability of becoming a teen father.
Source: Thornberry, Terence P., et al. "Teenage Fatherhood and Delinquent Behavior." Office of Juvenile Justice and Delinquency Prevention, U.S. Department of Justice, January 2000.

In a study of 506 boys in urban Pittsburgh, PA, those who later became teen fathers were more likely to have been raised on welfare, see others deal or use drugs, and be delinquent themselves.
Source: Thornberry, Terence P., et al. "Teenage Fatherhood and Delinquent Behavior." Office of Juvenile Justice and Delinquency Prevention, U.S. Department of Justice, January 2000.

Incarcerated Fathers

"In the beginning [my daughter and I] were close—all the way up to the age of eight or nine we were close. But after I kept getting myself in trouble [going back and forth to prison] I guess she kind of gave up on me. I was never around and I guess it hurt her. We just recently had a conversation on the phone. She cried and she explained [that] she feel that she didn't have no dad and it hurt me to hear that, but it was the truth. So now I have been trying to incorporate myself into her life again."

A 40-YEAR-OLD FATHER OF THREE CHILDREN, CURRENTLY SERVING A SENTENCE PAROLE VIOLATION IN A HALFWAY HOUSE. FROM EDIN, KATHRYN, TIMOTHY J. NELSON, AND RECHELLE PARANAL. "FATHERHOOD AND INCARCERATION AS POTENTIAL TURNING POINTS IN THE CRIMINAL CAREERS OF UNSKILLED MEN." INSTITUTE FOR POLICY RESEARCH, NORTHWESTERN UNIVERSITY, MAY 5, 2001.

When a family member is sent to prison, the impact is similar to a divorce. The concerns in the aftermath fall into five categories: individual, economic, legal, familial, and communal.
Source: Kaslow, F.W. "Divorce and its sequelae: A psychological perspective." Ed. F.W. Kaslow. *Handbook of Couple and Family Forensics.* New York, NY: John Wiley, 2000: 235-257.

A Department of Justice survey of 7,000 inmates revealed the number of jail inmates who lived in mother only households dropped from 43% to 39% between 1996 and 2002. The number of jail inmates who lived in a foster home, agency, or institution also dropped from 14% to 12% over the same period.

Approximately forty-six percent of jail inmates in 2002 had a previously incarcerated family member. One-fifth experienced a father in prison or jail.
Source: James, Doris J. *Profile of Jail Inmates, 2002.* (NCJ 201932). Bureau of Justice Statistics Special Report, Department of Justice, Office of Justice Programs, July 2004.

In a study of 531 incarcerated juvenile offenders, 28% reported becoming an adolescent father before the age of 20. Residing with a non-biological parent as a caretaker was identified as one of key predictors of adolescent fatherhood.
Source: Unruh, Deanne, Michael Bullis, and Paul Yovanoff. "Adolescent Fathers Who Are Incarcerated Juvenile Offenders: Explanatory Study of the Co-Occurrence of Two Problem Behaviors." *Journal of Child and Family Studies, 13* (December 2004): 405-419.

> Approximately forty-six percent of jail inmates in 2002 had a previously incarcerated family member.

In 1999, State and Federal prisons held an estimated 667,900 fathers of minor children, 44 percent of whom lived with their children prior to incarceration.
Source: Mumola, Christopher. *Incarcerated Parents and Their Children*. (NCJ 182335). Bureau of Justice Statistics Special Report, Department of Justice, Office of Justice Programs, August 2000.

"The typical male inmate grew up in a single parent home and has at least one family member who has been incarcerated."
Source: Brenner, Eric. *Fathers in Prison: A Review of the Data*. NCOFF Brief. Philadelphia: National Center on Fathers and Families, University of Pennsylvania, 1998.

1,372,700 minor children currently have a father in State or Federal prison, an increase of 58 percent since 1991.
Source: Mumola, Christopher. *Incarcerated Parents and Their Children*. (NCJ 182335). Bureau of Justice Statistics Special Report, Department of Justice, Office of Justice Programs, August 2000.

Ten million children have parents who have been imprisoned at some time in their lives.
Source: Jacobs, A. *Protecting Children and Preserving Families; A Cooperative Strategy for Nurturing Children of Incarcerated Parents*. New York: New York Women's Prison Association, 1995.

In 1999, fathers were missing from 300,900 households with minor children due to incarceration.
Source: Mumola, Christopher. *Incarcerated Parents and Their Children*. (NCJ 182335). Bureau of Justice Statistics Special Report, Department of Justice, Office of Justice Programs, August 2000.

While most incarcerated men are fathers, most are unmarried and did not live with their children at the time of their arrest.
Source: Hairston, Creasie Finney. "Fathers in Prison." In K. Gabel and D. Johnston (Eds.), *Children of Incarcerated Parents*. Pasadena, CA: Pacific Oaks Center for Children of Incarcerated Parents, 1995: 31-40; see also Brenner, Eric. *Fathers in Prison: A Review of the Data*. NCOFF Brief. Philadelphia: National Center on Fathers and Families, University of Pennsylvania, 1998.

African-American children are nearly 9 times more likely to have a parent in prison than white children. Hispanic children are 3 times as likely to have a parent in prison than white children.
Source: Mumola, Christopher. *Incarcerated Parents and Their Children*. (NCJ 182335). Bureau of Justice Statistics Special Report, Department of Justice, Office of Justice Programs, August 2000.

In 1997, 40 percent of fathers in State prison reported weekly contact with their children, by phone, mail or personal visits. Fifty-seven percent of fathers in State prison reported never having a personal visit with their children since their incarceration.
Source: Mumola, Christopher. *Incarcerated Parents and Their Children*. (NCJ 182335). Bureau of Justice Statistics Special Report, Department of Justice, Office of Justice Programs, August 2000.

Studies have shown that prisoners who maintain family ties have significantly greater success upon moving onto parole.
Source: Brenner, Eric. *Fathers in Prison: A Review of the Data*. NCOFF Brief. Philadelphia: National Center on Fathers and Families, University of Pennsylvania, 1998; see also Family and Corrections Network Report, Issue No. 1, 1994, p. 2.

Older fathers are more likely to use the event of incarceration to try to repair severed bonds with family than younger fathers.
Source: Edin, Kathryn, Timothy J. Nelson, and Rechelle Paranal. "Fatherhood and Incarceration As Potential Turning Points in the Criminal Careers of Unskilled Men." Institute for Policy Research, Northwestern University, May 5, 2001.

"The typical male inmate grew up in a single parent home and has at least one family member who has been incarcerated."

Ten million children have parents who have been imprisoned at some time in their lives.

About half of all fathers in State and Federal prisons had a personal income of less than $1,000 a month prior to incarceration.
Source: Mumola, Christopher. *Incarcerated Parents and Their Children.* (NCJ 182335). Bureau of Justice Statistics Special Report, Department of Justice, Office of Justice Programs, August 2000.

A study estimated that over half of male inmates in New Jersey are fathers, but that only 10 percent of the inmates lived with their children prior to incarceration.
Source: National Center on Fathers and Families. State Policy Series on Family Support and Father Involvement. (SPS-98-03). Philadelphia: National Center on Fathers and Families, University of Pennsylvania, 1998.

In Tennessee in 1995, 67.5% of male felons had children, and that each felon/father had an average of 2.4 children.
Source: Tennessee Department of Corrections. *The Children and Families of Incarcerated Felons: Status Report and Demographic Inquiry.* Nashville, TN: Tennessee Department of Corrections, 1995.

Of the 36,000 inmates incarcerated in Georgia state prisons, 88% had at least one child.
Source: National Governors' Association. *Governors' Bulletin.* Washington, D.C.: NGA, 1995.

A study estimated that over half of male inmates in New Jersey are fathers, but that only 10 percent of the inmates lived with their children prior to incarceration.

Single Fatherhood

"There have been a lot of professional opportunities I've had to let go by me. Yes, I was envious. I'd think, if that guy can do it, I could do the same thing, if not better. But I didn't have time to devote. I had to be gone by five o'clock, because I had to come home and make dinner."

JOHN CLARK, 39, AND A SINGLE FATHER. AS QUOTED IN MEN'S HEALTH MAGAZINE, NOVEMBER 1996.

"The last thing we need in our national discussion on families is to have abandoned denial and romanticism about single mothers, only to replace it with denial and romanticism about single fathers. The main question we face is not whether single fathers are as good as single mothers, but whether we want to continue to fragment married-couple homes into single-parent homes of either sex."

DAVID BLANKENHORN, PROPOSITIONS, NO. 11, SPRING/SUMMER 2001.

The Facts About Single Fathers

In 2000, there were 2 million single-father families with children, up from 1.3 million in 1990, a 51 percent increase. In 1970, there were only 393,000 single fathers.

- Currently, 3.1 million children under age 18 live with only their fathers, up from 2 million in 1990.
- Single fathers comprise 17 percent—one out of every six—of the nation's 11.7 million single parents.
- Among single fathers caring for children, 62 percent are divorced or separated, 34 percent are never married, and 4 percent are widowed.
- Sixty-four percent of single fathers care for only one child under 18, and 7 percent care for three or more such children.
- Sixty-five percent of single fathers are non-Hispanic white, 16 percent are African-American, and 15 percent are Hispanic.

Source: Fields, Jason, and Lynn M. Casper. *America's Families and Living Arrangements: March 2000.* Current Population Reports, P20-537. Detailed and Historical Tables. Washington, D.C.: U.S. Census Bureau, 2001.

Sixteen percent of children living with single fathers also lived with their father's cohabiting partner.

Source: *America's Children: Key National Indicators of Well-Being, 2001.* Table POP5.B. Washington, D.C.: Federal Interagency Forum on Child and Family Statistics, 2001.

The typical single father is 38 years old and has a median family income of $32,427.

Source: U.S. Census Bureau. *Household and Family Characteristics: March 1998.* Table 11. Washington, D.C.: U.S. Census Bureau, 1998; and U.S. Census Bureau. Historical Income Tables: Families. Table F-10. 1999.

Differences between Single Custodial Fathers and Single Custodial Mothers

Single-mother families are more than twice as likely to be poor as single-father families (35% vs. 16%, respectively). In 1999, the median income of single-father families with children was $32,427, compared to $19,934 for single-mother families with children.

Source: U.S. Census Bureau. "America's Families and Living Arrangements: March 2000." *Current Population Reports*, P20-537. Table FG-5. Washington, D.C.: U.S. Census Bureau, 2001. Historical Income Tables: Families. Table F-10. 1999.

Consequences of Single Fatherhood for Child Well-Being

In a study using a national probability sample of 1,250 fathers of school aged children, single fathers were found to spend significantly more time with their children than fathers in family structures where there are two biological parents. However, children of single fathers fared the worst academically of all children.
Source: Cooksey, Elizabeth C. and Michelle M. Fondell. "Spending Time with His Kids: Effects of Family Structure on Fathers' and Children's Lives." *Journal of Marriage and the Family 58* (August 1996): 693-707.

In a sample pulled from the NLAS, more than 30 percent of teens living with single fathers have been in violent encounters three or more times compared to 25% of teens living with single mothers and 15% of teens living with their biological parents.
Source: Cummins, H.J. "Living in a home with a single father can be treacherous for teens, according to a wide-ranging new study." *Minneapolis Star Tribune,* 5 August 2001: 1E.

Using three years of data from the National Household Survey on Drug Abuse, it was found that the risk that adolescents aged 12 to 17 would use illegal drugs was highest among adolescents in father-only and father-stepmother families, even after controlling for the effects of sex, age, race or ethnicity, family income, and residential mobility. The risk of drug use was lowest in intact, two-parent married households.
Source: Hoffman, John P., and Robert A. Johnson. "A National Portrait of Family Structure and Adolescent Drug Use." *Journal of Marriage and the Family, 60* (August 1998): 633-645.

Among children living in single-parent households, those living with only their fathers were approximately one and two-thirds times more likely to be physically abused than those living with only their mothers.
Source: Sedlak, Andrea J., and Diane D. Broadhurst. *Third National Incidence Study of Child Abuse and Neglect.* U.S. Department of Health and Human Services, Administration on Children, Youth, and Families, National Center for Child Abuse and Neglect, September 1996.

In a study of 16,000 adolescents pulled from the ADDHEALTH database, those in single-father families reported the highest level of delinquency followed by those in father-stepmother families and single-mother families. Two-married-biological parent families experienced the lowest levels of delinquency. Moreover, levels of parental involvement, supervision, monitoring, and closeness were higher on average in two-married-biological parent families as well. This relationship held even when taking income into account.
Source: Brown, Susan L. and Stephen Demuth. "Family Structure, Family Processes, and Adolescent Delinquency: The Significance of Parental Absence Versus Parental Gender." *Journal of Research in Crime and Delinquency, 41* (February 2004): 58-81.

In a longitudinal study of 6,403 boys, it was found that after controlling for family background variables such as mother's education level, race, family income, and number of siblings, as well as neighborhood variables such as unemployment rates and median income, boys who grew up in single-father families were no more likely to be incarcerated than those living with both parents.
Source: Harper, Cynthia, and Sara McLanahan. "Father Absence and Youth Incarceration." Paper presented at the annual meeting of the American Sociological Association, San Francisco, CA, 1998.

II. Father Time and Family-Work Conflict

"I think quality time is just a way of deluding ourselves into shortchanging our children. Children need vast amounts of parental time and attention. It's an illusion to think they're going to be on your timetable, and that you can say 'O.K. we've got half an hour, let's get on with it.' "

DR. RONALD LEVANT, AS CITED BY LAURA SHAPIRO, "THE MYTH OF QUALITY TIME," *NEWSWEEK*, MAY 12, 1997.

"Of course one of the big lessons of becoming a father is that you no longer see yourself as the sole protagonist of your movie: you are now just one of the cast, part of the ensemble."

WRITER RICH COHEN, "HOW MY SON GOT HIS NAME," *THE NEW YORK TIMES*, JANUARY 2, 2005.

"Parents are too busy spending their most precious capital—their time and their energy—struggling to keep up with MasterCard payments... They work long hours to barely keep up, and when they get home at the end of the day they're tired. And their kids are left with a Nintendo or a pair of Nikes or some other piece of crap. Big deal."

HARVARD PSYCHIATRIST ROBER T. COLES, 1991

"Kids spell love T-I-M-E."

AUTHOR KEN CANFIELD AT THE GOVERNOR'S SUMMIT ON FATHERS, CHARLESTON, SOUTH CAROLINA, SEPTEMBER 30, 1997.

Father Time

"The three most important things for children? To love and be loved by their mother and father. To have enduring relationships over time with others who care for them and care what kind of people they become. To learn what it means to live a good life."

DAVID BLANKENHORN IN *THE MISSISSIPPI CLARION-LEDGER*, AUGUST 2004.

Attitudes About Family Time

In a telephone survey of 200 12- to 15-year-olds and 200 parents, 21% of the children reported their top concern was not having enough time with their parents, whereas only 8% of parents said their top concern was not having enough time with their children.

Source: YMCA-2000 'Strong Families' Survey. Telephone survey conducted December 7-9, 1999 by Global Strategy Group of New York City for the YMCA of the USA.

Seventy percent of fathers and mothers feel they do not have enough time with their children.

Source: Bond, James T., Ellen Galinsky, and Jennifer E. Swanberg. *The 1997 National Study of the Changing Workforce*. New York: Families and Work Institute, 1998.

Seventy percent of fathers and mothers feel they do not have enough time with their children.

73% of kids say they spend less than one hour a day talking to their families. Only 20% said it's "very easy" to talk to parents about things that really matter. 26% said it's "somewhat difficult" or "very difficult" to talk about serious topics with their parents.
Source: Philips "Let's Connect" Family Communication Survey.

81% of youth ages 12-17 agreed that they can always trust their parents to be there for them when they need them. 62% said the same thing about their friends.
Source: Farkas, Steve et al. *Kids These Days: What Americans Really Think about the Next Generation*. Survey. Public Agenda. Ronald McDonald House Charities and the Advertising Council. June 1997.

A phone survey of over 3,200 adults and children found that over half of the parents surveyed say it is common for parents to equate buying things for their children to caring for them.
Source: Farkas, Steve et al. *Kids These Days: What Americans Really Think About the Next Generation*. Survey. Public Agenda. Ronald McDonald House Charities and the Advertising Council. June 1997.

Attitudes About Father Time

In 1999, 56.5% of those polled in a national survey (n = 928) agreed that "fathers today spend less time with children then their fathers did with them," up from 50.9% in 1996.
Source: Survey conducted by the Gallup Organization for The National Center for Fathering, as quoted in Today's Father, vol. 7 (2-3), 1999: 17.

According to a national survey of 1,010 adults and 500 teenagers, 61% of adults and 60% of teens agree that, "Youth are more likely to be violent and commit crimes when their fathers are living at home but not involved in their kids' lives."
Source: *Kids & Violence: A National Survey and Report*. Based on a national survey conducted by Wirthlin Worldwide between September 11-17, 1998 for Family First, Tampa, Florida.

A phone survey of over 3,200 adults and children found that 35% of parents think that fathers who act like their careers are more important than their families are very common, while only 22% of parents believe that fathers who are loving and affectionate toward their children are very common.
Source: Farkas, Steve et al. *Kids These Days: What Americans Really Think About the Next Generation. Survey*. Public Agenda. Ronald McDonald House Charities and the Advertising Council. June 1997.

The Facts About Father Time

In two-parent families, children under the age of 13 spend an average of 1.77 hours engaged in activities with their fathers and 2.35 hours doing so with their mothers on a daily basis in 1997. Children in single parent families spent .42 hours with their fathers and 1.26 hours with their mothers on daily basis.
Source: Lippman, Laura, et al. *Indicators of Child, Family, and Community Connections*. Office of the Assistant Secretary for Planning and Evaluation. Washington, DC: US Department of Health and Human Services, 2004 < http://aspe.hhs.gov/hsp/connections-charts04/>

In spite of increases in maternal labor force participation and college degrees, children age 3 to 12 spend about 4.3 hours more time with their parents per week in 1997 (about 28.6 hours) than in 1981 (about 24.3 hours). Father time increased by 2.0 hours per week over the same period.

The change was more pronounced for two-parent families. In fact, increases in the amount of time with fathers in two-parent families was offset by the increase in single mother families.
Source: Sandberg, John F. and Sandra L. Hofferth. "Changes in Children's Time With Parents: United States, 1981-1997." *Demography 38* (August 2001): 423-436; Conlin, Michelle. "Look Who's Barefoot in the Kitchen." *Business Week,* 17 September 2001: 76-77.

Fathers in intact families spend about 1 hour and 13 minutes on a weekday and 3.3 hours on a weekend day with children under age 13.
Source: Yeung, W. Jean, et al. "Children's Time With Fathers in Intact Families." *Journal of Marriage and Family, 63* (February 2001): 136-154.

> **Mothers, on average, spend five more hours per week with their children in comparison to fathers and also reported more role strain.**

From 1981 to 1997, father time increased by three hours a week for intact families. The change was not reflected overall due to the rise in single-parent and nonresidential families.
Source: Sandberg, John F. and Sandra L. Hofferth. "Changes in parental time with children." *Demography 38* (August 2001): 423-436.

In two surveys of 1,980 adults, fathers spend fewer total hours even though the matched mothers in terms of focused time. Fathers whose youngest child is an adolescent report the most strain.
Source: Milkie, Melissa A., Marybeth J. Mattingly, Kei M. Nomaguchi, Suzanne M. Bianchi, and John P. Robinson. "The Time Squeeze: Parental Statuses and Feelings About Time With Children." *Journal of Marriage and Family 66* (August 2004): 739-761.

Mothers, on average, spend five more hours per week with their children in comparison to fathers and also reported more role strain. Fathers' and mothers' estimates, however, were almost identical although fathers' assessment of the mothers' involvement was much lower than what mothers gave themselves. Moreover, fathers benefited most when roles in the household where clearly defined.
Source: Lee, Marceline, Lynne Vernon-Feagans, Arcel Vazquez and Amy Kolak. "The Influence of Family Environment and Child Temperament on Work/Family Role Strain for Mothers and Fathers." *Infant and Child Development, 12* (December 2003): 421-439.

Married fathers reported spending four hours a day with their children in 1998 compared to 2.7 hours in 1965. Sixty-nine percent of fathers say that they share the play with their children with their wives; 60 percent share the role of disciplinarian; and 54 percent share the role of caregiver.
Source: Gardyn, Rebecca. "Make Room for Daddy." *American Demographics* June 2000: 34-35.

> **Married fathers reported spending four hours a day with their children in 1998 compared to 2.7 hours in 1965.**

In a study of 799 families from the National Survey of Families and Households, fathers in two-parent biological families reported spending more time with their children and having higher family cohesion than did fathers in all other types of family structures.
Source: Lansford, Jennifer E., Rosario Ceballo, Antonia Abbey, and Abigail J. Stewart. "Does Family Structure Matter? A Comparison of Adoptive, Two-Parent Biological, Single-Mother, Stepfather, and Stepmother Households." *Journal of Marriage and the Family, 63* (August 2001): 840-851.

Children in two-parent families spent more time with their parents in 1997 than in 1981. Children's average time with their fathers increased from 19 hours a week in 1981 to 23 hours a week in 1997; the amount of time spent with mothers increased from 25 to 31 hours a week. Children's time with mothers in two-parent families increased over this period, regardless of whether mothers were employed outside of the home or not, but time with fathers increased significantly only in families in which mothers were working outside of the home.
Source: Sandberg, John F., and Sandra L. Hofferth. *Changes in Children's Time Spent with Parents*, U.S. 1981-1997. Population Studies Center Research Report 01-475. Institute for Social Research, University of Michigan, 2001.

On average, a child in a two-parent family spends 1.2 hours each weekday and 3.3 hours on a weekend day directly interacting with his or her father. Overall, the average total time fathers in two-parent families are engaged with or accessible to their children is 2.5 hours on weekdays and 6.3 hours on weekend days.
Source: Yeung, W. Jean, John F. Sandberg, Pamela E. Davis-Kean, and Sandra L. Hofferth. "Children's Time With Fathers in Intact Families." *Journal of Marriage and the Family, 63* (February 2000): 136-154.

According to a time-diary comparison study, married fathers spent an average of 3.8 hours a day with their children in 1998, up from 2.8 hours a day in 1965. Mothers' time with children basically remained the same, averaging 5.3 hours a day in 1965 and 5.5 hours a day in 1998.
Source: Bianchi, Suzanne M. "Maternal Employment and Time with Children: Dramatic Change or Surprising Continuity?" *Demography, 37.*4 (November 2000): 401-414.

In a study of 1,761 intact, two-parent households with children 12 years of age or younger, it was found that fathers do 65% as much childcare as mothers on weekdays and 87% as much on weekends.
Source: Yeung, W. Jean, John F. Sandberg, Pamela E. Davis-Kean, and Sandra L. Hofferth. "Children's Time With Fathers in Intact Families." *Journal of Marriage and the Family, 63* (February 2000): 136-154.

In a time-diary comparison study of married couples with children, fathers' share of childcare more than doubled between 1965 and 1998. In 1965, fathers spent 24% as much time as mothers did caring for their children. By 1998, that difference had narrowed considerably, with fathers spending 55% as much time as mothers did in direct childcare activities.
Source: Bianchi, Suzanne M. "Maternal Employment and Time with Children: Dramatic Change or Surprising Continuity?" *Demography, 37.*4 (November 2000): 401-414.

Sixty-eight percent of young people ages 12-17 report that they get a hug or kiss from a parent "every day" or "almost every day." Fifty-one percent say they get help or advice from parents with homework or school projects "every day" or "almost every day."
Source: Farkas, Steve et al. *Kids These Days: What Americans Really Think about the Next Generation*. Survey. Public Agenda. Ronald McDonald House Charities and the Advertising Council. June 1997.

...the average total time fathers in two-parent families are engaged with or accessible to their children is 2.5 hours on weekdays and 6.3 hours on weekend days.

...fathers' share of childcare more than doubled between 1965 and 1998.

In a study using a national probability sample of 1,250 fathers of school-aged children, it was found that fathers eat only half of their breakfasts and dinners together with their children. In addition, fathers who had no father figure present when they were growing up were less likely to participate in activities with their own children than men who had father figures during their own childhoods.
Source: Cooksey, Elizabeth C. and Michelle M. Fondell. "Spending Time with His Kids: Effects of Family Structure on Fathers' and Children's Lives." *Journal of Marriage and the Family, 58* (August 1996): 693-707.

Fathers and Childcare

A resounding 96% of respondents in a national survey agreed that parents should share equally in the caretaking of children.
Source: Radcliffe Public Policy Center. *Life's Work: Generational Attitudes toward Work and Life Integration*. Cambridge, MA: The Institute for Advanced Study, 2000.

A report on trends in paternal childcare found that there were 14.8 million fathers in married-couple families with children under 15 whose wives worked. Among these families:
- 2.9 million fathers provided care for at least one child while the mother was working.
- 1.9 million fathers were the primary caregiver, providing more hours of care than any other single provider while the mother was working.
- 1.6 million fathers were taking care of their preschool-aged children.
- 1 in 5 fathers were the primary care provider for their preschool-aged children compared to about
- 1 in 10 fathers who were the primary care provider for their school-aged children.
Source: Casper, Lynne M. "My Daddy Takes Care of Me! Fathers as Care Providers." United States Bureau of the Census P70-59. September 1997.

Family Time in Father-Absent Homes

Single mothers are more likely to struggle to spend time with their children compared to mothers in two-parent families. In 1997, mothers in two-parent families spent, on average, 31 hours a week with their children, compared to only 21 hours a week for mothers heading single-parent families.
Source: Sandberg, John F., and Sandra L. Hofferth. *Changes in Children's Time Spent with Parents*, U.S. 1981-1997. Population Studies Center Research Report 01-475. Institute for Social Research, University of Michigan, 2001.

Sixty-nine percent of poor, unmarried mothers and half of poor, unmarried fathers agreed that showing love and affection was the most important trait for a "good father." This was overwhelmingly the top selection.
Source: McLanahan, Sara. *The Fragile Families and Child Wellbeing Study: Baseline National Report*. Table 4. Princeton, NJ: Center for Research on Child Wellbeing, 2003: 10.

Children under age 13 living with single mothers were found to spend 12 to 14 fewer hours each week with parents than children living with married parents.
Source: Hofferth, Sandra L. "Women's Employment and Care of Children in the United States." In T. Van der Lippe and L. Van Dijk (Eds.), *Women's Employment in a Comparative Perspective*. New York: Aldine de Gruyter, 2001.

In a study of 383 African-American mothers and their adolescent children (ages 11 to 16) from poverty tracts and 163 African-American mothers and their adolescent children from middle-class tracts, it was found that youth in single-parent, welfare-dependent households were subject to less adult supervision than youth in any other family type.
Source: Quane, James M., and Bruce H. Ranking. "Neighborhood Poverty, Family Characteristics, and Commitment to Mainstream Goals: The Case of African American Adolescents in the Inner City." *Journal of Family Issues, 19* (1998): 769-794.

A resounding 96% of respondents in a national survey agreed that parents should share equally in the caretaking of children.

Married Fathers Providing Child Care While Mothers Are Working, 1988 to 1993*

	1988		1991		1993	
	Number	Proportion	Number	Proportion	Number	Proportion
Caring for Children 0-15						
Total number of married fathers whose wives are employed	14,278	100%	14,620	100%		100%
Providing some care	2,698	18.9%	3,331	22.8%	2,194	19.6%
Primary Provider of care	1,699	11.8%	2,032	13.9%	1,915	12.9%
Caring for Children Under 5						
Total number of married fathers whose wives are employed	6,536	100%	6,274	100%	6,274	100%
Providing some care	1,523	23.3%	1,901	30.2%	1,554	24.8%
Primary Provider of care	1,107	16.9%	1,407	22.4%	1,164	18.5%
Caring for Children 5-14						
Total number of married fathers whose wives are employed	10,720	100%	11,256	100%	11,412	100%
Providing some care	1,660	15.5%	1,975	17.5%	1,780	15.6%
Primary Provider of care	941	8.8%	1,015	9.0%	1,034	9.1%

*Numbers in thousands, proportion distribution within each age category.

1The number of fathers of children under 5 combined with the number of fathers of children 5-14 does not sum to the total number of fathers of children 0-14 because some fathers have children in both age groups.

Source: Casper, Lynne M. "My Daddy Takes Care of Me! Fathers as Care Providers." United States Bureau of the Census p70-59. September 1997.

Consequences of the Lack of Family Time

Teens with parents who are in the home at key times of the day, such as breakfast, after school, at dinner, and at bedtime, are less likely to try alcohol, tobacco, or marijuana.

Source: Resnick, Michael, et al. "Protecting Adolescents from Harm." *Journal of the American Medical Association, 278* (September 10, 1997): 823-832.

A study of 1,900 students in Mississippi found that children between the ages of 6 and 11 watch an average of 23 hours of television per week and teenagers 12-17 watch an average of 21 hours of television per week.

Source: Page, Randy M., et al. "Psychological and Health-Related Characteristics of Adolescent Television Viewers." *Child Study Journal, 26.*4 (1996): 319-331.

Family-Work Conflict

"Men's definition of success has changed. Where success was once defined by a father's ability to provide for his family, it's now divided equally between being involved with the kids and providing for them."

JAMES LEVINE QUOTED IN "SUPERDAD, MOMS AREN'T ALONE IN STRUGGLING TO BALANCE CAREERS AND FAMILIES," THE BOSTON HERALD, JULY 16, 2002.

"Our dads were not nearly involved as we are, and it's sort of difficult to figure out what my role is: breadwinner, diaper-changer, benevolent but a distant source of strength. [...] Popular culture isn't much help either. Dads are generally portrayed as complete boneheads."

LAWYER TOM DOLGENOS QUOTED IN "NO RESPECT: FATHERS SAY THEIR EFFORTS GO UNAPPRECIATED," THE WALL STREET JOURNAL, MAY 2005.

"The work place is much less hospitable than one would think. If a man shows too much interest in his other life he will be considered a less-than-serious worker. If he takes family leave, he puts himself on a 'daddy track' to nowhere."

FORMER EDITOR OF MS. AND COLUMBIA BUSINESS REVIEW, SUSANNE B. LEVINE, QUOTED IN "IT'S A LONG WAY FROM 'FATHER KNOW BEST' TO THE 21ST CENTURY," NEW ORLEANS TIMES-PICAYUNE, JUNE 18, 2000.

"'An awful lot of kids grow up nicely without both parents always being there,' I'd tell myself during intense periods of travel. And it's true. My kids survived the experience. They're good kids. But if anything had happened with them, I certainly would've blamed anything that went wrong on my career decision."

FATHER RICK TAVAN QUOTED IN "FATHERHOOD IN FLUX," THE SAN FRANCISCO CHRONICLE, JUNE 15, 2003.

Attitudes About Family-Work Conflict

A survey of 25,822 working men and women indicated equal rates of work-family conflict between men and women. Eighty-seven percent of men and 87 percent of women reported some work-family conflict.

Fathers, however, were less likely to report family-work conflict (42%) than working mothers (55%). Hence, there were less likely to feel drained at work due to pressures or problems at home than women were. Fathers were, however, just as likely to report feeling drained at home due to spillover from work.

Working fathers were also less like to report using their company's work-family programs (34%) compared to working mothers (58%).

Source: Hill, E. Jeffrey, et al. "Studying 'Working Fathers': Comparing Fathers' and Mothers' Work-Family Conflict, Fit, and Adaptive Strategies in a Global High-Tech Company." *Fathering, 1* (October 2003): 239-261.

Eighty-seven percent of men and 87 percent of women reported some work-family conflict.

Working fathers were also less like to report using their company's work-family programs (34%) compared to working mothers (58%).

In a 2004 survey of 946 full-time professionals, 39 percent said that they would accept a job paying 10 percent less in favor of a better corporate culture and more work-life balance.
Source: Koeppel, David. "When 'Job' Means Part Time, Life Becomes Very Different." *The New York Times* 10 October 2004: 10.

Four out of ten working fathers indicated they would leave their current job if their spouse earned enough for them to live. Sixty-five percent of all fathers work more than forty hours a week compared to 36 percent of working mothers; one quarter of working fathers work more than 50 hours a week compared to 11 percent of mothers.

Thirty-four percent of fathers cooked dinner four to five times a week as compared to 60 percent of mothers; 22 percent of fathers reported they never cooked dinner during the workweek compared to only 2 percent of working mothers.
Source: Sullivan, Jennifer. "Survey Shows 40 Percent of Working Fathers Willing to Relinquish Breadwinner Role." Chicago, IL: Careerbuilder.com, 2003. Acessed 11 May 2005 <http://www.careerbuilder.com/share/aboutus/pr/2003/061003.htm?cbRecursionCnt=1&cbsid=bfbeb2883e354abd9864c8f80b48d9bc-169137185-w3-2>

Sixty-two percent of fathers would sacrifice job opportunities and higher pay for more family time.
Source: Haralson, Daryl and Suzy Parker. "Dads want more time with family." *USA Today* 15 June 2005: D1.

In 2005, 60% of the 600 employees polled felt that flexibility to balance work-family issues was an important part of their job satisfaction, compared to 62% in 2003. Of human resource professionals, 53% considered work-family balance important, up from 46% in 2003.

An emphasis on work family balance was also highest (69%) for employees 35 and younger.
Source: Esen, Evren. *2005 Job Satisfaction: Survey Report.* Alexandria, VA: Society for Human Resource Management, 2005:10-11.

In a telephone survey of 200 12- to 15-year-olds and 200 parents, 34% of teens and 34% of parents reported that parental work obligations were the main reason families do not spend more time together.
Source: YMCA-2000 'Strong Families' Survey. Telephone survey conducted December 7-9, 1999 by Global Strategy Group of New York City for the YMCA of the USA.

Eighty-two percent of men ages 20-39 put family time at the top of their list compared with 85 percent of women in that age group. Seventy-one percent stated they would forego pay in favor of more time with their families. Surprisingly, young men in their 20's are seven percent more likely than young women to sacrifice their pay for family life.

Moreover, 96 percent of those polled thought that parents should share the child care-taking equally and 68 percent also said they thought one parent should stay home during a child's younger years.
Source: Radcliffe Public Policy Center. *Life's Work: Generational Attitudes toward Work and Life Integration.* Cambridge, MA: Radcliffe Institute for Advanced Study, 2000: 1-12.

In a 1998 survey, 71% of mothers and 65% of fathers said they would be likely to stay home with their children if they were financially able to do so.
Source: The Polling Company, survey of 1,000 registered voters, January/February, 1998.

...34% of teens and 34% of parents reported that parental work obligations were the main reason families do not spend more time together.

A MasterCard survey found that close to 85% of fathers polled said "the most priceless gift of all" was time spent with family.

Source: Harper, Jennifer. "Americans Celebrate Dad Today in All of His Different Guises." *Washington Times*, June 18, 2000: C1.

In a national survey of 2,000 adults, 55% agreed that "Employers giving parents more flexible work schedules so they can spend more time with their kids" was a "very effective" way of helping kids.

Source: Farkas, Steve, et al. Kids These Days: What Americans Really Think about the Next Generation. Survey. Public Agenda. Ronald McDonald House Charities and the Advertising Council. June 1997.

Survey Data Regarding Family-Work Stress

A survey of 546 working adults indicated that 59% did not think it was easier to find a balance between work and family now than it was five years ago. Thirty-two percent thought it was.

Source: USA Today. "Snapshots." *USA Today* 7 June 2005: B1.

In 1997, 31 percent of parents reported they experienced "a lot" of work-family conflict, up from just 16 percent in 1992.

Source: Bond, James T., Ellen Galinsky, and Jennifer E. Swanberg. *The 1997 National Study of the Changing Workforce*. New York: Families and Work Institute, 1998.

In a random sample survey of 32,000 officers and enlisted men and women in the U.S. Air Force, 55% of single fathers and 53% of single mothers reported being unable to successfully manage both the work stress and family stress in their lives.

Source: Heath, D. Terri, and Dennis K. Orthner. "Stress and Adaptation Among Male and Female Single Parents." *Journal of Family Issues, 20* (1999): 557-587.

National polling data reveals that in 1999, 58% of Americans believed employers do not recognize the strain fathers face when trying to balance the demands of family and the demands of work, up from 28% in 1996.

Source: The National Center for Fathering, *Today's Father,* 7(2-3), 1999: 18.

Empirical Studies of Family-Work Conflict

In a study of 447 fathers in dual-earner families, it was found that father involvement with children was primarily in pre-scheduled, non-emergency situations. Emergency situations, such as missing work because childcare was unavailable, had very low levels of father involvement.

Source: Berry, Judy O., and Julie Meyer Rao. "Balancing Employment and Fatherhood: A Systems Perspective." *Journal of Family Issues, 18* (July 1997): 386-402.

Corporate Barriers to Change

Proportion of Companies Offering Family-Friendly Benefits

Flextime	56%
Parental leave above state or federal FMLA	18%
Compressed workweeks	33%
Some form of telecommuting	40%
On-site childcare	6%
Emergency/sick childcare	6%

Data taken from sample of 370 human resource professionals.

Source: Burke, Mary Elizabeth. *2005 Benefits: Survey Report.* Alexandria, VA: Society of Human Resource Management, 2005: 3-10.

Twenty-seven countries provide paid paternity leave. Most of these (16 of 27) provide 100 percent wage replacement for at least some of the leave. Eighteen more countries that do not provide paternity leave offer paid parental leave for both fathers and mothers. In total, 45 countries offer either paid paternity leave or the right to paid paternity leave, including 16 countries that offer one year or more of paid leave to men.

The United States does not guarantee any paid leave to fathers.
Source: Heymann, Jody et al. "The Work, Family, and Equity Index: Where Does the United States Stand Globally?" Boston, MA: *The Project on Global Working Families at the Harvard School of Public Health, 2004*: 1, 25.

Almost half of U.S. fathers took some leave from work after the birth or adoption of a child, but these leaves were brief. The days used were not used as parental leave as very few fathers participated in formal parental leave programs. Fathers usually used paid vacation, sick days or personal days so as to minimize reductions of family income and avoid jeopardizing future career advancement.
Source: Seward, Rudy Ray, Dale E. Yeats, and Lisa K. Zottarelli. "Parental Leave and Father Involvement in Child Care: Sweden and the United States." *Journal of Comparative Family Studies, 33* (Summer 2002): 387-399.

Companies with 100 or more employees most frequently allow workers to return to work on a gradual basis following childbirth and adoption (81%). Only 18% of these companies view the costs of more flexible work arrangements as outweighing the benefits, while 36% view these programs as cost-neutral. Only 42% view these programs as a return on investment.
Source: Bond, James et al. *Highlights of the National Study of the Changing Workforce, 2003.* Executive Summary. New York, NY: Families and Work Institute: II.

Women, on average, receive three weeks more leave than men do. Only 13% of companies offer some replacement pay during leave to men, compared to 53% offered to women.
Source: Bond, James et al. *Highlights of the National Study of the Changing Workforce, 2003.* Executive Summary. New York, NY: Families and Work Institute, 2003: IV.

Effects of Family-Work Conflict

The odds of a reporting a drinking problem increased 45% for each unit increase of pressure on the job. Thus, midlife employees who report the highest levels of pressure at the office are four times more likely to report drinking problems than those with less demanding jobs. More negative spillover from work was also associated with higher odds of a drinking problem while positive spillover from family to work lowered those odds.
Source: Grzywacz, Joseph G. and Nadine F. Marks. "Family, Work, Work-Family Spillover, and Problem Drinking During Midlife." *Journal of Marriage and Family, 62* (May 2000): 336-348.

Although working fewer hours would alleviate some tension between work and family, many are unwilling to make that change. Family responsibilities and hour mismatches are more common for middle-aged workers than for young or old workers; middle-aged workers are 80% more likely to want fewer hours.
Source: Reynolds, Jeremy. "You Can't Always Get the Hours You Want: Mismatches between Actual and Preferred Work Hours in the U.S." *Social Forces, 81* (June 2003): 1171-1199.

> The United States does not guarantee any paid leave to fathers.

In a Harvard School of Public Health survey, 30 percent of respondents chose to cut back at least one day to meet the needs of family, 12 percent sacrificed two days and 5 percent three or more days.

Inflexibility of work schedules can have ill effects on children. Parents whose children were in the bottom quartile in math and reading tests scores were more likely to lack paid vacation leave, sick leave and/or work flexibility. Moreover, for every hour a parent works between 6 and 9 p.m., his or her child is 16 percent more likely to score in the bottom quartile on math tests. Children whose parents work at night are 2.7 times more likely to be suspended even when controlling for parents' income and education.
Source: Myron, Kevin. "Study Finds Work Interruptions to Care for Family Endemic; Lack of Paid Leave and Parents' Night Work Linked to School Children's Lower Test Scores." Harvard School of Public Health Press Release 15 November 2000. Accessed 8 March 2005 <http://www.hsph.harvard.edu/press/releases/press11152000.html>

Those who spend more time focused on work experienced the greatest amount of work-family stress. Those who engaged with the families more than their work experienced a higher quality of life.
Source: Greenhaus, Jeffrey H., Karen M. Collins, and Jason D. Shaw. "The relation between work-family balance and quality of life." *Journal of Vocational Behavior, 63* (December 2003): 510-531.

Employees with high work-to-family conflicts are more likely to leave work early.
Source: Boyar, Scott L., Carl P. Maertz Jr., and Allison W. Pearson. "The effects of work-family conflict and family-work conflict on nonattendance behaviors." *Journal of Business Research, 58* (July 2005): 919-925.

III. Consequences of Father Absence for Children

Child Abuse

"In the movies and on television, as well as in much of the print media, the portrayal of the sexual abuse of children follows a strict formula. It is never the butler. Always, the father did it... But the weight of the evidence is clear. What magnifies the risk of sexual abuse for children is not the presence of a married father but his absence."

DAVID BLANKENHORN, *FATHERLESS AMERICA*, NEW YORK, BASIC BOOKS, 1995.

"Fatal abuse, serious abuse, and neglect are lowest in households with married biological parents and highest in households in which the biological mother cohabits with someone who is not the parent... If American society continues to give equal standing to married family life, single-parent family life, and cohabitation, it must expect continued high levels of child abuse."

PATRICK F. FAGAN AND DOROTHY B. HANKS, *THE CHILD ABUSE CRISIS: THE DISINTEGRATION OF MARRIAGE, FAMILY AND THE AMERICAN COMMUNITY*, THE HERITAGE FOUNDATION, JUNE 3, 1997.

The Child Abuse-Father Absence Connection

In a study of first-graders in Baltimore public schools, being an African-American in a non-nuclear family structure was significantly associated with childhood sexual abuse.
Source: Menard, Christian, K.J. Bandeen-Roche, and H.D. Chilcoat. "Epidemiology of multiple childhood traumatic events: child abuse, parental psychopathology, and other family level stressors." *Social Psychiatry and Psychiatric Epidemiology 39* (2004): 857-865.

In a study of 263 adolescent females, never living with both parents was associated with not disclosing an unwanted sexual experience.
Source: Kogan, Steven M. "Disclosing unwanted sexual experiences: results from a national sample of adolescent women." *Child Abuse & Neglect, 28* (February 2004): 147-165.

In a study of 1,471 Canadian women, single mothers reported substantially lower incomes, higher rates of childhood abuse, and more psychiatric disorders. Almost half of the single mothers were poor compared with fewer than a tenth of married mothers. Reported child abuse was also twice as likely among single mothers when compared to married mothers.
Source: Lipman, Elaine L., Harriet L. MacMillan, and Michael H. Boyle. "Childhood abuse and psychiatric disorders among single and married mothers." *American Journal of Psychiatry. 158* (January 2001): 73-77.

Although levels of physical abuse did not differ by group, children reported that stepfathers were more emotionally abusive and they were more scared of their stepfathers. Children whose biological fathers had been physically abusive reported lower self-competency, but also indicated that their fathers were more emotionally available.
Source: Sullivan, Cris, Jennifer Juras, Deborah Bybee, Huong Nguyen, and Nicole Allen. "How Children's Adjustment Is Affected by Their Relationships to Their Mother's Abusers." *Journal of Interpersonal Violence, 15* (June 2000): 587-602.

Compared to living with both parents, living in a single-parent home doubles the risk that a child will suffer physical, emotional, or educational neglect.
Source: *America's Children: Key National Indicators of Well-Being.* Table SPECIAL1. Washington, D.C.: Federal Interagency Forum on Child and Family Statistics, 1997.

The overall rate of child abuse and neglect in single-parent households is 27.3 children per 1,000, whereas the rate of overall maltreatment in two-parent households is 15.5 per 1,000.
Source: *America's Children: Key National Indicators of Well-Being.* Table SPECIAL1. Washington, D.C.: Federal Interagency Forum on Child and Family Statistics, 1997.

In a longitudinal study of 644 families in upstate New York, children living with a single parent were two times more likely to be physically abused than children living with both parents.
Source: Brown, Jocelyn et al. "A Longitudinal Analysis of Risk Factors for Child Maltreatment: Findings of a 17-Year Prospective Study of Officially Recorded and Self-Reported Child Abuse and Neglect." *Child Abuse & Neglect, 22* (1998): 1065-1078

Compared to living with both parents, living in a single-parent home doubles the risk that a child will suffer physical, emotional, or educational neglect.

An analysis of child abuse cases in a nationally representative sample of 42 counties found that children from single-parent families are more likely to be victims of physical and sexual abuse than children who live with both biological parents. Compared to their peers living with both parents, children in single parent homes had:

- a 77% greater risk of being physically abused
- an 87% greater risk of being harmed by physical neglect
- a 165% greater risk of experiencing notable physical neglect
- a 74% greater risk of suffering from emotional neglect
- an 80% greater risk of suffering serious injury as a result of abuse overall, a 120% greater risk of being endangered by some type of child abuse.

Source: Sedlak, Andrea J. and Diane D. Broadhurst. *The Third National Incidence Study of Child Abuse and Neglect: Final Report.* U.S. Department of Health and Human Services. National Center on Child Abuse and Neglect. Washington, D.C., September 1996.

A national survey of nearly 1,000 parents found that 7.4% of children who lived with one parent had ever been sexually abused, compared to only 4.2% of children who lived with both biological parents.

Source: Finkelhor, David et al. "Sexually Abused Children in a National Survey of Parents: Methodological Issues." *Child Abuse and Neglect, 21* (1997): 1-9.

In a study of 269 Chicago children referred to a family preservation service provider due to child abuse or neglect, only 4.8% lived with both biological parents whereas 61% of the general population of children live with both biological parents.

Source: Quinn, Kevin P. et al. "Personal, Family, and Service Utilization Characteristics of Children Served in an Urban Family Preservation Environment." *Journal of Child and Family Studies, 5* (December 1996): 469-486.

Using data from 1000 students tracked from seventh or eighth grade in 1988 through high school in 1992, researchers determined that only 3.2 percent of the boys and girls who were raised with both biological parents had a history of maltreatment. However, a full 18.6 percent of those in other family situations had been maltreated.

Source: Smith, Carolyn and Terence P. Thornberry. "The Relationship Between Childhood Maltreatment and Adolescent Involvement in Delinquency." *Criminology, 33* (1995): 451-479.

In Iowa, rates of single-parent families were significantly associated with rates of child abuse, whereas medical and economic factors were not.

Source: Weissman, Alicia M., Gerald J. Jogerst, and Jeffrey D. Dawson. "Community characteristics associated with child abuse in Iowa." *Child Abuse & Neglect, 27* (October 2003): 1145-1159.

Father Absence and Adult Abuse

Adolescent women who have lived in a single parent household are more likely to be chronic victims of serious physical violence.

Source: Foshee, Vangie Ann, Thad Steven Benefield, Susan T. Ennett, Karl E. Bauman and Chirayath Suchindran. "Longitudinal predictors of serious physical and sexual dating violence victimization during adolescence." *Preventive Medicine, 39* (November 2004): 1007-1016.

In a study of 277 women, those who had been raised without a father during childhood were at greater risk for sexual assault victimization as an adult. Women who reported a close relationship with a father figure, however, reported lower risk for sexual assault victimization.

Source: Stermac, Lana, Donna Reist, Mary Addison, and Golden M. Millar. "Childhood Risk Factors for Women's Sexual Victimization." *Journal of Interpersonal Violence, 17* (June 2002): 647-670.

> In Iowa, rates of single-parent families were significantly associated with rates of child abuse, whereas medical and economic factors were not.

Crime

"Kids who grow up without a father never experience that special sense of security and the enhanced feeling of belonging that comes from having a father in the home. So they seek it elsewhere. They don't get that sweet feeling of triumph that comes from a father's approval, or the warmth of the old man's hug, or the wisdom to be drawn from his discipline."
BOB HERBERT, NEW YORK TIMES COLUMNIST, IN "DAD'S EMPTY CHAIR," JULY 7, 2005.

"Boys need same-sex role models to define themselves as male. When fathers are absent, young males are more likely to exaggerate their purported masculinity."
KATHLEEN HEIDE, PH.D., PROFESSOR OF CRIMINOLOGY, UNIVERSITY OF SOUTH FLORIDA (HEIDE, KATHLEEN M. "JUVENILE HOMICIDE IN AMERICA: HOW CAN WE STOP THE KILLING?" *BEHAVIORAL SCIENCES AND THE LAW 15* (1997): 203-220.)

"Every society must be wary of the unattached male, for he is universally the cause of numerous social ills. The good society is heavily dependent on men being attached to a strong moral order centered on families, both to discipline their sexual behavior and to reduce their competitive aggression."
JAMES Q. WILSON. QUOTED IN BRODER, DAVID. "BEWARE THE UNATTACHED MALE." *THE WASHINGTON POST*, FEBRUARY 16, 1994.

"From the wild Irish slums of the 19th century Eastern Seaboard to the riot-torn suburbs of Los Angeles, there is one unmistakable lesson in American history: A community that allows a large number of young men to grow up in broken families, dominated by women, never acquiring any stable relationship to male authority, never acquiring any rational expectations about the future — that community asks for and gets chaos."
DANIEL PATRICK MOYNIHAN, "THE NEGRO FAMILY: THE CASE FOR NATIONAL ACTION," U.S. DEPARTMENT OF LABOR, 1965

"The research is absolutely clear... the one human being most capable of curbing the antisocial aggression of a boy is his biological father."
CALIFORNIA-BASED FORENSIC PSYCHOLOGIST SHAWN JOHNSTON, AS QUOTED IN *THE PITTSBURGH TRIBUNE REVIEW*, MARCH 29, 1998.

Survey Data

According to a national survey of 1,010 adults and 500 teenagers, 73% of adults and 68% of teens agree that "Youth are more likely to be violent and commit crimes when their fathers are absent from home."
Source: *Kids & Violence: A National Survey and Report.* Based on a national survey conducted by Wirthlin Worldwide between September 11-17, 1998 for Family First, Tampa, Florida.

A 1994 survey of incarcerated youths aged 14-17 found that:
- the majority said they would like to father a child and thought they would be a good father.
- 26% had gotten a young woman pregnant.
- 63% said they would be pleased if they got a young woman pregnant.
- 78% thought they would be a good role model.
- 85% thought they would be able to get a good job and support a child.

Source: Nesmith, J.D et al. "Procreative Experiences and Orientations Toward Paternity Held by Incarcerated Adolescent Males." *Journal of Adolescent Health, 20* (1997): 198-203

Juvenile Delinquency and Father Absence

"Without two parents, working together as a team, the child has more difficulty learning the combination of empathy, reciprocity, fairness, and self-command that people ordinarily take for granted. If the child does not learn this at home, society will have to manage his behavior in some other way. He may have to be rehabilitated, incarcerated, or otherwise restrained. In this case, prisons will substitute for parents. […]

Family matters are first and foremost social matters because a family is a little society. The larger society is built in crucial ways upon the little society of the family. The family is more than a collection of individuals who make quasi-market exchanges with each other. And families are not miniature political institutions. The label of "social" also points us in the right direction for solutions. The most important tools for building up the family are not primarily economic and political, but social and cultural. Accurate information is a necessary educational tool in reversing the culture of despair around the institution of marriage."

Source: Morse, Jennifer Roback. "Parents or Prisons." *Policy Review* (August/September 2003): 49-60.

Attending a school with a higher percentage of two-parent households can reduce some of the risk associated with living in a single-parent household. Students living with two-parents who attend school where only 9 percent of the students have single-parents are at the lowest risk of delinquency. But living with one-parent and attending a school with 91% two-parent households yields risks only slightly higher than for students raised by two-parents and attending a school with 74% single families. Hence, children of two-parent households have a slight buffer effect on children from single-parent households.

Children raised in single-parent families and surrounded by children of single-parent families at school are at the greatest risk of delinquency.

Source: Anderson, Amy L. "Individual and contextual influences on delinquency: the role of the single-parent family." *Journal of Criminal Justice, 30* (November 2002): 575-587.

A Canadian study of 1,900 school children revealed that family structure was a significant predictor of self-reported delinquency. Researchers pointed to parental attachment as a probable reason for why certain family structures predict delinquent outcomes.

Source: Kierkus, Christopher A. and Douglas Baer. "A social control explanation of the relationship between family structure and delinquent behavior." *Canadian Journal of Criminology 44* (October): 425-458.

Problem behaviors were more frequent for children from unmarried families than from married families. Married caregivers also had twice the income of unmarried caregivers despite the relatively low status of the pool.

Source: Ackerman, Brian P. et al. "Family Structure and the Externalizing Behavior of Children From Economically Disadvantaged Families." *Journal of Family Psychology, 15* (June 2001): 288-300.

Problem behaviors were more frequent for children from unmarried families than from married families.

Particularly for males in five European cities, higher rates of disrupted family structure was correlated with delinquency and drug abuse.
Source: Mcardle, Paul et al. "International Variations in Youth Drug Use: The Effect of Individual Behaviours, Peer and Family Influences, and Geographical Location." *European Addiction Research, 6* (2000): 163-169.

A study of 109 juvenile offenders indicated that family structure significantly predicts delinquency.
Source: Bush, Connee, Ronald L. Mullis, and Ann K. Mullis. "Differences in Empathy Between Offender and Nonoffender Youth." *Journal of Youth and Adolescence, 29* (August 2000): 467-478.

In a longitudinal study of 6,403 males who were 14 to 22 years old, it was found that after controlling for family background variables such as mother's education level, race, family income, and number of siblings, as well as neighborhood variables such as unemployment rates and median income, boys who grew up outside of intact marriages were, on average, more than twice as likely as other boys to end up in jail. Each year spent without a dad in the home increased the odds of future incarceration by 5%. Boys raised by unmarried mothers were at greatest risk, mostly because they spent the most time in a home without a dad.

Overall, a boy born to an unwed mother was 2.5 times more likely to end up in prison, compared to boys reared in intact, two-parent households, whereas a boy whose parents split during his teenage years was 1.5 times more likely to eventually be imprisoned. Remarriage made things worse: Boys living in stepparent families were almost three times as likely to face incarceration. In contrast, boys living with their single fathers were no more likely to be incarcerated than those living with both parents.
Source: Harper, Cynthia C., and Sara S. McLanahan. "Father Absence and Youth Incarceration." Working Paper #99-03. Center for Research on Child Wellbeing, Princeton University, October, 1999.

In a study using a national probability sample of 1,636 young men and women, it was found that older boys and girls from female-headed households are more likely to commit criminal acts than their peers who lived with two parents.
Source: Heimer, Karen. "Gender, Interaction, and Delinquency: Testing a Theory of Differential Social Control." *Social Psychology Quarterly, 59* (1996): 39-61.

In a study of 194 white, urban boys, researchers found that being in a stepfamily or living with a single mother at the age of 10 more than doubled the odds that a boy would eventually be arrested, compared to children who lived with both biological parents.
Source: Coughlin, Chris and Samuel Vuchinich. "Family Experience in Preadolescence and the Development of Male Delinquency." *Journal of Marriage and the Family, 58* (May 1996): 491-501.

In a survey of parents of Montreal delinquents, 69 percent of the delinquent boys were from single-parent families, compared to only about a quarter of their peers in the larger society.
Source: Ambert, Anne-Marie. "The Effect of Male Delinquency on Mothers and Fathers: A Heuristic Study." *Sociological Inquiry 69* (Fall 1999): 621-640.

...older boys and girls from female-headed households are more likely to commit criminal acts than their peers who lived with two parents.

A study in the state of Washington using statewide data found an increased likelihood that children born out of wedlock would become juvenile offenders. Compared to their peers born to married parents, children born out of wedlock were:

- 1.7 times more likely to become an offender and 2.1 times more likely to become a chronic offender if male
- 1.8 times more likely to become an offender and 2.8 times more likely to become a chronic offender if female
- 10 times more likely to become a chronic juvenile offender if male and born to an unmarried teen mother

Source: Conseur, Amy et al. "Maternal and Perinatal Risk Factors for Later Delinquency." *Pediatrics, 99* (1997): 785-790.

In a study of 123 juvenile delinquents at the Wyoming Boys' School, it was found that the delinquent behavior of boys who grew up in two-parent households was significantly less severe than boys from single-parent households.

Source: Anderson, Bobbi Jo, Malcolm Holmes, and Erik Ostresh. "Male and Female Delinquents' Attachments and Effects of Attachments on Severity of Self-Reported Delinquency." *Criminal Justice and Behavior, 26* (1999): 435-452.

School Violence and Father Absence

"Teens from single-parent or stepparent homes are more likely to commit a school crime (possess, use or distribute alcohol or drugs; possess a weapon; assault a teacher, administrator, or another student) than teens from intact homes."

Source: Jenkins, Patricia H. "School Delinquency and School Commitment." *Sociology of Education, 68* (1995): 221-239.

> ...Florida counties with above average rates of father absence had nearly double the rate of school violence...

According to a statewide survey, Florida counties with above average rates of father absence had nearly double the rate of school violence compared to those counties with below average father absence rates.

Source: *Kids & Violence: A National Survey and Report.* Based on a national survey conducted by Wirthlin Worldwide between September 11-17, 1998 for Family First, Tampa, Florida.

A study of 1,800 middle-school students found that children who did not live with both biological parents were more likely to carry a gun than children who lived with both biological parents.

Source: Bailey, Susan L., Robert L. Flewelling, and Dennis P. Rosenbaum. "Characteristics of Students Who Bring Weapons to School." *Journal of Adolescent Health, 20* (1997): 261-270.

> Children living with one-parent were significantly more likely to have ever carried a gun to school.

In a study of more than 2,000 middle school students enrolled in 53 randomly selected middle schools in North Carolina, it was found that 3% reported ever having carried a gun to school. Children living with one-parent were significantly more likely to have ever carried a gun to school.

Source: DuRant, Robert, Daniel Krowchuk, Shelley Kreiter, et al. "Weapon Carrying on School Property Among Middle School Students." *Archives of Pediatric and Adolescent Medicine, 153* (January 1999): 21-26.

Violent Crime and Father Absence

In a study of INTERPOL crime statistics of 39 countries, it was found that single parenthood ratios were strongly correlated with violent crimes. This was not true 18 years ago.

Source: Barber, Nigel. "Single Parenthood As a Predictor of Cross-National Variation in Violent Crime." *Cross-Cultural Research, 38* (November 2004): 343-358.

In a study of neighborhoods in Prince George's County, MD, every one percent increase in female-headed households increased the odds of being murdered by 1.07.

Source: Dobrin, Adam, Daniel Lee, and Jamie Price. "Neighborhood structure differences between homicide victims and non-victims." *Journal of Criminal Justice, 33* (March/April 2005): 137-143.

"Family structure is one of the strongest, if not the strongest, predictor of variations of urban violence across cities in the United States . . . all else equal, in cities where family disruption is high the rate of violence is also high."
Source: Sampson, Robert J. "Unemployment and Imbalanced Sex Ratios: Race-Specific Consequences for Family Structure and Crime." *In The Decline in Marriage Among African Americans*. Ed. M. Belinda Tucker and Claudia Mitchell-Kernan. New York: Russell Sage Foundation, 1995: 229-254.

Adolescents who live in single-parent families were significantly more likely to commit status, property, or person delinquency when compared to adolescents living in two-parent families. This was consistent even when controlling for sex, minority group status, and mother's education (as a proxy for income).
Source: Anderson, Amy L. "Individual and contextual influences on delinquency: the role of the single-parent family." *Journal of Criminal Justice, 30* (November 2002): 575-587.

In an analysis of juvenile-committed homicide, forcible rape, aggravated assault, robbery, and weapons offenses in 264 non-metropolitan counties in Florida, South Carolina, Georgia, and Nebraska, higher levels of family disruption were strongly and consistently associated with higher rates of arrest for violent offenses.
Source: Osgood, D. Wayne, and Jeff M. Chambers. "Social Disorganization Outside the Metropolis: An Analysis of Rural Youth Violence." *Criminology, 38* (2000): 81-115.

In a study of preteens who committed murder, "the clearest finding pertain[ed] to family background": a high percentage of preteen homicide offenders come from homes where the child was consistently at risk for witnessing or experiencing violence, usually at the hands of the primary male caretaker.
Source: Shumaker, David M., and Ronald J. Prinz. "Children Who Murder: A Review." *Clinical Child and Family Psychology Review 3* (2000): 97-115.

A 10 percent increase in illegitimacy is associated with a 17 percent increase in violent teenage crime.
Source: Fagan, Patrick F. "The Real Root Causes of Violent Crime: The Breakdown of Marriage, Family and Community." *Heritage Foundation Backgrounder No. 1026*, March 17, 1995, pp. 9-10.

In an examination of national crime and social data, it was determined that high percentages of father-absent households were associated with lower rates of homicide among both black and white men.
Source: Cubbin, Catherine, Linda Williams Pickle, and Lois Fingerhut. "Social Context and Geographic Patterns of Homicide Among U.S. Black and White Males." *American Journal of Public Health, 90* (2000): 579-587.

Sexual Assault and Father Absence
In a study using national data on over 1600 juveniles in treatment for sex offenses, it was found that:
- only 27.8% were living with both biological parents
- 26.1% were living with a biological parent and a stepparent
- 23.1% were living with their mother only
- 3.2% were living with their father only
- 6.3% were living with a parent and that parent's housemate
- 15.1% were living with neither parent
Source: Ryan, Gail et al. "Trends in a National Sample of Sexually Abusive Youths." *Journal of the American Academy of Child Adolescent Psychiatry, 35* (January 1996): 17-25.

Adult Crime and Father Absence

Even after controlling for income, youths in father-absent households still had significantly higher odds of incarceration than those in mother-father families. Youths who never had a father in the household experienced the highest odds.

Source: Harper, Cynthia C. and Sara S. McLanahan. "Father Absence and Youth Incarceration." *Journal of Research on Adolescence 14* (September 2004): 369-397.

Drug and Alcohol Abuse
Substance Abuse and Father Absence

Of the 228 students studied, those from single-parent families reported higher rates of drinking and smoking as well as higher scores on delinquency and aggression tests when compared to boys from two-parent households.

Source: Griffin, Kenneth W., Gilbert J. Botvin, Lawrence M. Scheier, Tracy Diaz and Nicole L. Miller. "Parenting Practices as Predictors of Substance Use, Delinquency, and Aggression Among Urban Minority Youth: Moderating Effects of Family Structure and Gender." *Psychology of Addictive Behaviors, 14* (June 2000): 174-184.

Father closeness was negatively correlated with the number of a child's friends who smoke, drink, and smoke marijuana. Closeness was also correlated with a child's use of alcohol, cigarettes, and hard drugs and was connected to family structure. Intact families ranked higher on father closeness than single-parent families.

Source: National Fatherhood Initiative. "Family Structure, Father Closeness, & Drug Abuse." Gaithersburg, MD: National Fatherhood Initiative, 2004: 20-22.

Even after controlling for community context, there is significantly more drug use among children who do not live with their mother and father together.

Source: Hoffmann, John P. "The Community Context of Family Structure and Adolescent Drug Use." *Journal of Marriage and Family, 64* (May 2002): 314-330.

No matter what their gender, age, family income, and race/ethnicity, adolescents not living with both parents (biological or adoptive) are 50 to 150% more likely to use substances, to be dependent on substances, and to need illicit drug abuse treatment than adolescents living with two biological or adoptive parents.

Source: Substance Abuse and Mental Health Services Administration. *The Relationship between Family Structure and Adolescent Substance Use.* Rockville, MD: National Clearinghouse for Alcohol and Drug Information, 1996.

A child living in a two-parent family whose relationship with the father is fair or poor is 68% likelier to smoke, drink, and use drugs than teens living in an average two-parent household. A child living in a household with a single mother is at a 32% higher risk compared to teens living in average two-parent households.

Source: The National Center on Addiction and Substance Abuse at Columbia University. "National Survey of American Attitudes on Substance Abuse VI: Teens." Conducted by QEV Analytics, February 2001; see also The National Center on Addiction and Substance Abuse at Columbia University. "Back to School 1999 — National Survey of American Attitudes on Substance Abuse V: Teens and Their Parents." Conducted by The Luntz Research Companies and QEV Analytics, August 1999.

In a study involving 11,000 interviews with persons ranging in age from 18 to 89, it was found that children whose parents divorced had a one-third greater chance of becoming an adult smoker, and boys living with a single parent also had a one-third greater chance of developing a drinking problem as an adult.

Source: Wolfinger, Nicholas. "The Effects of Parental Divorce on Adult Tobacco and Alcohol Consumption." *Journal of Health and Social Behavior, 39* (September 1998): 254-270.

In a study of 630 predominantly African-American 10th graders at 9 urban high schools, it was found that the association between peer pressure to use drugs and actual drug use was strongest among adolescents in families without fathers or stepfathers. The association also increased as a function of the level of mother-adolescent distress among adolescents who were not living with fathers or stepfathers.

Source: Farrell, Albert D., and Kamila S. White. "Peer Influences and Drug Use Among Urban Adolescents: Family Structure and Parent-Adolescent Relationship as Protective Factors." *Journal of Consulting and Clinical Psychology 66* (April 1998): 248-258.

Alcohol Use and Father Absence

Females in "mother only" families are 1.9 times as likely to use alcohol as females in "mother/father" families. Males in "mother only" families are about 1.5 times as likely to use alcohol as males in "mother/father" families.

Source: Substance Abuse and Mental Health Services Administration. *The Relationship between Family Structure and Adolescent Substance Use.* Rockville, MD: National Clearinghouse for Alcohol and Drug Information, 1996.

"...the absence of the father from the home affects significantly the behavior of adolescents and results in greater use of alcohol and marijuana."

Source: Beman, Deane Scott. "Risk Factors Leading to Adolescent Substance Abuse." *Adolescence, 30* (1995): 201-206.

Tobacco Use and Father Absence

Smoking among 15-year-olds was significantly related to family structure in a cross-national survey of youth in 29 countries. Young people from single-parent families were more likely to be daily smokers than those in intact families. In most countries, children in stepfamilies are twice as likely to be daily smokers. This relationship holds independently in all countries except Wales. Young people in intact families were also less likely to have a smoking parent.

Source: Griesbach, Amanda Amos, and Candace Currie. "Adolescent smoking and family structure in Europe." *Social Science & Medicine, 56* (January 2003): 41-52.

In a study of 6,100 high schoolers, living in a non-intact family increased the likelihood of becoming a regular smoker during adolescence.

Source: Tucker, Joan S., Phyllis L. Ellickson, and David J. Klein. "Predictors of the Transition to Regular Smoking During Adolescence and Young Adulthood." *Journal of Adolescent Health, 32* (April 2003): 314-324.

A study conducted from a pool of 1,700 from the National Youth Survey identified family structure and family stress as significant predictors of adolescent cigarette smoking.

Source: Miller, Todd Q. and Robert J. Volk. "Family Relationships and Adolescent Cigarette Smoking: Results From a National Longitudinal Survey." *Journal of Drug Issues, 32* (Summer 2002): 945-972.

A study of 34,000 students in 11 countries determined that adolescents living with both biological parents smoke less than their peers from non-traditional family structures.

Source: Bjarnason, Thoroddur et al. "Family structure and adolescent cigarette smoking in eleven European countries." *Addiction, 98* (June 2003): 815-824.

Male teens in "mother only" families are 1.6 times as likely to use cigarettes as males in "mother/ father" families. Females in "mother only" families are 1.8 times as likely to use cigarettes as females in "mother/father" families.

Source: Substance Abuse and Mental Health Services Administration. *The Relationship between Family Structure and Adolescent Substance Use.* Rockville, MD: National Clearinghouse for Alcohol and Drug Information, 1996.

...adolescents living with both biological parents smoke less than their peers...

Using data from two national surveys, it was found that among white males — the group most likely to use smokeless tobacco — use of smokeless tobacco was almost a third more likely among those living in single-parent or stepparent families than among peers living with both biological parents.
Source: Tomar, Scott L., and Gary A. Giovino. "Incidence and Predictors of Smokeless Tobacco Use Among U.S. Youth." *American Journal of Public Health, 88* (1998): 20-26.

In an analysis of health data collected in a survey of 9,215 adults living in the San Diego, California area, respondents who had seen their parents divorce were almost twice as likely to have initiated smoking by age 14 compared to peers whose parents had not divorced.
Source: Anda, Robert, et al. "Adverse Childhood Experiences and Smoking During Adolescence and Adulthood." *Journal of the American Medical Association 282* (1999): 1652-1658.

Illegal Drug Use and Father Absence
Adolescents from homes with no parents or stepparents were more likely to admit marijuana use when compared to those in two-parent homes.
Source: Kim, Julia Yun Soo, Michael Fendrich, and Joseph S. Wislar. "The Validity of Juvenile Arrestees' Drug Use Reporting: A Gender Comparison." *Journal of Research in Crime and Delinquency 37* (November 2000): 419-432.

Researchers at Columbia University found that children living in two-parent household with a poor relationship with their father are 68% more likely to smoke, drink, or use drugs compared to all teens in two-parent households. Teens in single mother households are at a 30% higher risk than those in all two-parent households.
Source: "Survey Links Teen Drug Use, Relationship With Father." *Alcoholism & Drug Abuse Weekly* 6 September 1999: 5.

Using a sample of 22,237 adolescents ages 12-17 from 3 years of data from the National Household Survey on Drug Abuse, it was found that after controlling for the effects of sex, age, race-ethnicity, family income, and residential mobility, teens in mother-stepfather and mother-only households evidenced 1.5 to 2 times the risk of illegal drug use and teens in father-only and father-stepmother families evidenced over 2.5 times the risk of illegal drug use, compared to teens in mother-father families.
Source: Hoffmann, John P., and Robert A. Johnson. "A National Portrait of Family Structure and Adolescent Drug Use." *Journal of Marriage and the Family 60* (August 1998): 633-645.

Education
"One father is more than a hundred school masters."

17TH CENTURY ENGLISH PROVERB

"[I]f America's Dads got as involved as America's Moms in their children's education, America's children would be studying harder and getting a lot more A's. Dads make a powerful difference in defining expectations and challenging children to do their best."

FORMER U.S. SECRETARY OF EDUCATION RICHARD W. RILEY, 1997

Parental Involvement and Father Absence
Using data from the 1996 National Household Education Survey (n=20,702), it was found that 69% of non-resident fathers had no involvement in their children's school.
Source: *Nonresident Fathers Can Make a Difference in Children's School Performance* (NCES 98-117). Washington, D.C.: U.S. Department of Education, National Center for Education Statistics, 1998.

In a study of British households, spending time in a single mother household predicted a 14% lower level of achieving academically. It was also associated with a 14% higher probability of economic inactivity during young adulthood and higher risk of adolescent pregnancy and overall levels of psychological distress. Family dissolution was particularly harmful for children under five.
Source: Ermisch, John F. and Marco Francesconi. "Family structure and children's achievements." *Journal of Population Economics* (2001): 249-270.

Kindergarteners who live with single-parents are overrepresented in those lagging in health, social and emotional, and cognitive outcomes. Thirty-three percent of children who were behind in all three areas were living with single parents. Only 22 percent were not lagging behind in any areas.

Conversely, 45 percent of kindergarteners who were behind in all three areas came from two biological parent households, compared with 65 percent among other children.
Source: Wertheimer, Richard and Tara Croan, et al. *Attending Kindergarten and Already Behind: A Statistical Portrait of Vulnerable Young Children.* Child Trends Research Brief. Publication #2003-20. Washington, DC: Child Trends, 2003.

Only one-third of non-resident fathers who have had contact with their children in the past year continue to actively participate in school activities.
Source: Nord, Christine Winquist, DeeAnn Brimhall, and Jerry West. *Fathers' Involvement in Their Children's Schools* (NCES 98-091). Washington, D.C.: U.S. Department of Education, National Center for Education Statistics, 1997.

Students in single-parent families or stepfamilies are significantly less likely than students living in intact families to have parents involved in their schools. About half of students living in single-parent families or stepfamilies have parents who are highly involved, while 62 percent of students living with both their parents have parents who are highly involved in their schools.
Source: Nord, Christine Winquist, and Jerry West. *Fathers' and Mothers' Involvement in Their Children's Schools by Family Type and Resident Status.* (NCES 2001-032). Washington, D.C.: U.S. Department of Education, National Center for Education Statistics, 2001.

Children living with two parents are more likely to be read aloud to every day than are children who live with one or no parent. Fifty-eight percent of children in two-parent households were read to every day in 1999, compared with 43 percent of children living with one or no parent.
Source: *America's Children: Key National Indicators of Well-Being, 2001.* Washington, D.C.: Federal Interagency Forum on Child and Family Statistics, 2001.

Father Absence and Children's Attitudes Toward School
A study of 2,700 British children showed that those from intact and/or father involved families were more likely to report positive attitudes towards school than those from nonintact families or low father involvement.
Source: Flouri, Eirini, Ann Buchanan, and Victoria Bream. "Adolescents Perceptions of Their Fathers' Involvement: Significance to School Attitudes." *Psychology in Schools 39* (2002): 575-582.

In a study of 157 adolescents living in Utah, researchers found that boys in single-parent families spent an average of 3.5 fewer hours per week studying than boys who lived with both biological parents.
Source: Zick, Cathleen D. and Corinne Roylance Allen. "The Impact of Parents' Marital Status on the Time Adolescents Spend in Productive Activities." *Family Relations 45* (1996): 65-71.

A study on the effects of maternal depression on 44 eighth-grade girls found that those who lived with a single mother had lower educational expectations and grades than girls who lived with both biological parents.
Source: Silverburg, Susan B., Mary S. Marczak, and Dawn M. Gondoli. "Maternal Depressive Symptoms and Achievement Related Outcomes: Variations by Family Structure." *Journal of Early Adolescence 16* (1996): 90-109.

In a study of 383 African-American mothers and their adolescent children (ages 11 to 16) from poverty tracts and 163 African-American mothers and their adolescent children from middle-class tracts, it was found that youth from families headed by a single mother on welfare attached lower importance to academic performance and were less enthusiastic about their chances of finding a job in the future than youth in other family types.
Source: Quane, James M., and Bruce H. Ranking. "Neighborhood Poverty, Family Characteristics, and Commitment to Mainstream Goals: The Case of African American Adolescents in the Inner City." *Journal of Family Issues 19* (1998): 769-794.

School Achievement and Father Absence

Half of all children with highly involved fathers in two-parent families reported getting mostly A's through 12th grade, compared with 31.7% and 35.2% of children of single father and nonresident father families, respectively.
Source: National Center for Education Statistics. *The Condition of Education.* NCES 1999022. Washington, DC: U.S. Dept. of Education, 1999: 76.

A study of 1,330 children from the Panel Survey of Income Dynamics showed that fathers who are involved on a personal level with their child's schooling increases the likelihood of their child's achievement. When fathers assume a positive role in their child's education, students feel a positive impact.
Source: McBride, Brent A., Sarah K. Schoppe-Sullivan, and Moon-Ho Ho. "The mediating role of fathers' school involvement on student achievement." *Journal of Applied Developmental Psychology 26* (2005): 201-216.

In a study of 7,300 British children, father involvement by age 7 significantly predicted educational attainment and academic motivation when controlling for various factors like SES, parental education, and mother involvement.
Source: Flouri, Eirini and Ann Buchanan. "Early father's and mother's involvement and child's later educational outcomes." *British Journal of Educational Psychology 74* (2004): 141-153.

In a study using a national probability sample of 1,250 fathers of school-aged children, it was found that children who lived with both biological parents did better in school than children in all other family types. Children living with single, biological fathers and children living with stepfathers did significantly worse academically than children living with both biological parents.
Source: Cooksey, Elizabeth C. and Michelle M. Fondell. "Spending Time with His Kids: Effects of Family Structure on Fathers' and Children's Lives." *Journal of Marriage and the Family 58* (August 1996): 693-707.

According to data from the NSFH, greater care from a father is beneficial for difficult children. For fathers registering high on the care scale at the initial measurement, the child's problem behaviors were lower five years later. In contrast, children who received low levels of paternal care were not likely to be free of problems at the five year mark; they were most likely to be the most troubled. Hence, fathers' greater involvement when children are pre-schoolers decreased the likelihood of problem behavior in grade school.
Source: Aldous, Joan and Gail M. Mulligan. "Fathers' Child Care and Children's Behavior Problems: A Longitudinal Study." *Journal of Family Issues 23* (July 2002): 624-647.

Using data drawn from the 1990 test results of 18,000 10th graders who took the Louisiana Graduation Exit Examination, it was found that the percentage of students from single-parent families in schools had a strong negative relation to standardized test scores,

> ...children who lived with both biological parents did better in school than children in all other family types.

and that the prevalence of students from single-parent families in schools was a better predictor of academic outcomes than the racial composition of schools.
Source: Bankston, Carl L., and Stephen J. Caldas. "Family Structure, Schoolmates, and Racial Inequalities in School Achievement." *Journal of Marriage and the Family 60* (August 1998): 715-723.

A study of 1,700 seventh- and ninth-grade South Carolina students indicated that children whose parents were divorced had lower grades than their peers whose parents had stayed together, even after controlling for parental occupation, education, race, and family size.
Source: Smith, Thomas Ewin. "What a Difference a Measure Makes: Parental Separation Effect on School Grades, Not Academic Achievement." *Journal of Marriage and Divorce 23* (1995): 151-164.

Using a sample of 4,499 children ages 7-12 from the 1988 National Health Interview Survey, it was found that mobility (moving from one neighborhood to another) resulted in lower educational performance for children who were not living with both biological parents, but not for children living with their two biological, married parents.
Source: Tucker, C. Jack, Jonathan Marx, and Larry Long. "'Moving On': Residential Mobility and Children's School Lives." *Sociology of Education 71* (April 1998): 111-129.

Math and Reading Achievement and Father Absence

In 2001, 61 percent of 3- to 5-year olds living with two parents were read aloud to everyday by a family member, compared to 48% of children living in single- or no-parent families.
Source: Federal Interagency Forum on Child and Family Statistics. *America's Children: Key National Indicators of Well-Being, 2002.* Table ED1. Washington, DC: U.S. Government Printing Office, 2003.

Using longitudinal data taken in 1988 and 1992 on sibling pairs from the National Longitudinal Study of Youth, it was found that children who live in single-parent families, compared to those who live in two-parent households, score lower on mathematics and reading tests. Furthermore, the discrepancy in reading ability between children in two-parent and single-parent households increases over time.
Source: Teachman, Jay, et al. "Sibling Resemblance in Behavioral and Cognitive Outcomes: The Role of Father Presence." *Journal of Marriage and the Family 60* (November 1998): 835-848.

Using a sample of 940 children drawn from the National Longitudinal Survey of Youth, it was found that even after controlling for differences in income, children who were born out of wedlock and either remained in a single-parent family or whose mother subsequently married had significantly poorer math and reading scores and lower levels of academic performance than children from continuously married households.
Source: Cooksey, Elizabeth C. "Consequences of Young Mothers' Marital Histories for Children's Cognitive Development." *Journal of Marriage and the Family 59* (May 1997): 245-261.

In an analysis of data for more than 11,000 tenth graders included in the National Educational Longitudinal Study, whether or not a student grew up in an intact, two-parent household was a better predictor of math and reading achievement than either student/teacher ratios or racial segregation.
Source: Roscigno, Vincent J. "The Black-White Achievement Gap, Family-School Links, and the Importance of Place." *Sociological Inquiry 69* (1999): 159-186.

A study using a nationally representative sample of over 20,000 eighth graders from 970 schools found that students who attended schools with a high concentration of students from single-parent households had math and reading achievement scores that were 11% and 10% lower, respectively, than students who attended schools with a higher concentration of two-parent households, even after controlling for differences in student background and demographic characteristics.
Source: Pong, Suet-Ling. "Family Structure, School Context, and Eighth-Grade Math and Reading Achievement." *Journal of Marriage and the Family 59* (August 1997): 734-746.

An analysis on a random sample of 391 Baltimore first-graders found that single parents had lower educational expectations for their children than parents in two-parent households. Upon entering first grade, children who lived with both biological parents scored higher on math and reading tests than children in all other family types. As children progressed through school, the performance gap widened.
Source: Entwisle, Doris R. and Karl L. Alexander. "Family Type and Children's Growth in Reading and Math Over the Primary Grades." *Journal of Marriage and the Family 58* (1996): 341-355.

Grade Retention and Father Absence

Students living in father-absent homes are twice as likely to repeat a grade in school; 10 percent of children living with both parents have ever repeated a grade, compared to 20 percent of children in stepfather families and 18 percent in mother-only families.
Source: Nord, Christine Winquist, and Jerry West. *Fathers' and Mothers' Involvement in Their Children's Schools by Family Type and Resident Status.* (NCES 2001-032). Washington, D.C.: U.S. Department of Education, National Center for Education Statistics, 2001.

School Dropout Rates and Father Absence

Analyzing a group of eighth-graders who initially resided with both biological parents, children in households that had experienced a change in family structure had school dropout rates two to three times as high as their peers whose families did not change.
Source: Pong, Suet-Ling, and Dong-Beom Ju. "The Effects of Change in Family Structure and Income on Dropping Out of Middle and High School." *Journal of Family Issues 21* (March 2000): 147-169.

Data from the Montreal Longitudinal Study indicated that living in a two-parent household increases the likelihood of staying in school for children.
Source: Leung, Ambrose. "Delinquency, schooling, and work: time allocation decision of youth." *Applied Economics 36* (May 2004): 987-993.

Fifty-five percent of children in lower socioeconomic two-parent families drop out compared to 65% of children in lower SES one-parent families. If the two-parent family does not endure any stressful change, the percentage drops to 50%. One-parent families, however, are characterized by stressful change.
Source: Alexander, Karl L, Doris R. Entwisle, and Nader S. Kabbani. "The Dropout Process in Life Course Perspective: Early Risk Factors at Home and School." *Teachers College Record 103* (October 2001): 760-822.

"After taking into account race, socioeconomic status, sex, age, and ability, high school students from single-parent households were 1.7 times more likely to drop out than were their corresponding counterparts living with both biological parents."
Source: McNeal, Ralph B., Jr. "Extracurricular Activities and High School Dropouts." *Sociology of Education 68* (1995): 62-81.

Graduation Rates and Father Absence

More activities between absent parents and children produces better chances of postsecondary school attendance. At the median value of reported financial support ($1,920), a child who did not interact with their absent parent had only a 21% chance of attending a postsecondary institution. When the absent parent and child engaged in an activity several times a week, the child had a 50% chance of attending college. If an absent parent and child only participates in an activity once a year, financial support would have to increase 460% to $14,000 to make up for the lack of interaction.

Source: Menning, Chadwick L. "Absent Parents Are More Than Money: The Join Effect of Activities and Financial Support on Youth's Financial Attainment." *Journal of Family Issues 23* (July 2002): 648-671.

While family income could account for the rates of college attendance and completion rates between students from disrupted families and those from intact families, children from disrupted families were still less likely to attend college when grant aid was included in the model.

Source: Michele Ver Ploeg. "Children from disrupted families as adults: family structure, college attendance and college completion." *Economics of Education Review 21* (April 2002): 171-184.

Using data collected from three generations from a large sample of largely working-class and middle-class families from Southern California, it was found that 56 percent of males and 41 percent of females whose parents remained married had college degrees or advanced degrees, compared to only 23 percent of males and 25 percent of females whose parents divorced before they were 18 years old.

Source: Feng, Du, et al. "Intergenerational Transmission of Marital Quality and Marital Instability." *Journal of Marriage and the Family 61* (1999): 451-463.

A study of 549 young adults born out of wedlock found that their graduation rates correlated strongly with living arrangements during childhood. Graduation rates were:
- 96% for those raised by adoptive or biological parents who subsequently married
- 78% for those raised in stepfamilies
- 73% for those raised by their never-married mothers

Source: Aquilino, William S. "The Life Course of Children Born to Unmarried Parents: Childhood Living Arrangements and Young Adult Outcomes." *Journal of Marriage and the Family 58* (1996): 293-310.

School Disciplinary Problems and Father Absence

Students living with both their parents are less likely to have behavior problems in school that result in suspension or expulsion. Thirteen percent of 6th- through 12th-graders living with both their parents have ever been suspended or expelled, compared to 23 percent in stepfamilies and 27 percent in mother-only families.

Source: Nord, Christine Winquist, and Jerry West. *Fathers' and Mothers' Involvement in Their Children's Schools by Family Type and Resident Status.* (NCES 2001-032). Washington, D.C.: U.S. Department of Education, National Center for Education Statistics, 2001.

An analysis of a random sample of 391 Baltimore first-graders found that 30% of the children from single-parent homes had behavior described as "needing improvement," while only 15-20% of the children from two-parent homes had behavior described as "needing improvement."

Source: Entwisle, Doris R. and Karl L. Alexander. "Family Type and Children's Growth in Reading and Math Over the Primary Grades." *Journal of Marriage and the Family 58* (1996): 341-355.

A study of 28 families found that, according to teacher reports, children of single mothers had more behavior problems, poorer school performance, and were less adept socially than children of married mothers.

Source: Gringlas, Marcy and Marsha Weinraub. "The More Things Change...Single Parenting Revisited." *Journal of Family Issues 16* (1995): 29-52.

A study using a nationally representative sample of over 2,300 youths found that both black and white students from single-parent homes were more likely to have discipline problems than students who lived with both biological parents.

Source: Heiss, Jerold. "Effects of African American Family Structure on School Attitudes and Performance." *Social Problems 43* (1996): 246-264.

A longitudinal study on 326 adolescents showed that boys living with their single mothers were considered more aggressive by their teachers than boys who lived in a "mother and other" arrangement.

Source: Vaden-Kiernan, Nancy, et al. "Household Family Structure and Children's Aggressive Behavior: A Longitudinal Study of Urban Elementary School Children." *Journal of Abnormal Child Psychology 23* (1995): 553-568.

Emotional and Behavioral Problems

"Controlling for factors such as low income, children growing up in [single-parent] households are at a greater risk for experiencing a variety of behavioral and educational problems, including extremes of hyperactivity and withdrawal; lack of attentiveness in the classroom, difficulty in deferring gratification; impaired academic achievement, school misbehavior, absenteeism, dropping out, involvement in socially alienated peer groups, and the so-called 'teenage syndrome' of behaviors that tend to hang together — smoking, drinking, early and frequent sexual experience, and in the more extreme cases, drugs, suicide, vandalism, violence, and criminal acts."

PSYCHOLOGIST URIE BRONFENBRENNER, "DISCOVERING WHAT FAMILIES DO." IN *REBUILDING THE NEST: A NEW COMMITMENT TO THE AMERICAN FAMILY.* ED BLANKENHORN, ET AL. MILWAUKEE, WI: *FAMILY SERVICE AMERICA*, 1990: 27-38.

"The economic consequences of a parent's absence are often accompanied by psychological consequences, which include higher than average levels of youth suicide, low intellectual and education performance, and higher than average rates of mental illness, violence and drug use."

SOCIAL SCIENTISTS WILLIAM GALSTON AND ELAINE KAMARCK, 1993.

"'Father hunger' often afflicts boys ages one and two whose fathers are suddenly and permanently absent. Sleep disturbances, such as trouble falling asleep, nightmares, and night terrors frequently begin within one to three months after the father leaves home."

ALFRED A. MESSER, "BOYS' FATHER HUNGER: THE MISSING FATHER SYNDROME," *MEDICAL ASPECTS OF HUMAN SEXUALITY 23* (JANUARY 1989): 44-47.

> ...children of single mothers had more behavior problems, poorer school performance, and were less adept socially than children of married mothers.

Father Absence and Emotional and Behavioral Problems

Even though less than 10% of Swedish mothers can be considered poor and most were working, Swedish children of lone parents have more than double the risk of psychiatric disease, suicide and attempted suicide, and alcohol-related disease and more than three times the risk of drug-related disease compared to those in two-parent families. The study included one million children.
Source: Weitoft, Gunilla, et al. "Mortality, severe morbidity, and injury in children living with single parents in Sweden: a population-based study." *Lancet* 25 January 2003: 289-295.

According to a pool from the NLSY, the proportion of time spent in a female-headed household decreases the likelihood that a child will in engage in pro-social behavior or volunteerism. The difficulties of being raised in a single-mother household may diminish a child's social support and coping mechanism while assigning a sense of helplessness.
Source: Lichter, Daniel T., Michael J. Shanahan, and Erica L. Gardner. "Helping Others?: The Effects of Childhood Poverty and Family Instability on Prosocial Behavior." *Youth & Society 34* (September 2002): 89-119.

A study of 302 adolescent girls showed that those who feel connected with their biological father but have little contact are at higher risk of problematic psychosocial functioning. Poor school behavior also increases for girls with low contact levels with their father.
Source: Coley, Rebekah Levine. "Daughter-Father Relationship and Adolescent Psychosocial Functioning in Low-Income African American Families." *Journal of Marriage and Family 65* (November 2003): 867-875.

Fathers have a unique effect on their daughter's tendency towards anti-social behavior. A study of 325 families revealed that fathers who present their daughters more opportunities and reinforcement lessen the likelihood of their daughters poor behavior.
Source: Kosterman, Rick, et al. "Unique Influence of Mothers and Fathers on Their Children's Anti-Social Behavior." *Journal of Marriage and Family 66* (August 2004): 762-778.

After controlling for a variety of factors including parental income, a study of 7,415 from the ADDHEALTH sample established a link between the father-adolescent relationship and depression. Sons and daughters with satisfying relationships with their fathers demonstrate lower rates of depressive symptoms; decreased satisfaction increases depression.
Source: Videon, Tami M. "Parent-Child Relations and Children's Psychological Well-Being: Do Dad's Matter?" *Journal of Family Issues 26* (January 2005): 55-78.

A study of 3,400 middle schoolers indicated that not living with both biological parents quadruples the risk of having an affective disorder.
Source: Cuffe, Steven P., Robert E. McKeown, Cheryl L. Addy, and Carol Z. Garrison. "Family Psychosocial Risk Factors in a Longitudinal Epidemiological Study of Adolescents." *Journal of the American Academy of Child Adolescent Psychiatry 44* (February 2005): 121-129.

Arguments over staying out late are more common for single-parent families than for two-parent families. Twenty-two percent of single mothers recorded disagreements once a week or more on this subject compared to 8% of mothers in two-parent households. The percentages for fathers are 20% and 9%, respectively.
Source: *Child Trends*, "Charting Parenthood: A Statistical Portrait of Fathers and Mothers in America." Ed. Tamara Halle. Washington DC, 2004.

> Fathers have a unique effect on their daughter's tendency towards anti-social behavior.

> ...not living with both biological parents quadruples the risk of having an affective disorder.

British children of lone parents are twice as likely to have mental health problems than those from couple families. Even those from reconstituted families are twice as likely to have problems.
Source: "Figures Point to Lone Parent Problem." *Community Care* 14 February 2002: 12.

Using data from the National Longitudinal Survey of Children and Youth, it was found that children from single-mother families were 1.5 to 2 times more likely to have one or more behavioral or emotional problems compared to those living in two-parent, married households, whether or not the families were poor.
Source: *Growing Up In Canada.* National Longitudinal Survey of Children and Youth. Human Resources Development Canada, Statistics Canada, Catalogue no. 89-550-MPE, no. 1, November 1996.

Using longitudinal data taken in 1988 and 1992 on sibling pairs from the National Longitudinal Study of Youth, it was found that children who live in single-parent families have more behavior problems compared to those who live in two-parent households.
Source: Teachman, Jay, et al. "Sibling Resemblance in Behavioral and Cognitive Outcomes: The Role of Father Presence." *Journal of Marriage and the Family 60* (November 1998): 835-848.

A longitudinal study of 919 children indicated that family disruption during childhood, marital conflict, and low parental involvement increased the odds that a child would engage in anti-social behaviors such as fighting, lying, cheating, and criminal activity.
Source: Sim, Hee-Og, and Sam Vuchinich. "The Declining Effects of Family Stressors on Antisocial Behavior From Childhood to Adolescence and Early Adulthood." *Journal of Family Issues 17* (1996): 408-427.

In the only known study of the effect of divorce on twin-pairs, after controlling for genetic relatedness, parental separation or divorce increased the risk of major depression for female members of a twin-pair by 42%.
Source: Cherlin, Andrew J. "Going to Extremes: Family Structure, Children's Well-Being, and Social Science." *Demography 36* (November 1999): 421-428.

In a study of 18,000 children, it was found that children whose parents divorced when they were age 7-22 were 11% more likely to suffer "a wide variety of adult emotional disorders, such as depression, anxiety, phobias, and obsessions," with the likelihood of such problems doubling as the children entered adulthood. By the time these children had reached age 33, the children of divorce were 25% more likely to have emotional problems than children whose parents stayed married. Statistical analyses show that the harm divorce causes is not due to the income, race, or social status of the parents, but to the "divorce itself."
Source: Cherlin, Andrew J., P. Lindsay Chase-Lansdale, and Christine McRae. "Effects of Parental Divorce on Mental Health Throughout the Life Course." *American Sociological Review 63* (April 1998): 239-249.

Based on an unselected, general population sample of 11,017 persons, it was found that only 3.1% of those who grew up in two-parent, married households had a hospital-treated psychiatric disorder, compared to 5.4% of those who grew up in a single-parent household. In addition, the chances that someone would be diagnosed with a personality disorder in adulthood were 4.8 times more likely for those who experienced the loss of their father before the age of 14 years, 4.0 times more likely for those who experienced the loss of their father before birth, and 2.8 times more likely for those with a history of parental divorce anytime during childhood. Those who experience parental divorce as children also evidenced 3.7 times more adult alcoholism.
Source: Makikyro, Taru, et al. "Hospital-Treated Psychiatric Disorders in Adults with a Single-Parent and Two-Parent Family Background." *Family Process* (Fall 1998): 335-344.

A study of 648 children in New York indicated that children who lived with their single mother were more likely to develop disruptive and anxiety disorders than children who lived with both biological parents. Boys living with their single mother were more likely to be depressed than boys who lived with both biological parents.
Source: Kasen, Stephanie, et al. "A Multiple-Risk Interaction Model: Effects of Temperament and Divorce on Psychiatric Disorders in Children." *Journal of Abnormal Child Psychology 24* (1996): 121-150.

A study using a national sample of 482 adolescents showed that boys and girls whose fathers recently left them exhibited more behavior problems than their counterparts who lived with both biological parents. When a stepfather entered the home, the children exhibited more behavior problems compared to their peers who lived with both biological parents, and the impact was stronger for boys than for girls.
Source: Mott, Frank L., Lori Kowaleski-Jones, and Elizabeth G. Menaghen. "Paternal Absence and Child Behavior: Does a Child's Gender Make a Difference?" *Journal of Marriage and the Family 59* (February 1997): 103-118.

In a longitudinal study of 1,197 fourth-grade students, researchers observed "greater levels of aggression in boys from mother-only households than in boys from mother-father households."
Source: Vaden-Kiernan, N., et al. "Household Family Structure and Children's Aggressive Behavior: A Longitudinal Study of Urban Elementary School Children." *Journal of Abnormal Child Psychology 23.5* (1995): 553-568.

A study using a nationally representative sample of 6,287 children ages 4-11 years old indicated that children in single-parent homes are more likely to experience emotional problems and use mental health services than children who live with both biological parents.
Source: Angel, Ronald J. and Jacqueline L. Angel. "Physical Comorbidity and Medical Care Use in Children with Emotional Problems." *Public Health Reports 111* (1996): 140-145.

A study using data from a nationally representative sample of households found that adolescents in stepfamilies and divorced-mother households had higher levels of mother-adolescent disagreements, lower levels of interaction, and lower levels of overall socio-emotional well-being compared to adolescents who lived with both biological parents.
Source: Demo, David H. and Alan C. Acock. "Family Structure, Family Process, and Adolescent Well-Being." *Journal of Research on Adolescence 6* (1996): 457-488.

Peer Problems and Father Absence

A study of 40 middle school boys from a Midwest suburb found that those who lived without their father showed a poorer sense of masculinity and had poorer interpersonal relationships than boys who lived with their biological fathers.
Source: Beaty, Lee A. "Effects of Paternal Absence on Male Adolescents' Peer Relations and Self-Image." *Adolescence 30* (1995): 873-880.

A study of 60 college students found that students from divorced homes trusted their dating partners less than their peers who came from intact homes.
Source: Johnston, Stacy Glaser and Amanda McCombs Thomas. "Divorce Versus Intact Parental Marriage and Perceived Risk and Dyadic Trust in Present Heterosexual Relationships." *Psychological Reports 78* (1996): 387-390.

Suicide and Father Absence

In a survey of 272 high school students, family cohesion and marital status were the strongest protective factors against suicidal behavior, with students in intact families as the least likely to be suicidal and those in remarried families as the most likely to be suicidal. Thirty-eight percent of teens in stepfamilies reported suicidal behavior, compared to 20 percent of teens from single-parent homes, and just 9 percent of teens from intact families.
Source: Rubenstein, Judith L., et al. "Suicidal Behavior in Adolescents: Stress and Protection in Different Family Contexts." *American Journal of Orthopsychiatry 68* (1998): 274-284.

In a study of 146 adolescent friends of 26 adolescent suicide victims, teens living in single-parent families were not only more likely to commit suicide but also more likely to suffer from psychological disorders, when compared to teens living in intact families.
Source: Brent, David A. et al. "Post-traumatic Stress Disorder in Peers of Adolescent Suicide Victims: Predisposing Factors and Phenomenology." *Journal of the American Academy of Child and Adolescent Psychiatry 34* (1995): 209-215.

Physical Health

"Some of our nation's most urgent problems, ranging from infant mortality, to drug abuse, to AIDS, to teen pregnancy, to the disproportionately poor health and excess mortality afflicting the children of our minority citizens... arise precisely from an erosion of basic values, and the collapse of the institutions that teach them, like family and community."

FORMER DEPARTMENT OF HEALTH AND HUMAN SERVICES SECRETARY LOUIS W. SULLIVAN, 1991

General Health and Father Absence

In a longitudinal study of more than 10,000 families, researchers found that toddlers living in stepfamilies and single-parent families were more likely to suffer a burn, have a bad fall, or be scarred from an accident compared to kids living with both of their biological parents.
Source: O'Connor, T., L. Davies, J. Dunn, J. Golding, ALSPAC Study Team. "Differential Distribution of Children's Accidents, Injuries and Illnesses across Family Type." *Pediatrics 106* (November 2000): e68.

A fathers' body mass index (a measurement of the relative composition of fat and muscle mass in the human body) is directly related to a child's activity level. In a study of 259 toddlers, more active children were more likely to have a father with a lower BMI than less active children.
Source: Finn, Kevin, Neil Johannsen, and Bonny Specker. "Factors associated with physical activity in preschool children." *The Journal of Pediatrics 140* (January 2002): 81-85.

61% of children over a year old and living with both biological parents have had a medical check-up in the past year compared to only 46% of those who were living with a stepmother.
Source: "The Cinderella Syndrome." *The Economist* 28 October 2000. Accessed 15 May 2005. <http://www.economist.com/displaystory.cfm?story_id=S%26%28X%2C%28QA%27%27%0A>

Children who live apart from their fathers are more likely to be diagnosed with asthma and experience an asthma-related emergency even after taking into account demographic and socioeconomic conditions. Unmarried, cohabiting parents and unmarried parents living apart are 1.76 and 2.61 times, respectively, more likely to have their child diagnosed with asthma. Marital disruption after birth is associated with a 6-fold increase in the likelihood a children will require an emergency room visit and 5-fold increase of an asthma-related emergency.
Source: Harknett, Kristin. *Children's Elevated Risk of Asthma in Unmarried Families: Underlying Structural and Behavioral Mechanisms.* Working Paper #2005-01-FF. Princeton, NJ: Center for Research on Child Wellbeing, 2005: 19-27.

Prenatal Care, Infant Health and Father Absence

Babies born to married mothers are less likely to have a low birthweight. In 2002, 7 percent of births to married mothers were low birthweight, compared to 10 percent of births to unmarried mothers.

This relationship held for each race and ethnicity group as well. Six percent of infants born to married, White, non-Hispanic mothers were low birthweight, compared to 9% of infants in the unmarried mothers group. Similar figures were found for Black mothers (12% vs. 14%) and Hispanic mothers (6% vs. 7%).

Source: Federal Interagency Forum on Child and Family Statistics. *America's Children: Key National Indicators of Well-Being 2005*. Washington, D.C.: U.S. Government Printing Office, 2005: 66.

Infant mortality rates are 1.8 times higher for infants of unmarried mothers than for married mothers.

Source: Matthews, T.J., Sally C. Curtin, and Marian F. MacDorman. *Infant Mortality Statistics from the 1998 Period Linked Birth/Infant Death Data Set*. National Vital Statistics Reports, Vol. 48, No. 12. Hyattsville, MD: National Center for Health Statistics, 2000.

Based on birth and death data for 217,798 children born in Georgia in 1989 and 1990, infants without a father's name on their birth certificate (17.9 percent of the total) were 2.3 times more likely to die in the first year of life compared to infants with a father's name on their birth certificate.

Source: Gaudino, Jr., James A., Bill Jenkins, and Foger W. Rochat. "No Fathers' Names: A Risk Factor for Infant Mortality in the State of Georgia, USA." *Social Science and Medicine 48* (1999): 253-265.

"Unmarried mothers are less likely to obtain prenatal care and more likely to have a low birth-weight baby. Researchers find that these negative effects persist even when they take into account factors, such as parental education, that often distinguish single-parent from two-parent families."

Source: U.S. Department of Health and Human Services. Public Health Service. Center for Disease Control and Prevention. National Center for Health Statistics. Report to Congress on Out-of-Wedlock Childbearing. Hyattsville, MD (Sept. 1995): 12.

Pregnancies Ending in Live Birth to Women, and Months Pregnant When Prenatal Care Began, by Marital Status at Time of Birth, 1991-1995

Marital Status	Number (1,000)	Total (%)	Less than 3 Months Pregnant	3 to 4 Months Pregnant	5 Months Pregnant or More or No Prenatal Care
Never Married	3,940	100%	77.3%	9.6%	13.1%
Married	12,171	100%	91.5%	4.0%	4.5%
Formerly Married	942	100%	88.6%	5.3%	6.1%

Source: National Center for Health Statistics. "Fertility, Family Planning, and Women's Health: New Data from the 1995 Survey of Family Growth." *Vital and Health Statistics, Series 23, No. 19*. Washington, D.C., 1997.

Fathers and Breastfeeding

Expectant fathers can play a powerful role as advocates of breastfeeding to their wives. Three-fourths of women whose partners attended a breastfeeding promotion class initiated breastfeeding.

Source: Wolfberg, Adam J., et al. "Dads as breastfeeding advocates: results from a randomized controlled trial of an educational intervention." *American Journal of Obstetrics and Gynecology 191* (September 2004): 708-712.

Babies born to married mothers are less likely to have a low birthweight.

Expectant fathers can play a powerful role as advocates of breastfeeding to their wives.

Fathers' knowledge about breastfeeding increases the likelihood that a child will be breast-fed. Children whose fathers had more knowledge had a 1.76 higher chance of being breastfed at the end of the first month and 1.91 higher chance of receiving maternal milk at the end of the third month.

Source: Susin, Lulie R.O., et al. "Does Parental Breastfeeding Knowledge Increase Breastfeeding Rates?" *BIRTH 26* (September 1999): 149-155.

Long-Term Health and Father Absence

In a 35-year follow-up study of 126 healthy men randomly chosen from the Harvard University classes of 1952 to 1954, it was found that 82 percent of participants whose relationships with their fathers was characterized by low warmth and lack of closeness had diagnosed diseases in midlife compared to only 50 percent of those whose relationships with their fathers were characterized by high warmth and emotional closeness.

Source: Russek, L., and Schwartz, G. E. "Perceptions of Parental Love and Caring Predict Health Status in Midlife: A 35-year Follow-up of the Harvard Mastery of Stress Study." *Psychosomatic Medicine 59* (1997): 144-149.

Father Absence and Longevity

Children whose parents divorced before they are 21 years old have shorter average life spans than children whose parents do not divorce. For men, one of the causes for the increased risk of mortality is a higher frequency of accidental and violent deaths.

Source: Peterson, C., M.E.P. Seligman, K.H. Yurko, L.R. Martin, and H.S. Friedman. "Catastrophizing and Untimely Death." *Psychological Science 9* (1998): 127-130.

A longitudinal study of over 1500 California adults found that those whose parents divorced died an average of four years sooner than their counterparts whose parents remained married.

Source: Tucker, Joan, et al. "Parental Divorce: Effects on Individual Behavior and Longevity." *Journal of Personality and Social Psychology 73* (1997): 381-191.

"...men and women who experienced parental divorce or separation as children (before the age of 21) tend to have a shorter life span, by more than 4 years, than children who did not experience parental divorce."

Source: Schwartz, Joseph E., et al. "Sociodemographic and Psychosocial Factors in Childhood as Predictors of Adult Mortality." *American Journal of Public Health 85* (1995): 1237-1245.

Poverty

"Promoting responsible fatherhood is the critical next phase of welfare reform and one of the most important things we can do to reduce child poverty."

FORMER VICE PRESIDENT AL GORE, SPEAKING AT THE NATIONAL FATHERHOOD INITIATIVE'S 3RD ANNUAL NATIONAL SUMMIT ON FATHERHOOD IN WASHINGTON, D.C., JUNE 2, 2000.

"There's a very simple lesson here that many people do not seem to understand, and that is that poverty, especially in married-couple households, is almost always flat. It doesn't change much. And it's much lower, sometimes by a factor of 5 or 6, than poverty in female-headed families. So if you want to make progress against poverty, the key target is female-headed families.

RON HASKINS AT THE BROOKINGS WELFARE REFORM & BEYOND PRESS BRIEFING, AUGUST 26, 2004.

...men and women who experienced parental divorce or separation as children... tend to have a shorter life span...

"The vast majority of children who are raised entirely in a two-parent home will never be poor during childhood. By contrast, the vast majority of children who spend time in a single-parent home will experience poverty."
HARVARD PROFESSOR DAVID ELLWOOD, *POOR SUPPORT* , NEW YORK: BASIC BOOKS, 1988, P. 46.

"Child poverty rates today would be one-third lower if family structure had not changed so dramatically since 1960. Fifty-one percent of the increase in child poverty observed during the 1980s is attributable to changes in family structure during that period."
UNIVERSITY OF MARYLAND POLITICAL SCIENTIST WILLIAM GALSTON, 1993

"Much of the income differential between whites and blacks today, perhaps as much as two thirds, can be attributed to differences in family structure."
AUTHOR DAVID POPENOE, *LIFE WITHOUT FATHER*, 1996.

"What is the poorest group of Americans today? The children of single mothers, that's who."
WILLIAM RASPBERRY, COLUMNIST, *THE WASHINGTON POST*, DECEMBER 31, 1995

Poverty and Family Structure
A simulation increased the marriage rate to what it was in 1970. Between 1970 and 2001, the overall marriage rate had declined by 17 percent and by 34 percent for blacks. If marriage had stayed at the same level, poverty would drop from 13.0 percent to 9.5 percent, a 27 percent decrease. Education, for example, would only decrease poverty by 15 percent.
Source: Haskins, Ron. Speech. Testimony before the Social Security and Family Policy Subcommittee on Finance. 5 May 2004.; Thomas, Adam and Isabel Sawhill. "For Richer or for Poorer: Marriage as an Antipoverty Strategy." *Journal of Policy Analysis and Management 21* (Autumn 2002): 587-599.

Children in father-absent homes are five times more likely to be poor. In 2002, 7.8 percent of children in married-couple families were living in poverty, compared to 38.4 percent of children in female-householder families.
Source: U.S. Census Bureau, *Children's Living Arrangements and Characteristics: March 2002*, P20-547, Table C8. Washington D.C.: GPO, 2003.

In 2002, 5.3 percent of married-couple families with children were poor, compared to 26.5 percent of mother-only families.
Source: U.S. Census Bureau, *Children's Living Arrangements and Characteristics: March 2002*, P60-222, Washington D.C.: GPO, 2003.

The poverty rate for children under age six living in single-mother families was 48.6 percent in 2002. The poverty rate for children under age six in married-couple families in 2002 was 9.7 percent.
Source: U.S. Census Bureau, *Children's Living Arrangements and Characteristics: March 2002*, P60-222, Washington D.C.: GPO, 2003.

Children in father-absent homes are five times more likely to be poor.

In a cross-national study of 8 countries, single mothers suffered from a higher poverty rate in all countries except Sweden. In all countries, including Sweden, single mothers fared worse than married mothers in families. Even in Sweden, single mothers were at least 5 times more likely to be poor than married parents. The difference between single and married parents was greater in all other cases.

Source: Christopher, Karen, Paula England, Timothy M. Smeeding, and Katherin Ross Phillips. "The Gender Gap in Poverty in Modern Nations: Single Motherhood, The Market, and the State." *Sociological Perspectives 45* (Fall 2002): 219-242.

In a study of 14 wealthy nations, it was found that very few children living in two-parent families in any country were extremely poor. Italy had the highest rate with 10 percent and the United States had the next highest rate at 4%. Children in single-mother families fare comparatively worse. With the exception of Sweden (52 percent), Spain (56 percent), Belgium and Finland (64 percent), and Italy (65 percent), some 70 percent or more of children in single-mother families have incomes that place them in the lower third of the distribution of all persons' income. Indeed, 80 percent or more of such children in the United Kingdom, Australia, Germany, and the Netherlands are in the lower third of the total distribution.

Source: Rainwater, Lee and Timothy M. Smeeding. "Dooing Poorly: U.S. Child Poverty in Cross-National Context." *Children, Youth and Environments 13* (2003). Accessed 9 May 2005. <http://www.colorado.edu/journals/cye/13_2/RainwaterSmeedingPaper/DoingPoorly.htm>

The average difference in poverty rates between lone and two-parent households in the US, UK, Germany, France, Sweden, and Italy is about 20%. The split in the United States is the highest at 42.9%.

Source: Daniela Del Boca. "Mothers, fathers and children after divorce: The role of institutions." *Journal of Population Economics 16* (2003): 399-422.

Forty-five percent of unmarried mothers in large U.S. cities are poor...

Forty-five percent of unmarried mothers in large U.S. cities are poor and another 28% are "near poor," with incomes below 200% of the poverty line. Twenty seven and 29% of fathers are poor or "near poor," respectively.

Source: McLanahan, Sara. *The Fragile Families and Child Wellbeing Study: Baseline National Report.* Figure 3. Princeton, NJ: Center for Research on Child Wellbeing, 2003: 11.

During the year before their babies were born, 43% of unmarried mothers received welfare or food stamps, 21% received some type of housing subsidy, and 9% received another type of government transfer (unemployment insurance etc.). For women who have another child, the proportion who receive welfare or food stamps rises to 54%.

Source: McLanahan, Sara. *The Fragile Families and Child Wellbeing Study: Baseline National Report.* Princeton, NJ: Center for Research on Child Wellbeing, 2003: 13.

Compared to children in married-couple families, children in female householder families with no husband experience a poverty rate more than four times higher (40% vs. 9%). Children living in two-parent families were also more likely to have a parent working full-time, year round (89%) as compared to children living with a single mother or single father (49% and 70%, respectively).

Source: *America's Children in Brief: Key National Indicators of Well-Being.* Washington, DC: Federal Interagency Forum on Child and Family Statistics, 2004: 7.

When compared by family structure, 45.9% of poor families reported material hardship compared to 38.6% of poor two parent families. For unpoor families who did not experience material hardship, 23.3% were single-parent families compared to 41.2% of two-parent families.

Source: Beverly, Sondra G., "Material hardship in the United States: Evidence from the Survey of Income and Program Particpation." *Social Work Research 25* (September 2001): 143-151.

Although their collective poverty rate did not change, the number of families with a female householder and no husband increased from 3.5 million in 2001 to 3.6 million in 2002. Half of all families in poverty are comprised of this arrangement.
Source: Proctor Bernadette D. and Joseph Dalaker. *Poverty in the United States: 2002.* Current Population Reports, P60-222. Washington DC: U.S. Census Bureau, 2003: 7.

In 1997, 65 percent of poor children lived in households that did not include their biological fathers, compared to 25 percent of children who were not poor.
Source: Feeley, Theresa J. "Low Income Noncustodial Fathers: A Child Advocate's Guide to Helping Them Contribute to the Support of Their Children." *National Association of Child Advocates Issue Brief*, National Association of Child Advocates, Washington, D.C., February, 2000.

In a 1997 nationally representative survey of 44,461 households, it was found that 59% of children born outside of marriage were poor, compared to 37% of those born within marriage. Of those currently residing in a two-parent family, only 11% were living below the poverty line, compared to 44% of those living in a single-parent household.
Source: Ehrle, Jennifer, and Kristin Moore. *Assessing the New Federalism: Snapshots of America's Families.* Washington, D.C.: Urban Institute, 1999: Snapshot C-2 (Children's Environment and Behavior: Children Born Outside of Marriage); also see Halpern, Ariel. "Poverty among Children Born Outside of Marriage: Preliminary Findings from the National Survey of America's Families." Washington, D.C.: *The Urban Institute*, December 1999.

Using data from the National Longitudinal Survey of Youth, it was found that for children living in near poverty, those whose mothers were married fared better than those whose mothers were not married.
Source: Miller, Jane E., and Diane Davis. "Poverty History, Marital History, and the Quality of Children's Home Environments." *Journal of Marriage and the Family 59* (November 1997): 996-1007.

"Eighty-eight percent of women who had children out of wedlock and did not finish high school are living in poverty, compared to just 8 percent of women who finished school, married, and had a baby after the age of twenty."
Source: Popenoe, David. *Life Without Father.* New York: Martin Kessler Books, The Free Press, New York, 1996. 55.

Poverty, Family Structure, and Race and Ethnicity

In 1999, 5 percent of white children in married-couple families lived in poverty, compared to 29 percent of those in single-mother households. Eleven percent of black children in married-couple families lived in poverty, compared to 52 percent of those living with their mother only. Twenty-two percent of Hispanic children in married-couple families lived in poverty, compared with 52 percent in mother-only families.
Source: *America's Children: Key National Indicators of Well-Being, 2001.* Table ECON1.A. Washington, D.C.: Federal Interagency Forum on Child and Family Statistics, 2001.

Earnings and Family Structure

In 2001, the median income for married-couple families with children was $60,471, compared to only $28,142 for mother-only families with children.
Source: Money Income in the United States: 2001. Current Population Reports, P60-218. Table 1. Washington, D.C.: U.S. Census Bureau, 2002.

In 1999, the median income for black female-headed families was $18,244, compared to $50,656 for black married couples. For Hispanic families, the corresponding figures were $18,701 and $37,132; for white families, $26,529 and $57,089.
Source: Money Income in the United States: 1999. Current Population Reports, P60-209. Table 4. Washington, D.C.: U.S. Census Bureau, 2000.

Eighty-eight percent of women who had children out of wedlock and did not finish high school are living in poverty...

An analysis of county-level economic data from 1970 to 1990 found that female-headship was significantly related to higher levels of income inequality.
Source: Nielsen, Francois and Arthur S. Alserson. "The Kuznets Curve and the Great U-Turn: Income Inequality in U.S. Counties, 1970 to 1990." *American Sociological Review 62* (February 1997): 12-33.

A study using the Public Use Microdata Sample found that children who live with two married parents are more likely to live with an employed male, compared to children who live with a single parent and that parent's cohabiting partner.
Source: Manning, Wendy D. and Daniel T. Lichter. "Parental Cohabitation and Children's Economic Well-Being." *Journal of Marriage and the Family 58* (November 1996): 998-1010.

Consequences of Family Structure for Later Earnings
Based on a national sample of 3,523 30- to 59-year-old women and men derived from the 1989 Panel Study of Income Dynamics, it was found that both men and women who grew up in two-parent households earned more as adults than those from other family structures. The positive effect on earnings of growing up in a two-parent household is stronger for women than for men.
Source: Powell, Mary Ann, and Toby L. Parcel. "Effects of Family Structure on the Earnings Attainment Process: Differences by Gender." *Journal of Marriage and the Family 59* (May 1997): 419-433.

The results from a study of 1,731 young men indicated that living in a broken home at the age of 14 increased the likelihood that a man would leave the labor force at some point by 30% to 50% compared to a man who lived with both parents at the age of 14. They were also 30% to 50% more likely to experience a spell of idleness (unemployed and not in school) compared to men who lived with both biological parents at the age of 14.
Source: Powers, Daniel A. "Social Background and Social Context Effects on Young Men's Idleness Transitions." *Social Science Research 25* (1996): 50-72.

Homelessness and Family Structure
In a recent investigation of homeless families in St. Louis, researchers found that "single mothers accounted for fully 90 percent of the homeless families. In contrast, married-couple households only accounted for 8 percent of the homeless population."
Source: Young McChesney, Kay. "A Review of the Empirical Literature on Contemporary Urban Homeless Families." *Social Service Review* (September 1995): 428-434.

Distressed Neighborhoods and Family Structure
A longitudinal study of 17,000 households indicated that marriage almost doubles the chances of moving from a poor to a non-poor neighborhood. Conversely, divorce more than doubles the chances of moving from a non-poor to a poor neighborhood. For blacks, divorce increases the risk of moving from a non-poor neighborhood to a poor neighborhood nearly six times.
Source: South, Scott J. and Kyle D. Crowder. "Escaping Distressed Neighborhoods: Individual, Community, and Metropolitan Influences." *American Journal of Sociology 102* (1997): 1040-1084.

Welfare Participation and Family Structure
More than 75 percent of all unmarried teen mothers go on welfare within 5 years of the birth of their first child.
Source: *When Teens Have Sex: Issues and Trends*. Baltimore, MD: The Annie E. Casey Foundation, 1998: 13.

Of children living in TANF households, more than 7 out of 10 children (71.8 percent) lived with a single parent in 1998, and fewer than one in 10 (7.4 percent) lived with two parents.
Source: Committee on Ways and Means, U.S. House of Representatives. 2000 Green Book. Washington, D.C.: U.S. Government Printing Office, 2000.

> Of children living in TANF households, more than 7 out of 10 children... lived with a single parent in 1998...

In 1993, 48% of all AFDC recipients had never been married and in 1995, 88% of the mothers who received AFDC payments were single mothers.
Source: Bachu, Amara. "Mothers Who Receive AFDC Payments: Fertility and Socioeconomic Characteristics." U.S. Bureau of the Census. Statistical Brief SB/95-2. Washington, D.C.: GPO, March 1995.

An analysis using the Public Use Microsample Data indicated that nearly one quarter of children in cohabiting families and 30% of children in families headed by a single female have mothers who receive public assistance.
Source: Manning, Wendy D. and Daniel T. Lichter. "Parental Cohabitation and Children's Economic Well-Being." *Journal of Marriage and the Family 58* (November 1996): 998-1010.

Sexual Activity

"Fatherless boys (as a general rule) become ineligible to be husbands --- though no less likely to become fathers — and their children fall into patterns that render them ineligible to be husbands. The absence of fathers means, as well, that girls lack both a pattern against which to measure the boys who pursue them and an example of sacrificial love between a man and a woman."
WILLIAM RASPBERRY, WASHINGTON POST COLUMNIST, "WHY OUR BLACK FAMILIES ARE FAILING," JULY 7, 2005.

"If our daughters are to flower, they need optimal growing conditions. Almost always this means being lovingly cared for by mother and father. It is from her mother that a girl learns to be a woman; it is from her father that she learns what to expect from men in the way of love and respect."
EVELYN BASSOFF, PH.D., *CHERISHING OUR DAUGHTERS: HOW PARENTS CAN RAISE GIRLS TO BECOME STRONG AND LOVING WOMEN*, 1998.

"Today with the rise in illegitimacy and divorce, fewer fathers are around to protect and defend their daughters' safety and honor. With more girls lacking the love and attention that only a father can give, more of them are willing to settle for perverse alternatives, namely, seeking intimacy with predatory adult men."
GRACIE S. HSU, "LEAVING THE VULNERABLE OPEN TO ABUSE," *PERSPECTIVE*, SEPTEMBER 9, 1996.

"Having loving parents you can talk to can help reduce teen pregnancy. Fathers [especially] are very influential in the decision to have sex."
SURVEY OF TEENAGE GIRLS CONDUCTED BY MARK CLEMENTS RESEARCH, AS CITED IN *PARADE*, FEBRUARY 2, 1997.

Survey Data

In a national sample of 10,847 women, 20 percent of women surveyed responded "yes" to a question asking if they had ever been forced to have sexual intercourse. For women who grew up in intact two-parent families, 17 percent reported being forced to have intercourse, compared to 27 percent of those from single-parent or stepparent homes.
Source: Abma, J., A. Chandra, W. Mosher, L. Peterson, and L. Piccinino. "Fertility, Family Planning, and Women's Health: New Data from the 1995 National Survey on Family Growth." Table 20. National Center for Health Statistics. Vital Health Stat 23(19), 1997: 31.

In UCLA's annual national survey of the attitudes of college freshmen, 39.6% of students agreed that "If two people really like each other, it's alright for them to have sex even if they've known each other for a very short time," down from 51.9% in 1987 and a record low since the question first was asked three decades ago.
Source: UCLA annual survey of college freshmen, 1998, as cited in Leo, John, "Reversal in the Sex Revolution." The Washington Times, February 27, 1999.

In a survey of 1,172 children ages 6 to 14, 76% of those ages 12 to 14 said it's "somewhat or very important" to wait until marriage before having sex. When the other 24% were asked to name an appropriate age for premarital sex, the average age mentioned was 23 years. When their parents were asked the same question, the average age given was 18 years.
Source: Peen, Shoen & Berland Associates poll conducted for *Nickelodeon* and *Time* magazine; July 5, 1999.

A survey of 720 teenage girls found:
- 97% of girls said that having parents they could talk to could help reduce teen pregnancy.
- 93% said having loving parents reduced the risk of teen pregnancy.
- 76% said that their fathers were very or somewhat influential on their decision to have sex.
Source: Clements, Mark. *Parade.* February 2, 1997.

Teenage Sexual Activity and Father Absence
Seventy percent of British youth polled who had not had sex came from married, two-parent households compared with only half of the teens who were sexually active. Twenty-three percent of teens whose parents were divorced had underage sex compared to 14 percent from similar backgrounds but different family structures who had not.

Data from the National Health Interview Survey indicated that both male and female adolescents who come from nonintact families are more likely to have had sexual intercourse.
Source: Santelli, John S. et al. "The Association of Sexual Behaviors With Socioeconomic Status, Family Structure, and Race/Ethnicity Among US Adolescents." *American Journal of Public Health 90* (October 2000): 1582-1588.

Being raised by a single mother raises the risk of teen pregnancy, marrying with less than a high school degree, and forming a marriage where both partners have less than a high school degree.
Source: Teachman, Jay D. "The Childhood Living Arrangements of Children and the Characteristics of Their Marriages." *Journal of Family Issues 25* (January 2004): 86-111.

Separation or frequent changes increase a woman's risk of early menarche, sexual activity and pregnancy. Women whose parents separated between birth and six years old experienced twice the risk of early menstruation, more than four times the risk of early sexual intercourse, and two and a half times higher risk of early pregnancy when compared to women in intact families. The longer a woman lived with both parents, the lower her risk of early reproductive development.

Women who experienced three or more changes in her family environment exhibited similar risks but were five times more likely to have an early pregnancy.
Source: Quinlan, Robert J. "Father absence, parental care, and female reproductive development." *Evolution and Human Behavior 24* (November 2003): 376-390.

> 76% of teenage girls said that their fathers were very or somewhat influential on their decision to have sex.

In pool from the NSFG, being born out-of-wedlock, the number of transitions experienced, and the type of childhood living arrangement were shown to increase the risk of teenage premarital intercourse for Whites and Blacks. Each change in family living arrangement increases the risk by 23% to 41% for Whites. These effects are substantially larger for Blacks.
Source: Albrecht, Chris and Jay D. Teachman. Childhood Living Arrangements and Risk of Premarital Intercourse." *Journal of Family Issues 24* (October 2003): 867-894.

Father's interactions with their children differ depending on the familial context. Young men who live in a two-parent household and spend a lot of time with their father were more likely to delay sexual activity than those who spent time with their fathers but lived in a single-parent household.
Source: Ramirez-Valles, Jesus, Marc A. Zimmerman, and Lucia Juarez. "Gender Differences of Neighborhood and Social Control Processes: A Study of the Timing of First Intercourse Among Low-Achieving, Urban, African American Youth." Youth & Society 33 (March 2002): 418-441.

Although researchers using a pool from both the U.S. and New Zealand did not find a connection between father absence and other behavioral, mental, or academic problems, they did find strong evidence that father absence has an effect on early sexual activity and teenage pregnancy. Teens without fathers were twice as likely to be involved in early sexual activity and seven times more likely to get pregnant as an adolescent.
Source: Ellis, Bruce J., et al. "Does Father Absence Place Daughters at Special Risk for Early Sexual Activity and Teenage Pregnancy?" Child Development 74 (May/June 2003): 801-821.

Teens whose parents were separated or cohabiting were twice as likely to have had sex.
Source: Meikle, James. "Underage sex linked to single-parent families: Study stresses home environment as key to forming youthful attitudes." The Guardian 23 July 2001: 12.

Although the odds of sexual initiation for teenage males increases with age, living with both parents decreases the odds by 70%. Conversely, having a mother who gave birth as a teen increases the odds by 40%.
Source: Forste, Renata and David W. Haas. "The transition of adolescent males to first intercourse: anticipated or delayed?" Perspectives on Sexual & Reproductive Health 34 (July/August 2002): 184-190.

In an analysis of data collected from 26,023 adolescents ages 13 to 18, the teens living in single-parent households were more likely to engage in premarital sex than those living in two-parent households.
Source: Lammers, Christina, et al. "Influences on Adolescents' Decision to Postpone Onset of Sexual Intercourse: A Survival Analysis of Virginity Among Youths Aged 13 to 18 Years." Journal of Adolescent Health 26 (2000): 42-48.

In a study of 870 adolescents, boys and girls who lived with both biological parents had the lowest risk of becoming sexually active, and teens living in single-parent and stepfamilies were particularly at risk of becoming sexually active at younger ages.
Source: Upchurch, Dawn M., Carol S. Aneshensel, Clea A. Sucoff, and Lene Levy-Storms. "Neighborhood and Family Contexts of Adolescent Sexual Activity." *Journal of Marriage and the Family, 61* (November 1999): 920-933.

Among women from intact two-parent families, the mean age at first intercourse is 18.2 years. For women from single-parent or stepparent families, the mean age at first intercourse is 16.6 years.
Source: Abma, J., A. Chandra, W. Mosher, L. Peterson, and L. Piccinino. "Fertility, Family Planning, and Women's Health: New Data from the 1995 National Survey on Family Growth." Table 20. National Center for Health Statistics. Vital Health Stat 23(19), 1997: 31.

> Teens whose parents were separated or cohabiting were twice as likely to have had sex.

"A white teenage girl from an advantaged background is five times more likely to become a teen mother if she grows up in a single-mother household than if she grows up in a household with both biological parents."
Source: Whitehead, Barbara Dafoe. "Facing the Challenges of Fragmented Families." *The Philanthropy Roundtable, 9.1* (1995): 21.

A study using a nationally representative sample of 2,300 young people found that those who had experienced family disruption, including divorce or separation, were at a heightened risk of experiencing early intercourse.
Source: Moore, Kristin A., Donna Ruane Morrison, and Dana A. Glei. "Welfare and Adolescent Sex: The Effects of Family History, Benefit Levels, and Community Context." *Journal of Family and Economic Issues 16* (1995): 207-230.

A five-year study on 800 African-American and Hispanic adolescents found that boys and girls who did not live with both biological parents were significantly more likely to engage in sexual intercourse than their peers who lived with both biological parents.
Source: Smith, Carolyn A. "Factors Associated with Early Sexual Activity Among Urban Adolescents." *Social Work, 42.4* (July 1997): 334-346.

A study of 200 middle-school and high-school-aged boys from high-crime areas found that of those who were virgins, 59% lived in intact families. In contrast, only 18% of those who had sexual intercourse by the eighth grade were from intact families.
Source: Capaldi, Deborah M., Lynn Crosby, and Mike Stoolmiller. "Predicting the Timing of First Sexual Intercourse for At-Risk Adolescent Males." *Child Development, 67* (1996): 344-359.

IV. Positive Effects of Father Presence

"Don't ever doubt the impact that fathers have on children. Children with strongly committed fathers learn about trust early on. They learn about trust with their hearts. They learn they're wanted, that they have value, that they can afford to be secure and confident and set their sights high. They get the encouragement they need to keep going through the rough spots in life. Boys learn from their fathers how to be fathers. I learned all those things from my own father, and I count my blessings."

FORMER VICE PRESIDENT AL GORE, SPEAKING AT THE NATIONAL FATHERHOOD INITIATIVE'S 3RD ANNUAL NATIONAL SUMMIT ON FATHERHOOD IN WASHINGTON, D.C., JUNE 2, 2000.

"Fatherhood is no simple phenomenon, but a complex tapestry of things [...] the reality [is] that fatherhood is not a static phenomenon, but more like a moving target, only some of which has constant meaning."

GARY PETERSON AND SUZANNE STEINMETZ IN "THE DIVERSITY OF FATHERHOOD: CHANGE, CONSTANCY, AND CONTRADICTION," *MARRIAGE AND FAMILY REVIEW,* 2000.

"Fathers' involvement has a unique impact on children's outcomes, including cognitive development, achievement, math and reading scores, as well as behavioral problems. The fact that this benefit is here should raise concern to those who do not have these resources."

W. JEAN YEUNG, SOCIOLOGIST, UNIVERSITY OF MICHIGAN, AS QUOTED IN *REUTERS HEALTH NEWS,* JUNE 12, 1999

"We asked [poor, unwed fathers] what their lives would be like without their children. We expected them to say their lives would be so much easier, but they said, 'I'd be dead or in jail.' Children have tremendous importance for fathers."

KATHRYN EDIN, SOCIOLOGIST, UNIVERSITY OF PENNSYLVANIA, AS QUOTED IN *THE WALL STREET JOURNAL*, AUGUST 16, 1998.

"Attempts to understand the 'active ingredient' in fathers' play that promotes peer competence have revealed that children learn critical lessons about how to recognize and deal with highly charged emotions in the context of playing with their fathers. Fathers, in effect, give children practice in regulating their own emotions and recognizing others' emotional cues."

JOSEPH H. PLECK, ASSOCIATE PROFESSOR OF HUMAN DEVELOPMENT AND FAMILY STUDIES, UNIVERSITY OF ILLINOIS, 1993.

"Children with an involved father are exposed to more varied social experiences and are more intellectually advanced than those who only have regular contact with their mother. Infants with two involved parents can cope better with being alone with strangers and also seem to attend more effectively to novel and complex stimuli. Well-fathered children have a greater breadth of positive social experiences than those exclusively reared by their mothers."

HENRY B. BILLER, *FATHERS AND FAMILIES: PATERNAL FACTORS IN CHILD DEVELOPMENT*, AUBURN HOUSE, WESTPORT, CONNECTICUT, 1993.

"At the end of the day when I go to bed, Daddy tucks me in. We talk together about our day. He reads me a story to help me sleep. We pray together. That is my favorite part."

AMANDA, AGE 6, AS QUOTED BY MARY KAY SHANLEY IN *WHEN I THINK ABOUT MY FATHER*

"Dad is my buddy."

JOSH, AGE 10, AS QUOTED BY MARY KAY SHANLEY IN *WHEN I THINK ABOUT MY FATHER*

...97% felt that fathers were just as important as mothers for the proper development of children.

Attitudes About Positive Father Involvement

In a poll of 1,503 adults, 97% felt that fathers were just as important as mothers for the proper development of children.

Source: National Fatherhood Initiative. *With This Ring...: A National Survey On Marriage in America*. Gaithersburg, MD: National Fatherhood Initiative, 2005: 4.

In a poll of 1,031 adults, most Americans still expect father figures to assist with specific parenting practices. A high majority feel that mothers and fathers should equally share the responsibilities for bathing the children and changing diapers (83%), caring for the children when they are sick or hurt (82%), playing with the kids (95%), helping with schoolwork (93%), and disciplining children (92%).

Source: Fetto, John. "Does Father Really Know Best?" *American Demographics* June 2002: 10-11.

A resounding 96% of respondents in a national survey agreed that parents should share equally in the caretaking of children.
Source: Radcliffe Public Policy Center. *Life's Work: Generational Attitudes toward Work and Life Integration.* Cambridge, MA:Radcliffe Institute of Advanced Study, 2000.

A survey of over 500 Baby Boomer men found that 84% said that being a good father was a very important factor in their definition of success.
Source: Goldstein, Dr. Ross. "The New American Adulthood." National Survey. Consumer Survey Center. Half Moon Bay, California, 1996.

A survey of Kentucky fathers found:
- 44% didn't feel included in decisions regarding their families.
- 45% said they didn't think their ideas were taken seriously.
- 38% said the services they received helped them become better fathers.

Source: Musgrave, Beth. "Fathers are feeling left out, state study shows." *Lexington Herald-Ledger* 29 April 2005.

The Positive Impact of Father Involvement on Child Well-Being

A literature review of fatherhood in the twenty-first century revealed five effects of father absence:
- the lack of a coparent
- the economic loss that accompanies single motherhood and its correlative effect on educational and psychosocial wellbeing
- emotional distress from social disapproval and lack of support
- psychological distress from perceived or actual father abandonment
- conflict between parents

Source: Cabrera, Tamera and Catherine S. Tamis-Lemonda, et al. "Fatherhood in the Twenty-First Century." *Child Development, 71* (January/February 2000): 127-136.

In an analysis of nearly 100 studies on parent-child relationships, father love (measured by children's perceptions of paternal acceptance/rejection, affection/indifference) was as important as mother love in predicting the social, emotional, and cognitive development and functioning of children and young adults:
- Having a loving and nurturing father was as important for a child's happiness, well-being, and social and academic success as having a loving and nurturing mother.
- Withdrawal of love by either the father or the mother was equally influential in predicting a child's emotional instability, lack of self-esteem, depression, social withdrawal, and level of aggression.
- In some studies, father love was actually a better predictor than mother love for certain outcomes, including delinquency and conduct problems, substance abuse, and overall mental health and well-being.
- Other studies found that, after controlling for mother love, father love was the sole significant predictor for certain outcomes, such as psychological adjustment problems, conduct problems, and substance abuse.

Source: Rohner, Ronald P., and Robert A. Veneziano. "The Importance of Father Love: History and Contemporary Evidence." Review of General Psychology, 5.4 (December 2001): 382-405.

A survey of 723 fathers identified nine dimensions of father involvement: providing, supporting the mother, disciplining and teaching responsibility, encouraging success in school, giving praise and affection, spending time together and talking, being attentive to their child's needs, reading to their children, and encouraging children to develop their talents.
Source: Bradford, Kay P. and Alan Hawkins, et al. "The Inventory of Father Involvement: A Pilot Study of a New Measure of Father Involvement." *Journal of Men's Studies, 10* (Winter 2002): 183-196.

...96% of respondents in a national survey agreed that parents should share equally in the caretaking of children.

In a review of the literature published since 1980 examining the impact of father involvement on child well-being in two-parent families, it was determined that 56 of 68 studies (82%) found significant and positive associations between father involvement and child well-being.
Source: Amato, Paul R., and Fernando Rivera. "Paternal Involvement and Children's Behavior Problems." *Journal of Marriage and the Family, 61* (1999): 375-384.

A consistent finding from research on adolescence is that early onset of puberty in girls is associated with negative health and psychosocial outcomes, such as higher rates of teenage pregnancy, depression, alcohol consumption, and disturbances in body image. In an 8-year prospective study of 173 girls and their families, it was found that fathers' presence in the home, more time spent by fathers in child care, greater supportiveness in the parental dyad, more father-daughter affection, and more mother-daughter affection, as assessed prior to kindergarten, each predicted later pubertal timing by daughters in 7th grade. In total, the quality of fathers' investment in the family emerged as the most important feature of the proximal family environment relative to daughters' pubertal timing.
Source: Ellis, B. J., S. McFadyen-Ketchum, K.A. Dodge, G.S. Pettit, and J.E. Bates. "Quality of Early Family Relationships and Individual Differences in the Timing of Pubertal Maturation in Girls: A Longitudinal Test of an Evolutionary Model." *Journal of Personality and Social Psychology, 77* (1999): 387-401.

When married fathers are more involved in childrearing, their marriages are more likely to be stable because wives tend to be happier if the husband is strongly involved with the children.
Source: Kalmijn, Matthijs. "Father Involvement in Childrearing and the Perceived Stability of Marriage." *Journal of Marriage and the Family, 61* (May 1999): 409-421.

In a study of 175 low-income, 3-year-old African American children, researchers concluded that where fathers lived with the child, "the home was more child-centered."
Source: Black, M.M., H. Dubowitz, and R.H. Starr. "African American Fathers in Low Income, Urban Families: Development, Behavior, and Home Environment of their Three-Year-Old Children." *Child Development, 70* (1999): 967-978.

A study using a nationally representative sample of children showed that children whose fathers showed little emotional involvement were more likely to have experienced poverty than children whose fathers were emotionally involved with their children.
Source: Mullan Harris, Kathleen and Jeremy K. Marmer. "Poverty, Paternal Involvement, and Adolescent Well-Being." *Journal of Family Issues, 17* (1996): 614-640.

A study using a nationally representative sample of 1,600 10-13 year olds found that children who shared important ideas with their fathers and who perceived the amount of time they spent with their fathers as excellent had fewer behavior problems and lived in more cognitively stimulating homes than their peers who did not share important ideas or view the amount of time they spent with their fathers as excellent.
Source: Williams, Malcolm V. "Reconceptualizing Father Involvement." Masters Thesis, Georgetown University, 1997.

In a study of 254 African-American male adolescents, boys living with both biological parents were most likely to cite their fathers as role models (96 percent), compared to only 44 percent of those not living with their fathers, and were more likely to stay in school.
Source: Zimmerman, Marc, Deborah Salem and Kenneth Maton. "Family Structure and Psychosocial Correlates among Urban African-American Adolescent Males." *Child Development, 66* (1995): 1598-1613..

...56 of 68 studies... found significant and positive associations between father involvement and child well-being.

POSITIVE EFFECTS OF FATHER PRESENCE

A longitudinal study of 584 children from intact families indicated that children whose fathers are highly involved with them attain higher levels of education and economic self-sufficiency than children whose fathers are not highly involved. A high level of paternal involvement and improved father-child relations throughout adolescence were associated with lower levels of delinquency and better psychological well-being.
Source: Mullan Harris, Kathleen, Frank F. Furstenberg, and Jeremy K. Marmer. "Paternal Involvement with Adolescents in Intact Families: The Influences of Fathers over the Life Course." American Sociological Association. New York. 16-20 Aug. 1996.

A longitudinal study on over 1,000 children who lived with both biological parents found that children whose fathers wore seat belts, had car insurance, and had precautionary savings were more successful as adults than their peers whose fathers did not engage in these activities. In addition, the fathers' educational attainment and wage rate were positively associated with higher outcomes for the children when they entered the labor market.
Source: Yeung, Wei-Jun J., Greg J. Duncan, and Martha S. Hill. "Putting Fathers Back in the Picture: Parental Activities and Children's Adult Attainments." Conference on Father Involvement. Bethesda, Maryland, 10-11 Oct. 1996.

Using nationally representative data on over 2,600 adults born in the inner city, it was found that children who lived with both parents were more likely to have finished high school, be economically self-sufficient, and to have a healthier life style than their peers who grew up in broken homes.
Source: Hardy, Janet B., et al. "Self Sufficiency at Ages 27 to 33 Years: Factors Present between Birth and 18 Years that Predict Educational Attainment Among Children Born to Inner-city Families." Pediatrics, 99 (1997): 80-87.

Educational Attainment and Positive Father Involvement

Children whose fathers were highly involved in their schools were more likely to do well academically, to participate in extracurricular activities, and to enjoy school, and were less likely to have ever repeated a grade or been expelled compared to children whose fathers were less involved in their schools. This effect held for both two-parent and single-parent households, and was distinct and independent from the effect of mother involvement.
Source: Nord, Christine Windquist. Students Do Better When Their Fathers Are Involved at School (NCES 98-121). Washington, D.C.: U.S. Department of Education, National Center for Education Statistics, 1998; see also Nonresident Fathers Can Make a Difference in Children's School Performance (NCES 98-117). Washington, D.C.: U.S. Department of Education, National Center for Education Statistics, 1998; Nord, Christine Winquist, and Jerry West. Fathers' and Mothers' Involvement in Their Children's Schools by Family Type and Resident Status. (NCES 2001-032). Washington, D.C.: U.S. Department of Education, National Center for Education Statistics, 2001.

Utilizing a sample of 1,052 children born between 1956 and 1962 and followed until 1985, it was found that the children whose fathers were substantially involved in parent-teacher activities completed more schooling and enjoyed higher wages and family income as adults compared to those whose fathers had little or no involvement in parent-teacher activities.
Source: Duncan, Greg J., Martha Hill, and W. Jean Yeung. "Fathers' Activities and Children's Attainments." Paper presented at the Conference on Father Involvement, October 10-11, 1996, Washington, D.C., pp. 5-6.

Fathers' reports of time spent with their children were found to be positively associated with fathers' reports of children's grades.
Source: Cooksey, E.C., and M.M. Fondell. "Spending Time with His Kids: Effects of Family Structure on Fathers' and Children's Lives." Journal of Marriage and the Family, 58 (1996): 693-707.

In a study of 111 third- and fourth-graders, fathers' provision of warmth and control was positively related to higher academic achievement. Girls and black children were more positively affected by relations with fathers than were boys and white children. Divorced fathers were more influential in children's achievement than never-married fathers.
Source: Coley, Rebekah Levine. "Children's Socialization Experiences and Functioning in Single-Mother Households: The Importance of Fathers and Other Men." Child Development, 69 (February 1998): 219-230.

Children whose fathers were highly involved in their schools were more likely to do well academically...

158   **FATHER FACTS, 5TH EDITION** • © 2007 National Fatherhood Initiative

In a study of 29 fathers of academically successful African-American males, six childrearing practices were observed: child-focused love (consistent concern and showing interest); setting limits and discipline; high expectations; open, consistent, and strong communication ("talking with" rather than lecturing); positive racial and male gender identification; and drawing from community resources (especially the church).

Source: Greif, Geoffrey L., Freeman A. Hrabowski, and Kenneth I. Maton. "African-American Fathers of High-Achieving Sons: Using Outstanding Members of an At-Risk Population to Guide Intervention." *Families in Society, 79* (January/February 1998): 45-52.

In a study of 175 3-year-old African American children (89% in families receiving welfare and 92% with unmarried mothers), fathers' financial contributions and nurturing behaviors were associated with children's receptive language skills.

Source: Black, M.M., H. Dubowitz, and R.H. Starr. "African American Fathers in Low Income, Urban Families: Development, Behavior, and Home Environment of their Three-Year-Old Children." *Child Development, 70* (1999): 967-978.

A study using a national probability sample of 1,250 fathers showed that children whose fathers share meals, spend leisure time with them, or help them with reading or homework do significantly better academically than those children whose fathers do not.

Source: Cooksey, Elizabeth C. and Michelle M. Fondell. "Spending Time with His Kids: Effects of Family Structure on Fathers' and Children's Lives." *Journal of Marriage and the Family, 58* (August 1996): 693-707.

Development of Empathy and Positive Father Involvement

A study of 47 first-grade boys and their married parents found that fathers who participated more in childcare had sons who were more empathetic than sons whose fathers did not participate often in childcare.

Source: Bernadett-Shapiro, Susan, Diane Ehrensaft, and Jerold Lee Shapiro. "Father Participation in Childcare and the Development of Empathy in Sons: An Empirical Study." *Family Therapy, 23* (1996): 77-93.

Pro-Social Behavior and Positive Father Involvement

Father involvement has a direct effect on a child's externalizing and internalizing behavior. Differences in the level of involvement have significant effects on the behavioral outcomes of the child, but overall is more beneficial when the father lives with the child.

Source: Carlson, Marcia J. *Family Structure, Father Involvement and Adolescent Behavioral Outcomes.* Working Paper #05-10. Princeton, NJ: Center for Research on Child Well-Being, 2005: 2, 20-23.

In a study of 6,500 children from the ADDHEALTH database, "father closeness" ranked highest in intact, two-parent families followed by single-father families and no-parent families. Blended families ranked the lowest.

Family structure was also a significant predictor of violence (which father closeness helps ameliorate) and running away from home.

Source: National Fatherhood Initiative. "Family Structure, Father Closeness & Delinquency." Gaithersburg, MD: National Fatherhood Initiative, 2004: 16-24.

In a study of 1,300 British boys, low father involvement and peer victimization was linked to low levels of life satisfaction. Higher levels of father involvement did indicate a buffering effect to protect adolescents from extreme bullying.

Source: Flouri, Eirini and Ann Buchanan. "Life Satisfaction in Teenage Boys: The Moderating Role of Father Involvement and Bullying." *Aggressive Behavior, 28* (2002): 126-133.

> Differences in the level of [father] involvement have significant effects on the behavioral outcomes of the child...

Low to medium amounts of warmth and medium to high amounts of control in father involvement was associated with lower child internalizing behaviors. Moreover, father involvement can help heal mothers who experience depression after birth.

Source: Mezulis, Amy H., Janet Shibley Hyde, and Roseanne Clark. "Father Involvement Moderates the Effect of Maternal Depression During a Child's Infancy on Child Behavior Problems in Kindergarten." *Journal of Family Psychology, 18* (December 2004): 575-588.

Fathers' emotional involvement in the lives of their child can lead to less gendered roles. Traditionally feminine activities such as sewing, cooking, jumping rope, and art were more common for both boys and girls when the father was involved. Hence, a fathers' approval may be effective in removing the stigma attached to femininity in any form, particularly for boys.

Source: Deutsch, Francine M., Laura J. Servis, and Jessica D. Payne. "Paternal Participation in Child Care and Its Effects on Children's Self-Esteem and Attitudes Toward Gendered Roles." *Journal of Family Issues, 22* (November 2001): 1000-1024.

Children who have involved fathers expressed emotions in ways in non-traditional gender patterns. Girls express more aggression, competition, and less intense fear and sadness whereas boys expressed more warmth and fear as well as less aggression. Also, 3 to-5-year-old children with highly involved fathers had less traditional views of future employment possibilities when they became adolescents than did their peers whose fathers were more aloof.

Source: Rivers, Caryl and Rosalind Chait Barnett. "Father Figures a Slew of New Studies Applaud Dads." *The Boston Globe* 18 June 2000: E1.

Higher levels of father involvement in activities with their children, such as eating meals together, helping with homework, and going on family outings, has been found to be associated with fewer child behavior problems, higher levels of sociability, and higher levels of academic performance in children and adolescents.

Source: Mosley, J., and E. Thomson. "Fathering Behavior and Child Outcomes: The Role of Race and Poverty." In W. Marsiglio (Ed.), *Fatherhood: Contemporary Theory, Research and Social Policy*. Thousand Oaks, CA: Sage Publications, 1995: 148-165.

Using a national probability sample, father involvement correlates with fewer behavior problems exhibited by their children. This finding holds after controlling for the level of maternal involvement.

Source: Amato, Paul R., and Fernando Rivera. "Paternal Involvement and Children's Behavior Problems." *Journal of Marriage and the Family, 61* (1999): 375-384.

Children who have fathers who regularly engage them in physical play are more likely to be socially popular with their peers than children whose fathers do not engage them in this type of play.

Source: Carson, J., V. Burks, & R.D. Parke. "Parent-child Play: Determinants and Consequences." In K. MacDonald (Ed.), *Parent-child Play: Descriptions and Implications*. Albany, NY: State University of New York Press, 1993: 197-220; see also Parke, R.D. "Fathers and Families." In M.H. Bornstein (Ed.), Handbook of Parenting: Vol. 3, Status and Social Conditions of Parenting. Mahwah, NJ: Erlbaum, 1995: 27-63.

In a study of 64 African American 6th-graders, it was found that even after controlling for demographic variables, including socioeconomic status, children whose fathers were more involved in their care tended to have fewer teacher reports of negative "acting out" behavior.

Source: McCabe, Kristen M., Rodney Clark, and Douglas Barnett. "Family Protective Factors Among Urban African American Youth." *Journal of Clinical Child Psychology, 28* (1999): 137-150.

Using a sample of 994 two-parent married households from the National Survey of Families and Households, it was found that even after controlling for mothers' involvement, when fathers were highly involved in their children's lives, the child evidenced fewer behavior problems.

Source: Amato, Paul R., and Fernando Rivera. "Paternal Involvement and Children's Behavior Problems." *Journal of Marriage and the Family, 61* (1999): 375-384.

Fathers' emotional involvement in the lives of their children can lead to less gendered roles.

Using a representative household sample of over 600 adolescents and their parents, researchers found that white adolescents in single-mother families who were involved with their non-resident fathers had lower levels of delinquency, heavy drinking, and drug use than their peers living with a single mother with no father involvement.
Source: Thomas, George, Michael P. Farrell, and Grace M. Barnes. "The Effects of Single-Mother Families and Nonresident Fathers on Delinquency and Substance Abuse in Black and White Adolescents." Journal of Marriage and the Family 58 (November 1996): 884-894.

A survey of 564 adolescent young women in rural South Carolina revealed that "being from a two-parent family increased the likelihood of not engaging in premarital sexual intercourse."
Source: Lock, Sharon E. and Murray L. Vincent. "Sexual Decision Making Among Rural Adolescent Females." *Health Values, 19.1* (1995): 47-58.

Self-Esteem and Positive Father Involvement
In a study of 116 fifteen-year-old African American students, boys with married parents were found to be higher in self-esteem, self-control, and feelings of personal power compared with boys who had only their mothers in the home, even when income, parental education, and the number of people living in the home were controlled.
Source: Mandara, Jelani, and Carolyn B. Murray. "Effects of Parental Marital Status, Income, and Family Functioning on African American Adolescent Self-Esteem." *Journal of Family Psychology, 14* (2000): 475-490.

For predicting a child's self-esteem, it is sustained contact with the father that matters for sons, but physical affection from fathers that matters for daughters.
Source: Duncan, Greg J., Martha Hill, and W. Jean Yeung. "Fathers' Activities and Children's Attainments." Paper presented at the Conference on Father Involvement, October 10-11, 1996, Washington, D.C., pp. 5-6

A study of 90 Oklahoma college students found that a strong attachment to fathers had a larger impact on young adult self-esteem than attachment to their mothers.
Source: McCurdy, Susan J. and Avraham Scherman. "Effects of Family Structure on the Adolescent Separation-Individuation Process." *Adolescence, 31* (1996): 307-318.

In a sample of 455 adolescents ages 14 to 19, "students who have higher self-esteem and lower depression reported having greater intimacy with their fathers."
Source: Field, Tiffany, et al. "Adolescents' Intimacy With Parents and Friends." *Adolescence, 30.117* (Spring 1995): 133-140.

Effects of Early Father Involvement on Child Well-Being
In a study of 60 fathers and mothers, engagement in caregiving entered as the most significant predictor of attachment security in their infants. Moreover, children whose fathers reported having a secure attachment relationship with their father had mothers with higher self esteem. They also had higher attachments to their mothers.
Source: Caldera, Yvonne M. "Paternal Involvement and Infant-Father Attachment: A Q-Set Study." *Fathering, 2* (Spring 2004): 191-210.

A study of Swedish infants found that those who were securely attached to their fathers were more sociable with strangers than their peers who were less attached to their parents.
Source: Lamb, M.E., et al. "Security of Mother- and Father-Infant Interaction Involving Play and Holding in Traditional and Nontraditional Swedish Families, Infant Behavior and Development." (1982): 355-367. "The Development of Father-Infant Relationships." *The Role of the Father in Child Development.* Ed. Michael E. Lamb. New York: Wiley, 1997.

...boys with married parents were found to be higher in self-esteem, self-control, and feelings of personal power...

"Premature infants whose fathers spent more time playing with them had better cognitive outcomes at age 3."
Source: Yogman, M.W., D. Kindlon and F.J. Earls. "Father Involvement and Cognitive Behavioral Outcomes of Premature Infants." *Journal of the American Academy Child and Adolescent Psychology, 34* (1995): 58-66.

Avoidance of High-Risk Behaviors and Positive Father Involvement

Youths are more at risk of first substance use without a highly involved father. Each unit increase in father involvement is associated with 1% reduction in substance use. Living in an intact family also decreases the risk of first substance use.
Source: Bronte-Tinkew, Jacinta, Kristin A. Moore, Randolph C. Capps, and Jonathan Zaff. "The influence of father involvement on youth risk behaviors among adolescents: A comparison of native-born and immigrant families." Article in *Press*. Social Science Research December 2004.

Children with "hands-on" fathers (fathers who are involved, set reasonable household rules, monitor TV and internet use, etc.) are much less likely to use drugs than children with "hands-off" or absent fathers.
Source: The National Center on Addiction and Substance Abuse at Columbia University. "National Survey of American Attitudes on Substance Abuse VI: Teens." Conducted by QEV Analytics, February 2001.

In a study of 584 children who lived with both biological parents during three waves (1976, 1981, and 1987) of the National Survey of Children, it was found that adolescents who experienced increasing closeness with their fathers experienced less delinquency and psychological distress, whereas deteriorating father-adolescent relations resulted in more delinquency and depression.
Source: Harris, Kathleen Mullan, Frank F. Furstenberg, Jr., and Jeremy K. Marmer. "Paternal Involvement with Adolescents in Intact Families: The Influence of Fathers Over the Life Course." *Demography, 35* (May 1998): 201-216.

In a survey of 870 adolescents, boys who reported high levels of emotional support from parents have significantly lower rates of early sexual behavior than those reporting low levels of support. In addition, boys and girls who perceive their parents to be overcontrolling are likely to initiate sex at younger ages than do those reporting less controlling parents.
Source: Upchurch, Dawn M., Carol S. Aneshensel, Clea A. Sucoff, and Lene Levy-Storms. "Neighborhood and Family Contexts of Adolescent Sexual Activity." *Journal of Marriage and the Family, 61* (November 1999): 920-933.

The Positive Impact of Father Involvement on Men

A qualitative study of young fathers and mothers found that mothers received their primary parenting information from their own mother, the mothers of their partners, television and health care providers. Young fathers learned about child development from their own observations and memories of their relatives.

Young fathers also stressed the importance of good paternal role models. They reported that their own biological fathers' behavior influenced their own expectations for being a father. They identified their own fathers as poor models for how to raise a child.
Source: Dallas, Constance, Tony Wilson, and Vanessa Salgado. "Gender Differences in Teen Parents' Perceptions of Parental Responsibilities." *Public Health Nursing 17* (Nov./Dec. 2000): 423-433.

Men who live with their biological children are more involved in community and service organizations, more connected to their own siblings, adult children and aging parents, and they invest more hours per week in work and career than non-fathers and fathers of adult children.
Source: Eggebeen, David J., and Chris Knoester. "Does Fatherhood Matter for Men?" *Journal of Marriage and the Family, 63* (May 2001): 381-393.

Youths are more at risk of first substance use without a highly involved father.

...adolescents who experienced increasing closeness with their fathers experienced less delinquency and psychological distress...

In a study of fathers' interaction with their children in intact two-parent families, nearly 90% of the fathers surveyed said that being a father is the most fulfilling role a man can have.
Source: Yeung, W. Jean, et al. "Children's Time with Fathers in Intact Families." Paper presented at the Annual Meeting of the American Sociological Association, Chicago, IL, August, 2000.

Based on an analysis of longitudinal data between 1968 and 1993 on more than 1,200 men from the U.S. Panel Study of Income Dynamics, men, on average, worked 122 hours more a year after the birth of a son, and 56 more hours per year after the birth of a daughter. As a result, even after controlling for age, men's wages increased, on average, by about 4.5 percent every time they father a child.
Source: Lundberg, Shelly, and Elaina Rose. "The Effects of Sons and Daughters on Men's Labor Supply and Wages." Paper presented at Canadian Employment Research Forum conference on Families, Labour, Markets, and the Well-Being of Children, Vancouver, Canada, June 1-2, 2000.

Predictors of Father Involvement

Fathers perceptions' of their own fathering abilities are not always as important as their wives'. A study of 28 families suggested that fathers who are more involved in their children's lives have wives who see them as more invested in the parenting role, even though these involved fathers do not see themselves in the same supportive way.
Source: McBride, Brent A., et al. "Paternal Identity, Maternal Gatekeeping, and Father Involvement." *Family Relations, 54* (July 2005): 360-372.

A study of 186 married fathers indicated that fathers viewed their role as a dad as psychologically central and are involved in the lives of their child. Those who see their father role identity as prominent also report higher levels of involvement. Moreover, the more positively he perceives his spouse's evaluations of him as a father and the more extensive his social support network, the more he was involved with his child.
Source: Pasley, Kay, Ted G. Futris, and Martie L. Skinner. "Effects of Commitment and Psychological Centrality on Fathering." *Journal of Marriage and Family, 64* (February 2002): 130-138.

A study of 1,088 parents showed that egalitarian fathers (those more involved in child care and housework) demonstrated greater involvement in their child's lives than those with traditional views. The mother's belief's about a father's role, however, had no effect on the father's involvement.
Source: Bulanda, Ronald. "Paternal Involvement with Children: The Influence of Gender Ideologies." *Journal of Marriage and Family, 66* (February 2004): 40-45.

When a group of 181 mothers perceived that they had a significant role for the father of their child, they were more likely to report satisfaction with father involvement over time.
Source: Krishnakumar, Ambika and Maureen M. Black. "Family Processes Within Three-Generation Households and Adolescent Mothers' Satisfaction With Father Involvement." *Journal of Family Psychology, 17* (December 2003): 488-498.

A pool of 289 fathers said that they were more involved when they viewed their fathering identities as satisfying, when they were more invested in their identities, when their interparental relationships had less indirect conflict and were more cooperative, and when they were married.
Source: Henley, Kari and Kay Pasley. "Conditions Affecting the Association between Father Identity and Father Involvement." *Fathering, 3* (Winter 2005): 59-80.

...90% of the fathers surveyed said that being a father is the most fulfilling role a man can have.

...egalitarian fathers... demonstrated greater involvement in their child's lives than those with traditional views.

A study of 107 adolescents indicated that subjective closeness in relationships was positively correlated with frequency of interaction with fathers, the diversity of their activities, a positive emotional relationship, and the strength of the father's influence.
Source: Repinski, Daniel J. and Joan M. Zook. "Relationship Features and Adolescents' Experience of Closeness in Relationships with Mothers, Fathers, and Friends." Poster presented at the Biennial Meeting of the Society for Research in Child Development, April 2000, Minneapolis, Minnesota.

Fathers who consider the nurturing role as the central piece of their self-identity were more involved with their children in a study of 89 families. They average 40 minutes more interacting with their children during a workday than fathers who did not view nurturing highly.
Source: Rane, Thomas R. and Brent A. McBride. "Identity Theory as a Guide to Understanding Fathers' Involvement With Their Children." *Journal of Family Issues, 21* (April 2000): 347-366.

In a study of 41 adolescent fathers and mothers, self esteem, the father's age at birth, and social support satisfaction were connected to the father's parenting satisfaction. Mothers' parenting satisfaction scores, however, were higher overall.
Source: Thompson, Stacy D. and Andrea C. Walker. "Satisfaction With Parenting: A Comparison Between Adolescent Mothers and Fathers." *Sex Roles, 50* (May 2004): 677-687.

Men who value the father's role, reject the biological basis of gender differences, and who perceive their caregiving skills as adequate are more likely to be involved with their infants.
Source: Beitel, A.H., and R.O. Parke. "Paternal Involvement in Infancy: The Role of Maternal and Paternal Attitudes." *Journal of Family Psychology, 12* (1998): 268-288.

Fathers with a more traditional orientation toward sex roles are less involved in childrearing than fathers who hold more liberal, egalitarian views of gender roles.
Source: Kalmijn, Matthijs. "Father Involvement in Childrearing and the Perceived Stability of Marriage." *Journal of Marriage and the Family, 61* (May 1999): 409-421.

In an analysis of white, two-parent families drawn from the 1987-1988 and 1992-1993 National Surveys of Families and Households with at least one child younger than five years of age at the time of the first survey, it was found that the more hours the mother spends in child care, the more hours the father spends in child care as well. Fathers were also found to play a greater role with their sons than with their daughters.
Source: Aldous, Joan, Gail M. Mulligan, and Thoroddur Bjarnason. "Fathering Over Time: What Makes the Difference?" *Journal of Marriage and the Family, 60* (November 1998): 809-820.

In a longitudinal study (n = 184) of father-child interaction when their children were 6, 15, 24, and 36 months of age, fathers were more involved in caregiving when they worked fewer hours, were younger, had more positive personalities, reported greater marital intimacy, and when their children were boys.
Source: NICHD Early Child Care Research Network. "Factors Associated with Fathers' Caregiving Activities and Sensitivity With Young Children." *Journal of Family Psychology, 14* (June 2000): 200-219.

In a study of 89 predominately white two-parent families with preschool-aged children, it was found that fathers' perception of spouses' confidence in their own parental roles and their shared parental philosophy were significant predictors of father involvement in childrearing activities.
Source: McBride, Brent A., and Thomas R. Rane. "Parenting Alliance as a Predictor of Father Involvement: An Exploratory Study." *Family Relations, 47* (1998): 229-236.

In a study of 120 dual-earner couples with children between the ages of 1 and 4, higher levels of marital satisfaction and mothers' perception of their husbands' competence were associated with higher levels of father involvement in child-care tasks.
Source: Bonney, Jennifer F., Michelle L. Kelley, and Ronald F. Levant. "A Model of Fathers' Behavioral Involvement in Child Care in Dual-Earner Families." *Journal of Family Psychology, 13* (1999): 401-415.

...higher levels of marital satisfaction and mothers' perception of their husbands' competence were associated with higher levels of father involvement in child-care tasks.

Predictors of Involvement by Stepfathers

Stepfathers are more likely to be involved with their stepchildren if their biological children are also living with them, their stepchild was relatively young at the time the stepfamily was formed, the stepfather and his wife have a good relationship, and the stepchild has a good relationship with the stepfather.

Source: Marsiglio, W. "Stepfathers with Minor Children Living at Home: Parenting Perceptions and Relationship Quality." Journal of Family Issues 13(1992): 195-214; see also Pasley, K., and C.L. Healow. "Adolescent Self-Esteem: A Focus on Children in Step-families." In E.M. Hetherington and J.D. Arasten (Eds.), *Impact of Divorce, Single Parenting, and Step Parenting on Children*. Hillsdale, NJ: Lawrence Erlbaum, 1987: 263-277; Hetherington, M., and S.H. Henderson. "Fathers in Step Families." In M.E. Lamb (Ed.), *The Role of the Father in Child Development*. New York: John Wiley & Sons, Inc., 1997: 212-226.

V. Differences in Maternal and Paternal Behavior

"Involved fathers typically initiate more active play and are more tolerant of physical exploration by infants than are mothers... In their efforts to encourage infant competence, mothers are generally more concerned with verbal-intellectual teaching, whereas fathers are more oriented toward active, arousing play and fostering autonomy and independence."

HENRY B. BILLER, FATHERS AND FAMILIES: PATERNAL FACTORS IN CHILD DEVELOPMENT, AUBURN HOUSE, WESTPORT, CONNECTICUT, 1993.

"Moms and dads tend to specialize. Mother becomes more of a caregiver, manager, as well as a playmate. Father's specialty seems to be play. Play [of fathers] has serious consequences. It teaches some serious lessons. It teaches kids how to regulate their emotions. [Kids] gotta learn to signal to dad saying, 'Hey, Dad, that's enough. Shut it down, slow it down.' It's important because the kids are learning through dad how to modulate their play effectively, stop when it gets too rough."

DR. ROSS PARKE, CHILD PSYCHOLOGIST AS SEEN ON "COMMON SENSE" WITH JOHN STOSSEL, AN ABC NEWS TELEVISION PRODUCTION, 1996.

"The best mom in the world cannot be a father."

AUTHOR DAVID BLANKENHORN, AS SEEN ON "COMMON SENSE," WITH JOHN STOSSEL, AN ABC NEWS TELEVISION PRODUCTION, 1996.

Not Just Another Pair of Hands

A study of 56 parents of preschoolers revealed divergent views of parenting from each spouse. Fathers perceive themselves as being less authoritative, less permissive, and more authoritarian than their spouses whereas mothers only perceive themselves as more authoritative than fathers.

Source: Winsler, Adam, Amy L. Madaigan, and Sally Aquilino. "Correspondence between maternal and paternal parenting styles in early childhood." *Early Childhood Research Quarterly, 20* (1st Quarter 2005): 1-12.

According to a 1,200 child sample from the Panel Study of Income Dynamics, the proportion of children who learned to parent from their mother is about 70%. 63% of Whites, 45% of African-Americans, and 38% of Hispanics claimed to have learned from their fathers.

Source: Hofferth, Sandra L. "Race/Ethnic Differences in Father Involvement in Two-Parent Families: Culture, Context, or Economy?" *Journal of Family Issues, 24* (2003): 185-216.

The majority of mothers and fathers reported equal, shared responsibility for playing with their children (77 and 91 percent, respectively) and for discipline (70 and 89 percent). Perceptions of fathers' involvement in choosing a child care program, preschool, or school was hardly less equitable from both sexes' opinions.

Source: *Child Trends*, "Charting Parenthood: A Statistical Portrait of Fathers and Mothers in America." Ed. Tamara Halle. Washington DC, 2004.

Thirty-nine percent of children's engaged time with their fathers is spent in play and companionship during the week. Time spent with fathers on educational activities is relatively small (3 to 5%).

Source: Yeung, W. Jean and John F. Sandberg, et al. "Children's Time With Fathers in Intact Families." *Journal of Marriage and Family, 63* (February 2001): 136-154.

A Canadian study of 87 parents of newborns found gendered differences in child interaction. Mothers tend to vocalize and make more requests. Fathers, on the other hand, increase their conventional play over time as mothers decrease their play.

Source: Laflamme, Darquise, Andrée Pomerleau, and Gérard Malcuit. "A Comparison of Fathers' and Mothers' Involvement During Free-Play With Their Infants at 9 and 15 Months." *Sex Roles, 47* (December 2002): 507-518.

A study of parents and infants showed that an infants' attachment to their mother will increase the quality of their friendship at age 4, but only if the infant is securely connected to the father as well.

Source: McElwain, Nancy L. and Brenda L. Volling. "Attachment security and parental sensitivity during infancy: Associations with friendship quality and false-belief understanding at age four." *Journal of Social and Personal Relationships, 21* (October 2004): 639-667.

Fathers often experience depression in conjunction with their wives. A literature review revealed that incidence of paternal depression ranged from 1.5% to 25% in community samples and 24% to 50% for fathers whose partners were experiencing postpartum depression.

Source: Goodman, Janice H. "Paternal postpartum depression, its relationship to maternal postpartum depression, and implications for family health." *Journal of Advanced Nursing, 45* (January 2004): 26-35.

A study of 41 adolescent parents revealed that perceived paternal warmth was tied to the mothers' satisfaction with the fathers' parenting. Fathers' parenting satisfaction was correlated with self-esteem, age at first birth, and depression.

Source: Thompson, Stacy D. and Andrea C. Walker. "Satisfaction With Parenting: A Comparison Between Adolescent Mothers and Fathers." *Sex Roles, 50* (May 2004):

In a qualitative study of 52 parents, fathers connected parental identity to their caregiving more than mothers did. Promoting development, arranging and planning, and the relationship with the child were relatively more co-parental and solo-parental activities.

Source: Stueve, Jeffrey L. and Joseph H. Pleck. "'Parenting voices': Solo parent identity and co-parent identities in married parents' narratives of meaningful parenting experiences." *Journal of Social and Personal Relationships, 18* (October 2001): 691-708.

> The majority of mothers and fathers reported equal, shared responsibility for playing with their children... and for discipline...

With Infants

An analysis of parental interactions with their premature infants found that fathers responded more to gross motor cues of their infants and touched their children with rhythmic pats while mothers were more responsive to social cues and spoke to their children with soft, repetitive, and imitative sounds.
Source: Marton, P. and K. Minde. "Paternal and Maternal Behavior with Premature Infants." Orthopsychiatric Association, Toronto. April 1980 as cited in Michael E. Lamb, "The Development of Father-Infant Relationships." *The Role of the Father in Child Development*. Ed. Michael E. Lamb. New York: Wiley, 1997.

In a study of 94 mothers, fathers, and their healthy 4-month-old infants, moms and dads showed similar levels of sensitivity toward and mutual engagement with their infants. When the infants were distressed, however, they showed more object orientation when they were with their mothers and more parent orientation when they were with their fathers.
Source: Braungart-Rieker, Julia, Molly Murphy Garwood, Bruce P. Powers, and Paul C. Notaro. "Infant Affect and Affect Regulation During the Still-Face Paradigm With Mothers and Fathers: The Role of Infant Characteristics and Parental Sensitivity." *Developmental Psychology, 34* (1998): 1428-1437.

With Preschoolers

A 16-year study of 44 families reported high scores to fathers who understand, stimulate, and encourage their toddler, specifically those who avoid criticism and make suggestions for how a child should play. The quality of this bond rivals the mother-infant bond in its ability to predict the child's relationships with others and actually surpasses the mother-infant bond at age 16.
Source: Grossman, Karin, Klaus E. Grossman, Elisabeth Fremmer-Bombik, Heinz Kindler, Hermann Scheuerer-Englisch, and Peter Zimmerman. "The Uniqueness of the Child-Father Attachment Relationship: Fathers' Sensitive and Challenging Play as a Pivotal Variable in a 16-year Longitudinal Study." *Social Development, 11* (August 2002): 307-331.

With young children, fathers tend to engage their children in physical and stimulating play activities, whereas mothers tend to spend more time in routine caregiving activities.
Source: Parke, Ross D., and B.J. Tinsley. "Family Interaction in Infancy." In J. Osofsky (Ed.), *Handbook of Infant Development, 2nd Edition*. New York: Wiley, 1987: 579-641; see also Parke, Ross D. Fatherhood. Cambridge, MA: Harvard University Press, 1996.

In an observational study of 36 preschool children and their parents, it was found that mothers' social coaching and father-child play increased children's skillfulness with peers.
Source: Pettit, Gregory S., Elizabeth Glyn Brown, Jacquelyn Mize, and Eric Lindsey. "Mothers' and Fathers' Socializing Behaviors in Three Contexts: Links with Children's Peer Competence." *Merrill-Palmer Quarterly, 44* (April 1998): 173-193.

In a study of the disciplinary strategies of 38 parents (19 couples) with hard-to-manage toddlers, it was found that mothers were more over-reactive in their discipline than fathers; however, no differences in lax childrearing were found.
Source: Arnold, Elizabeth Harvey, and Susan G. O'Leary. "Mothers' and Fathers' Discipline of Hard-to-Manage Toddlers." *Child and Family Behavior Therapy, 19* (1997): 1-12.

With Older Children

Fathers tend to play games with their children that involve more physical activity, teamwork, and mental skills. Often their games involve more competition, independence, risk-taking, and initiative. Fathers may act as if they are teachers and their children are apprentices. They focus on the long-term development and well-being of their children.
Source: Popenoe, David. *Life Without Father*. New York: Martin Kessler Books, The Free Press, 1996. 143-145.

In an observational study of 369 three-, five-, and seven-year-old children and their parents, it was found that mothers issued more instructions to their children than did fathers.
Source: Fagot, Beverly I. "Social Problem Solving: Effect of Context and Parent Sex." *International Journal of Behavioral Development, 22* (1998): 389-401.

71% of teens report having an excellent or very good relationship with their mothers; only 58% have such a relationship with their fathers. Consequently, teens are three times more likely to rely solely on mom when they have to make important decisions (27% vs. 9%).
Source: The National Center on Addiction and Substance Abuse at Columbia University. "Back to School 1999 — National Survey of American Attitudes on Substance Abuse V: Teens and Their Parents." Conducted by The Luntz Research Companies and QEV Analytics, August 1999.

Differences in the Way Fathers Relate to Sons versus Daughters

A father's work involvement is connected to the quality of the relationship with his daughter. Fathers tend to increase their workload and hours in response to less accepting relationships with their daughters.
Source: Fortner, Melissa R., Ann C. Crouter, and Susan M. McHale. "Is Parents' Work Involvement Responsive to the Quality of Relationships With Adolescent Offspring?" *Journal of Family Psychology 18* (September 2004): 530-538.

Fathers tend to engage in relatively more companionship with sons but express relatively more physical affection to daughters.
Source: Duncan, Greg J., Martha Hill, and W. Jean Yeung. "Fathers' Activities and Children's Attainments." Paper presented at the Conference on Father Involvement, October 10-11, 1996, Washington, D.C., pp.

VI. Marriage

"If we are serious about renewing fatherhood, we must be serious about renewing marriage."
PRESIDENT GEORGE W. BUSH, SPEAKING AT THE NATIONAL FATHERHOOD INITIATIVE'S 4TH ANNUAL NATIONAL SUMMIT ON FATHERHOOD IN WASHINGTON, D.C., JUNE 7, 2001.

"The disappearance of marriage in large sections of our community, poor and middle class, means that elected officials are mopping up while the faucet is still on. We've got to talk about marriage again. We've got to make it fashionable."
CONGRESSWOMAN ELEANOR HOLMES NORTON (D-D.C.) AS QUOTED IN FARAI CHIDEYA , "SHAPING THE BLACK AGENDA: AFRICAN AMERICAN WOMEN IN POLITICS," *ESSENCE*, MAY 2000.

"Marriage remains the best solution we have ever come up with for helping to ensure children the protection, love and support of their mother and father. Marriage is neither a conservative nor a liberal idea."
ELIZABETH MARQUARDT IN "THE OTHER KIND OF RELATIONSHIP," *CHICAGO TRIBUNE*, DECEMBER 19, 2004.

"If there is one thing in this life I know, it's that children need mothers and fathers. This is my whole public life, that children deserve, as a sort of birthright, mothers and fathers -- preferably the mothers and fathers who brought them into this world."
DAVID BLANKENHORN IN "REASONS FOR MARRIAGE," *THE WASHINGTON POST*, FEBRUARY 23, 2004.

71% of teens report having an excellent or very good relationship with their mothers; only 58% have such a relationship with their fathers.

Fathers tend to engage in relatively more companionship with sons but express relatively more physical affection to daughters.

FATHER FACTS, 5TH EDITION • © 2007 National Fatherhood Initiative

"Like all human institutions, marriage is far from perfect. And getting married does not turn people into saints. Yet the fact remains: despite its acknowledged problems and imperfections, marriage remains an indispensable source of social goods, individual benefits, mutual caregiving, affectionate attachments, and long-term commitments. And people who are married, though not saints, tend to behave in ways that benefit themselves, their children, families and communities."

BARBARA DAFOE WHITEHEAD SPEAKING BEFORE THE SENATE COMMITTEE ON HEALTH, EDUCATION, LABOR, AND PENSIONS SUBCOMMITTEE ON CHILDREN AND FAMILIES, APRIL 28, 2004.

"While marriage may not be a cure for poverty, it does turn out to be a fairly reliable preventative. Isn't it worthwhile to spend more time and resources helping young people to understand the economic implications of single parenthood before they become single parents? Wouldn't it make sense to rethink our relatively easy acceptance of out-of-wedlock parenting?"

WILLIAM RASPBERRY, *WASHINGTON POST* COLUMNIST, "POVERTY AND THE FATHER FACTOR," AUGUST 1, 2005.

Attitudes About Marriage

Most of respondents in a 1,503 person telephone survey expressed favorable views of marriage. Eighty-eight percent of respondents said that marriage was a lifelong commitment. Seventy-one percent disagreed that "Either spouse should be allowed to terminate a marriage at any time for any reason."
Source: National Fatherhood Initiative. *With This Ring…: A National Survey on Marriage in America.* Gaithersburg, MD: National Fatherhood Initiative, 2005: 4.

Younger respondents were more likely than older respondents to view marriage as an outmoded and outdated institution. They were also more likely to approve of cohabitation as preparation for marriage, believe divorced parents can parent as effectively as married ones, and reject the idea that parents should stay in marriage for the children's sake if there is no threat of violence or extreme conflict.
Source: National Fatherhood Initiative. *With This Ring…: A National Survey on Marriage in America.* Gaithersburg, MD: National Fatherhood Initiative, 2005: 4.

A survey of 8,800 teens revealed that two-thirds expressed a positive attitude toward marriage. Fifty-seven percent, however, felt that they were unprepared for marriage. But they did believe though that they had the skills for a good marriage (67.7%). Only 28.9% had negative attitudes towards marriage counseling. Fifty-one percent expressed negative attitudes towards divorce. Eight-three percent agreed that marriage is "a lifelong commitment." Half of respondents viewed cohabitation positively and 48.7% wanted to live with someone before they got married.
Source: Martin, Paige, Gerald Specter, Don Martin, and Maggie Martin. "Expressed Attitudes of Adolescents Toward Marriage and Family Life." *Adolescence, 38* (Summer 2003): 359-367.

FATHER FACTS, 5TH EDITION • © 2007 National Fatherhood Initiative   169

Only 16% of twentysomethings said that the main purpose of marriage is having children. Sixty-two percent felt that it was OK for a woman to have a child even if she lacked a soul mate.

Two-thirds (68%) said that a good marriage is tougher to achieve today than in the past. Half (52%) said they see so few happy marriages that they question marriage as an option.
Source: Peterson, Karen S., "At 20, a soul mate is a cool concept but majority fear eventual divorce." USA TODAY 13 June 2001: 13A.; Whitehead, Barbara Dafoe and David Popenoe. *Who Wants to Marry A Soul Mate?* Piscataway, NJ: The National Marriage Project, 2001. Accessed 12 May 2005. <http://marriage.rutgers.edu/ Publications/SOOU/TEXTSOOU2001.htm>

According to a national survey of 1,010 adults and 500 teenagers, 72% of adults and 72% of teens agreed that "Mothers and fathers with strong marriages are less likely to have children or teenagers who are violent and commit crimes."
Source: *Kids & Violence: A National Survey and Report.* Based on a national survey conducted by Wirthlin Worldwide between September 11-17, 1998 for Family First, Tampa, Florida.

Eighty-six percent of men and more than 90 percent of women age 60 or older agree that "people who want to have children should get married." In contrast, only 62 percent of men and 50 percent of women ages 18-29 agreed with this statement. Only 15 percent of men and 23 percent of women 60 or older agree that "one parent can bring up a child as well as two parents." In contrast, 35 percent of men and fully 62 percent of women ages 18-29 agreed with this statement. Only 33 percent of men and 25 percent of women ages 18-29 agree that "married people are generally happier than unmarried people."
Source: 1994 General Social Survey. Cited in Whitehead, Barbara Dafoe. "Clueless Generation." In Wade F. Horn, David Blankenhorn, and Mitch Pearlstein (Eds.) *The Fatherhood Movement: A Call to Action.* Lanham, MD: Lexington Books, 1999: 65-75.

In a 1997 USA Today poll of over 1,000 adults, 70% of those surveyed stated that they believe that, in general, children raised in a two-parent family fare better than children raised in a single-parent family.
Source: *USA Today.* "We Hold These Truths..." 4 July 1997.

Of all ethnicities, Black cohabiting women have the lowest odds of expecting marriage.
Source: Manning, Wendy D. and Pamela J. Smock. "First Comes Cohabitation and Then Comes Marriage?" *Journal of Family Issues, 23* (November 2002): 1065-1087.

The Facts About Marriage

According to demographers, 85% of young people today will marry at some point in their lives, compared to 94% in 1960.
Source: Schoen, Robert, and Nicola Standish. "The Retrenchment of Marriage: Results from Marital Status Life Tables for the United States, 1995." Unpublished manuscript. Department of Sociology, Pennsylvania State University, University Park, PA; Cited in Popenoe, David, and Barbara Dafoe Whitehead. *The State of Our Unions 2001: The Social Health of Marriage in America.* Piscataway, NJ: National Marriage Project, 2001.

In 2003, about 117 million adult Americans, or 52 percent of Americans age 20 and older, were married and living with their spouses. This is a decrease of 6% from 2000.
Source: Fields, Jason. *America's Families and Living Arrangements: 2003.* Table 6. Current Population Reports, P20-553. Washington, D.C.: U.S. Census Bureau, 2004; Fields, Jason, and Lynn M. Casper. America's Families and Living Arrangements: March 2000. Table 5. Current Population Reports, P20-537. Washington, D.C.: U.S. Census Bureau, 2001.

The median age at first marriage has been rising since the mid-1950s, to 25.3 years for women and 27.1 years for men in 2003.
Source: Fields, Jason. *America's Families and Living Arrangements: 2003.* Current Population Reports, P20-553. Washington, D.C.: U.S. Census Bureau, 2004: 12.

According to a United Nations survey, nine out of ten people worldwide will still choose to marry at least once in their lives. In the developed world, the overall average of each

---

> Only 16% of twentysomethings said that the main purpose of marriage is having children.

nation's mean age at first marriage is 27.9 years for men and 25.2 years for women. Among developing nations, the overall average is 24.9 years for men and 21.4 years for women.

Source: *World Marriage Patterns 2000*. United Nations, Population Division, Department of Economic and Social Affairs.

Sixty-four percent of poor, unmarried mothers and 77 percent of poor, unmarried fathers agree that marriage is better for the kids.

Source: McLanahan, Sara, et al. *The Fragile Families and Child Wellbeing Study: Baseline National Report*. Table 2. Princeton, NJ: Center for Research and Child Wellbeing, 2003: 8.

The Decline in Marriage

In 2000, 56% of American men fifteen years and older were married, down from 59% in 1990, 61% in 1980, and 65% in 1970. The number is now 52%.

Source: Fields, Jason. *America's Families and Living Arrangements: 2003*. Table 6. Current Population Reports, P20-553. Washington, D.C.: U.S. Census Bureau, 2004.

The proportion of Americans fifteen years and older who have never been married rose from 24.9% to 29.6% between 1970 and 2003. One-quarter of 30- to 34-year-olds today are never married, up from 8% in 1970.

Source: Fields, Jason and Lynn M. Casper. *America's Families and Living Arrangements: 2003*. Table 6. Current Population Reports, P20-553. Washington, D.C.: U.S. Census Bureau, 2004.

The percentage of married couples with children fell from 40 percent of all households in 1970 to 31 percent in 1980, 26 percent in 1990, and 24.3 percent of all households in 2003.

Source: Fields, Jason, and Lynn M. Casper. *America's Families and Living Arrangements: March 2000*. Figure 1. Current Population Reports, P20-537. Washington, D.C.: U.S. Census Bureau, 2001; Fields, Jason and Lynn M. Casper. America's Families and Living Arrangements: 2003. Table 1. Current Population Reports, P20-553. Washington, D.C.: U.S. Census Bureau, 2004.

Families, defined by two or more people living together who are related by birth, marriage or adoption, made up 90 percent of households in 1940, 81 percent in 1970, and just 67.8 percent in 2003.

Source: Fields, Jason, and Lynn M. Casper. *America's Families and Living Arrangements: March 2000*. Figure 1. Current Population Reports, P20-537. Washington, D.C.: U.S. Census Bureau, 2001; Fields, Jason and Lynn M. Casper. America's Families and Living Arrangements: 2003. Table 1. Current Population Reports, P20-553. Washington, D.C.: U.S. Census Bureau, 2004.

From 1980 to 2003, the percentage of married adults has decreased from:
- 67% to 56% for whites
- 51% to 34% for blacks
- 66% to 51% for Hispanics

Source: Fields, Jason and Lynn M. Casper. *America's Families and Living Arrangements: 2003*. Detailed Tables A1. Current Population Reports, P20-553. Washington, D.C.: U.S. Census Bureau, 2004.

Between 1970 and 2003, the percentage of households comprised of a woman living alone grew from 11.5 percent to 17.6 percent, while the percentage of "man living alone" households doubled, from 5.6 percent to 14.3 percent.

Source: Fields, Jason, and Lynn M. Casper. *America's Families and Living Arrangements: March 2000*. Figure 1. Current Population Reports, P20-537. Washington, D.C.: U.S. Census Bureau, 2001; Fields, Jason and Lynn M. Casper. America's Families and Living Arrangements: 2003. Table 1. Current Population Reports, P20-553. Washington, D.C.: U.S. Census Bureau, 2004.

From 1970 to 1993, the percentage of white males ages 25-29 who had ever been married decreased from 82% to 54%. For African-Americans in this age group, the percentage decreased from 72% to 39%. The study found that being unemployed greatly reduces the odds of marriage for both blacks and whites.

Source: Kincade Oppenheimer, Valerie, Matthijs Kalmign, and Nelson Lim. "Men's Career Development and Marriage Timing During a Period of Rising Inequality." *Demography, 34.3* (August 1997): 311-330.

According to a United Nations survey, nine out of ten people worldwide will still choose to marry at least once in their lives.

Sixty-four percent of poor, unmarried mothers and 77 percent of poor, unmarried fathers agree that marriage is better for the kids.

Predictors of Marriage

A study of 273 college students indicated that those from intact homes had more favorable expectations about the quality of their future marriage than those who came from single or multiple divorce families.

Source: Boyer-Pennington, Michelle E., John Pennington, and Camille Spink. "Students' Expectations and Optimism Toward Marriage as a Function of Parental Divorce." *Journal of Divorce & Remarriage, 34* (2001): 71-88.

Research from the Fragile Families Study indicated that women's trust of men, parents' positive attitudes towards marriage, and both parents' assessment of the supportiveness of the relationship encourage couples to get married.

Source: Carlson, Marcia, Sara McLanahan, and Paula England. "Union Formation in Fragile Families." *Demography, 41* (May 2004): 237-261.

In an analysis of data from a survey of 415 low-income men in Chicago, employed men were determined to be twice as likely to marry in the event of a non-marital pregnancy as were unemployed men.

Source: Testa, M., Astone, N.M., Krogh, M., and Neckerman, K.M. "Employment and Marriage Among Inner-City Fathers." *Annals of the American Academy of Political and Social Sciences, 501* (1989): 79-91; see also Testa, Mark, and Marilyn Krogh. "The Effect of Employment on Marriage Among Black Males in Inner-City Chicago." *In The Decline in Marriage Among African Americans.* Ed. M. Belinda Tucker and Claudia Mitchell-Kernan. New York: Russell Sage Foundation, 1995: 59-95.

In a longitudinal study of the marriage behavior of cohabiting Swedish women ages 23 to 45 using the Swedish Family Survey and register data of marriages and births, the likelihood of moving from cohabitation to marriage was greater if the couple pooled resources, the woman grew up in a family with two biological or adoptive parents, and the woman participated in religious activity.

Source: Duvander, Ann-Zofie. "The Transition from Cohabitation to Marriage: A Longitudinal Study of the Propensity to Marry in Sweden in the Early 1990s." *Journal of Family Issues, 20* (September 1999): 698-717.

Marriage and Father Involvement

Of adolescents with residential fathers, eighty-one percent agreed or strongly agreed that they think highly of their father. Almost two-thirds (61 percent) agreed or strongly agreed that they wanted to be like their father. More than three-quarters (76 percent) reported that they enjoy time spent with their father.

Children from biological and stepparent families, however, feel differently from each other. In mid-adolescence, 82% of teens living with biological parents thought highly of their fathers, compared to 67% of teens from stepparent families. Sixty-three percent of teens with biological fathers agreed with "I want to be like my [father figure]," compared to only 39% of children with stepfathers. For the statement, "I enjoy spending time with my [father figure]," the proportions were 78% and 59%, respectively.

Source: Moore, Kristin A., et al. *Parent-Teen Relationships and Interactions: Far More Positive Than Not.* Child Trends Research Brief. Publication # 2004.25. Washington, DC: Child Trends, 2004.

In an analysis of data from both waves of the National Survey of Families and Households, a national probability sample of over 13,000 households, it was found that the most important determinant of whether the father lived with his children was marital status at the time of the child's birth. Fully 80% of men who were married to the child's mother at the child's birth were living with all of their biological children as compared to only 22.6% of men who were not in a co-residential union relationship with the child's mother at the time of the child's birth.

Source: Clarke, L., E.C. Cooksey, and G. Verropoulou. "Fathers and Absent Fathers: Sociodemographic Similarities in Britain and the United States." *Demography, 35* (1998): 217-228.

While unhappily married men may be less involved in childrearing than their wives, they are far more involved, on average, than are single, non-custodial fathers.
Source: Coiro, Mary Jo, and Robert E. Emery. "Do Marriage Problems Affect Fathering More Than Mothering? A Quantitative and Qualitative Review." *Clinical Child and Family Psychology Review, 1* (1998): 23-40.

Impact of Marital Quality on Parenting

In an ethnically diverse sample of 113 families, fathers were more rejecting and coercive and less emotionally supportive of their children when their relationships with their wives were characterized by destructive conflict.
Source: Lindahl, Kristin M., and Neena M. Malik. "Observations of Marital Conflict and Power: Relations with Parenting in the Triad." *Journal of Marriage and the Family, 61* (1999): 320-330.

Marital distress disrupts fathering more than mothering, although the parenting of both mothers and fathers is negatively associated with marital conflict.
Source: Crockenberg, S., and S.L. Covey. "Marital Conflict and Externalizing Behavior in Children." In D. Cicchetti & S. Toth (Eds.), *Rochester Symposium on Developmental Psychopathology: Vol. 3. Models and Integrations.* Rochester, NY: University of Rochester Press, 1991; see also Coiro, Mary Jo, & Robert E. Emery. "Do Marriage Problems Affect Fathering More Than Mothering? A Quantitative and Qualitative Review." *Clinical Child and Family Psychology Review, 1* (1998): 23-40.

Marital distress is associated with hostile-competitive coparenting (particularly with boys) and with a greater discrepancy in the amount of mother versus father involvement.
Source: McHale, J.P. "Coparenting and Triadic Interactions During Infancy: The Roles of Marital Distress and Child Gender." *Developmental Psychology, 31* (1995): 985-996.

Using data from a nationally representative panel of parents interviewed in 1988 and 1992, childrearing satisfaction was found to be significantly higher for married parents with high marital quality and for those who were rearing their own biological children.
Source: Rogers, Stacy J., and Lynn K. White. "Satisfaction with Parenting: The Role of Marital Happiness, Family Structure, and Parents' Gender." *Journal of Marriage and the Family, 60* (May 1998): 293-308.

In a study of 195 black urban households and 73 Latino urban households with sons between the ages of 10 and 15, it was found that two-parent, married families had higher cohesion and parental monitoring scores than did single-parent families. As a result, boys in single-mother families were, on average, at greater risk for behavior problems.
Source: Florsheim, Paul, Patrick Tolan, and Deborah Gorman-Smith. "Family Relationships, Parenting Practices, the Availability of Male Family Members, and the Behavior of Inner-City Boys in Single-Mother and Two-Parent Families." *Child Development, 69* (1998): 1437-1447.

In a survey of 200 students ages 17 to 47 at the University of Dundee in Scotland, married mothers were more likely to be judged to be more nurturing and to have better family relations and parenting skills compared to divorced and never-married parents. All mothers, regardless of their own status, perceived married mothers to be significantly more satisfied with motherhood than single mothers.
Source: Bennett, Mark, and Lynne Jamieson. "Perceptions of Parents as a Function of their Marital Status and Sex." *Infant and Child Development, 8* (1999): 149-154.

While unhappily married men may be less involved in childrearing than their wives, they are far more involved, on average, than are single, non-custodial fathers.

Using data from a nationally representative sample of about 1,900 children between the ages of six and nine, it was found that after controlling for income, children in married households received significantly more emotional support in the home environment than children who lived with a divorced mother or other marital statuses.
Source: Miller, Jane E., and Diane Davis. "Poverty History, Marital History, and Quality of Children's Home Environments." *Journal of Marriage and the Family, 59* (1997): 996-1007.

In an analysis of data from the National Commission on Children's 1990 Survey of Parents and Children, marital happiness was found to be significantly and positively related to parental wellbeing.
Source: Voydanoff, Patricia, and Brenda W. Donnelly. "Parents' Risk and Protective Factors as Predictors of Parental Well-Being and Behavior." *Journal of Marriage and the Family, 60* (May 1998): 344-355.

Importance of Marriage to the Well-Being of Children

Children with married parents have the lowest odds of poverty out of all family arrangements.
Source: Kreider, Rose M. and Jason Fields. *Living Arrangements of Children: 2001.* Current Population Studies, P70-104. Table 2. Washington, D.C.: US Census Bureau, 2005.

Eighty-six percent of adolescents ages 15-17- living with their biological married parents reported to be in excellent or very good health, compared to 80 percent of those living in married stepfamilies, 76 percent of those living with a single parent, and 67 percent of those living with neither parent. This held even for income. Among the adolescents ages 15-17 who lived in families with incomes more than twice the poverty line, those in married, biological household reported excellent or very good health ratings more often (87 percent).

By comparison, 81 percent of adolescents in married stepfamilies, 79 percent of those living with a single parent, and 69 percent of those living with neither parent reported enjoying the same healthiness.
Source: Federal Interagency Forum on Child and Family Statistics. *America's Children: Key National Indicators of Well-Being 2005.* Washington, D.C.: U.S. Government Printing Office, 2005: 70.

In a study of 118 mothers and fathers, the quality of the marital relationship during infancy predicted the frequency of behavior problems that the father reported. The connection held even after accounting for socioeconomic status.
Source: Benzies, Karen M., Margaret J. Harrison, and Joyce Magill-Evans. "Parenting Stress, Marital Quality, and Child Behavior Problems at Age 7 Years." *Public Health Nursing ,21* (March/April 2004): 111-121.

In a study 9,024 from the General Social Survey, intact families had the highest average scores in terms of life satisfaction, followed by reconstituted families. Among the four marital groups, married people are the most satisfied with their lives whereas divorce/separated/widowed people are the least satisfied.
Source: Louis, Vincent V. and Shanyang Zhao. "Effects of Family Structure, Family SES, and Adulthood Experiences on Life Satisfaction." *Journal of Family Issues, 23* (November 2002): 968-1005.

Using data from the National Longitudinal Study of Youth, children living in intact, married households, compared to those living in disrupted nuclear families, had lower rates of delinquency, youth crime, and use of alcohol and drugs. Later, during adulthood, they also had higher educational attainments, job statuses, and marital stability. As the respondents entered their thirties, they also were less likely to report symptoms of depression.
Source: Feigelman, William. "Adopted Adults: Comparisons with Persons Raised in Conventional Families." *Marriage and Family Review, 25* (1997): 199-223.

> Children with married parents have the lowest odds of poverty out of all family arrangements.

> ...children living in intact, married households... had lower rates of delinquency, youth crime, and use of alcohol and drugs...

In a longitudinal study of 53 two-parent families, warm marital engagement between husband and wife was associated with more secure father-child attachment among preschoolers.
Source: Frosch, Cynthia A., Sarah C. Mangelsdorf, and Jean L. McHale. "Marital Behavior and the Security of Preschooler-Parent Attachment Relationships." *Journal of Family Psychology, 14* (2000): 144-161.

In an analysis of longitudinal data from the Panel Study of Income Dynamics, it was found that marriage, but not cohabitation, facilitated moving from a poor to a non-poor neighborhood.
Source: South, Scott J., and Kyle D. Crowder. "Avenues and Barriers to Residential Mobility Among Single Mothers." *Journal of Marriage and the Family, 60* (November 1998): 866-877.

A study of 70 children living with their married, biological parents found that children whose parents were happily married had higher grades, and their teachers reported that they were better students than children whose parents were not happily married.
Source: Westerman, Michael and Edgar J. La Luz. "Marital Adjustment and Children's Academic Achievement." *Merrill-Palmer Quarterly, 41* (1995): 453-470.

Importance of Marriage to the Well-Being of Adults

Data from the NSFH showed that married people report less depression and fewer alcohol problems than do never-married, separated, divorced or widowed persons. Individuals who marry for the first time or remarry experience a decrease in depression while those who separate or divorce become more depressed.
Source: Simon, Robin W. "Revisiting the Relationships Among Gender, Marital Status and Mental Health." *American Journal of Sociology, 107* (January 2002): 1065-1096.

Married individuals have a higher level of psychological well-being than members of any other marital status. Remarriage also had a positive effect although the effect of first-marriage was higher and divorce/separation were correlated with depressive symptoms. Cohabitation did not decrease depressive symptoms.
Source: Kim, Hyoun K. and Patrick C. McKenry. "The Relationship Between Marriage and Psychological Well-Being: A Longitudinal Analysis." *Journal of Family Issues, 23* (November 2002): 885-911.

Young people between the ages of 18-35 who marry are much less likely to experience depression and also have the largest decrease in depressive symptoms when compared to their cohabiting peers. Selection bias was ruled out as a possible cause.
Source: Lamb, Kathleen et al. "Union Formation and Depression: Selection and Relationship Effects." *Journal of Marriage and the Family, 65* (November 2003): 953-962.

More than seventy-percent of married, two parent families had an adult with more than a high school diploma compared with 54% of cohabiting couples and 48% of single parents.
Source: Lerman, Robert I. "Impacts of Marital Status and Parental Presence on the Material Hardship of Families with Children." Washington, DC: Urban Institute and American University, 2002: 12.

Of the 838 couples studied, those who married and remained together experienced an overall decrease in depressive symptoms. Prolonged cohabitation had no such effect.
Source: Lamb, Kathleen A., Gary R. Lee, and Alfred DeMaris. "Union Formation and Depression: Selection and Relationship Effects." *Journal of Marriage and Family, 65* (November 2003): 953-962.

> Married individuals have a higher level of psychological well-being than members of any other marital status.

Marital quality and job satisfaction are intimately connected, according to a study of 1,065 adults. In an effect known as "positive spillover," increases in marital satisfaction increased job satisfaction over a period of 12 years.
Source: Rogers, Stacy J. and Dee C. May. "Spillover Between Marital Quality and Job Satisfaction: Long-Term Patterns and Gender Differences." *Journal of Marriage and Family, 65* (May 2003): 482-495.

With the exception of obesity, married adults tended to be healthier than adults in other marital status categories. This was consistent across all population subgroups (age, sex, race, income etc.) and other health indicators (smoking, fair or poor health, serious psychological stress etc.). The difference between married adults and other groups was most profound in the 18-44 age group.
Source: Schoenborn, Charlotte A. *Marital Status and Health: United States, 1999-2002.* Advance Data From Vital and Health Statistics, No. 351. Hyattsville, MD: Center for Disease Control, 2004: 10.

...married adults tended to be healthier than adults in other marital status categories.

In a seven-year longitudinal study of 600 adults, it was found that married men and women were less depressed and have fewer alcohol problems than people who remain single, even after controlling for premarital levels of depression and alcohol problems. Furthermore, marriage significantly reduces alcohol problems for women and depression among men.
Source: Horwitz, A.V., H.R. White, and S. Howel-White. "Becoming Married and Mental Health: A Longitudinal Study of a Cohort of Young Adults." *Journal of Marriage and the Family, 58* (1996): 895-907.

A survey of 18,000 adults in 17 industrialized nations found that married persons have a significantly higher level of happiness than unmarried adults, even after controlling for health and financial status, which are also linked to marriage.
Source: Sack, Steven, and J. Ross Eshleman. "Marital Status and Happiness: A 17 Nation Study." *Journal of Marriage and the Family, 60* (May 1998): 527-536.

...married persons have a significantly higher level of happiness than unmarried adults...

According to a survey of 35,000 adults, married people are more likely to be happier than their non-married counterparts, with 40% of the currently married rating their lives as very happy, compared with 20% of the divorced, separated, or never-married population. In addition, married people are happier in their marriages (62% very happy) than they are about life as a whole (40% very happy). Nevertheless, people today are less likely to rate marriages in general as happy and are more likely to say there are few good marriages compared to the past.
Source: Smith, Tom W. "The Emerging 21st Century Family." *GSS Social Change Report No. 42.* Chicago, IL: University of Chicago, National Opinion Research Center, 1999: 5-6

In a national study of 930 Norwegian persons married in 1980 or 1983, it was found that persons who subsequently separated or divorced experienced a significant increase in psychological distress both short-term (less than 4 years post-divorce) and long-term (4 to 8 years post-divorce).
Source: Mastekaasa, A. "Marital Dissolution and Subjective Distress: Panel Evidence." *European Sociological Review, 11* (1995): 173-185.

In a five-year longitudinal study using a nationally representative sample of 5,991 people ages 19 to 75, it was found that after taking into account mental health at the start of the study as well as age, education, number of children in the household, and other factors known to affect mental health, getting married or staying married was associated with significantly fewer symptoms of depression compared with being single, divorced, or cohabiting. Even unhappily married partners had fewer symptoms of depression compared to never-married or divorced individuals. Remarriage was found to improve mental health, but not as much as first marriage.
Source: McKenry, Patrick. "The Relationship between Marriage and Psychological Well-being: A Longitudinal Analysis." Paper presented at American Sociological Association meeting, August, 2000, Washington, D.C.; see also Elias, Marilyn. "Marriage Makes for a Good State of Mind." *USA Today,* August, 14, 2000: D6.

Using a sample of 9,643 respondents from the National Survey of Families and Households, it was found that the transition from marriage to separation or divorce was associated with an increase in depression, a decline in happiness, less personal mastery, less positive relations with others, and less self-acceptance. These associations were stronger for women than for men. Becoming married, on the other hand, was associated with a "considerable well-being boost" evident in both women and men.
Source: Marks, Nadine F., and James D. Lambert. "Marital Status Continuity and Change Among Young and Midlife Adults: Longitudinal Effects on Psychological Well-Being." *Journal of Family Issues, 19* (1998): 652-686.

In a study of 140 young adults (aged 21-28 years), it was found that being married and having one or more children was associated with decreased participation in risky behaviors, including risky driving, substance use, and risky sexual behavior.
Source: Arnett, Jeffrey Jensen. "Risk Behavior and Family Role Transitions During the Twenties." Journal of Youth & Adolescence 27 (June 1998): 301-320.

Using data from Statistics Canada, it was found that married persons, compared to single or unmarried persons, have lower death rates for a variety of causes of death, including suicide, motor vehicle accidents, lung cancer, cirrhosis of the liver, ischaemic heart disease, and diabetes.
Source: Trovato, Frank. "Nativity, Marital Status and Mortality in Canada." *Canadian Review of Sociology and Anthropology, 35* (February 1998): 65-91.

Single men have almost six times the probability of being incarcerated as married men.
Source: Akerlof, George A. "Men Without Children." *The Economic Journal, 108* (1998): 287-309.

In a study of 162 junior-high and high-school teachers in Great Britain, evening blood pressure rates dropped significantly for married adults, and especially for married adults with children, but not for unmarried adults. This pattern did not differ in men and women, and was not due to variations between groups in levels of subjective pressure, physical activity, or location.
Source: Steptoe, Andrew, Karen Lundwall, and Mark Cropley. "Gender, Family Structure and Cardiovascular Activity During the Working Day and Evening." *Social Science and Medicine 50* (2000): 531-539.

Studies on marriages have found that married people live longer, have higher incomes and wealth, engage less in risky behaviors, eat more healthily, and have fewer psychological problems than unmarried people.
Source: Waite, Linda J. "Why Marriage Matters." *Strengthening Marriage Roundtable.* Washington, D.C., 23 June 1997.

Single men have almost six times the probability of being incarcerated as married men.

A study of over 800 young adults living in New Jersey found that those who were married had lower levels of depression and fewer alcohol problems than their single counterparts.
Source: Horwitz, Allan V., Helene Raskin White, and Sandra Howell-White. "Becoming Married and Mental Health: A Longitudinal Study of a Cohort of Young Adults." *Journal of Marriage and the Family 58* (1997): 895-907.

In a study using a nationally representative sample of 3,098 Mexican and African Americans, marital status was strongly linked to personal happiness and life satisfaction. Marital status was a better predictor of happiness than income, education, church attendance, gender, or ethnicity.
Source: Parker, Keith D., Suzanne T. Ortega, and Jody VanLaningham. "Life Satisfaction, Self-Esteem, and Personal Happiness Among Mexican and African Americans." *Sociological Spectrum 15* (1995): 131-145.

In a study on 6,203 married and cohabiting couples, married couples reported significantly higher levels of happiness than cohabiting couples.
Source: Nock, Steven L. "A Comparison of Marriages and Cohabiting Relationships." *Journal of Family Issues 16* (January 1995): 53-76.

Of violent acts against women committed by acquaintances, 42% involved a close friend or partner, 29% involved a current spouse, and 12% involved an ex-spouse. Only 12.6 of every 1000 married women are victims of violent acts, while 43.9 of every 1000 never-married women are victims of violent acts, and 66.5 of every 1000 divorced or separated women are victims of violent acts.
Source: Popenoe, David. "A World without Fathers." *Wilson Quarterly* (Spring 1996): 12-29.

Importance of Marriage to the Well-Being of Men

Marriage has a unique effect on men's productivity. While cohabiting men earn more than single men alone, their wage advantage is only 13% compared to 22% for married men. This difference increases over time.
Source: Koretz, Gene. "Marriage's 'Unique Effect'" Business Week 13 May 2002: 32.; Stratton, Leslie. "Examining the Wage Differential For Married and Cohabiting Men." *Economic Inquiry, 40* (April 2002): 199-212.

Married men are twice as likely to be affluent at age 45 than nonmarried men. Over the age of 45, married men are even more likely (2.4 times) to be affluent compared to non-married men.
Source: Hirschl, Thomas A., Joyce Altobelli, and Mark R. Rank. "Does Marriage Increase the Odds of Affluence? Exploring the Life Course Probability." *Journal of Marriage and Family, 65* (November 2003): 927-938.

Married men experience an income premium compared to unmarried men, depending on their wife's work status. Men whose wives do not work earn 31.5% more than never married-men, whereas men whose wives work the average amount (25.6 hours) experience a premium of 12.6%.
Source: Chun, Hyunbae and Injae Lee. "Why Do Married Men Earn More: Productivity or Marriage Selection?" *Economic Inquiry, 39* (April 2001): 307-319.

A sample of 300 boys indicated that those who felt close to their father (biological custodial, biological noncustodial, or stepfather) were less likely to divorce at later life than boys who lacked father closeness.
Source: Risch, Sharon C., Kathleen M. Jodl, and Jaquelynne S. Eccles. "Role of the Father-Adolescent Relationship in Shaping Adolescents' Attitudes Toward Divorce." *Journal of Marriage and Family, 66* (February 2004): 46-58.

Of the 1,010 men polled, 94% said they enjoyed being married more than being single. Seventy-three percent say that their sex life is better since getting married and 68 percent say that marriage has helped them become more financially stable.
Source: Whitehead, Barbara Dafoe and David Popenoe. *The State of Our Unions 2004.* The National Marriage Project. Piscataway, NJ: The National Marriage Project, 2004: 9.

Married men are twice as likely to be affluent at age 45 than nonmarried men.

A study on the effects of marriage and divorce found that divorced men are twice as likely to die prematurely from hypertension, four times as likely to die prematurely from throat cancer, and seven times as likely to die prematurely from pneumonia. In addition, divorced men have higher rates of depression, substance abuse, auto accidents, and suicide than their married peers.

Source: *American Journal of Public Health, 1995*. "Stay Married, Go to Church, Live Longer. No Sweat." by Gracie S. Hsu. Washington, D.C.: Family Research Council, August 1995.

Importance of Marriage to the Well-Being of Women

Compared to other living arrangements, women who grew up in homes with their two biological parents married later, had more education at marriage, had husbands with more education, were less likely to have a premarital birth or conception, and were less likely to cohabit before marriage.

Moreover, women who grew up in biological two-parent households were less likely to form high risk marriages. They were less likely to marry as teenagers, were more likely to have more than a high school education, were more likely to form a marriage in which both spouses have more than a high school education, were less likely to marry someone 5 or more years older, were less likely to marry as a teen and marry someone 5 or more years older, and had fewer total risk factors.

Source: Teachman, Jay D. "The Childhood Living Arrangements of Children and the Characteristics of Their Marriages." *Journal of Family Issues, 25* (January 2004): 86-111.

Married mothers received much higher scores in supportiveness and positivity with their infants when compared to single and cohabiting mothers. Married mothers created more positive home environments and the infants were more likely to be attached to their mothers.

Married mothers also had social advantages. They had more education, financial security, and psychological adjustments.

Source: Aronson, Stacey Rosenkrantz and Aletha C. Huston. "The Mother-Infant Relationship in Single, Cohabiting, and Married Families: A Case for Marriage?" *Journal of Family Psychology, 18* (March 2004): 5-18.

In a study of 500 women, those in satisfied marriages were healthier overall than women in unmarried arrangements. They even experienced an advantage over women in moderately healthy marriages who were exposed to higher risk of psychosocial problems and cardiovascular risk. Divorced women had higher BMIs and lower rates of physical activity.

Source: Gallo, Linda et al. "Marital Status and Quality in Middle-Aged Women: Associates With Levels and Trajectories of Cardiovascular Risk Factors." *Health Psychology, 22* (September 2003): 453-463.

The effect of never being married had no effect on the wages of Black women in the 80s, but played a role in the downward decline of earnings in the 90s. Having children negatively effected earnings in both decades. Although Black women had fewer children in 1990, both fertility and marriage contributed negatively to the change in Black women's earning over that period.

Source: Newsome, Yvonne D and F. Nii-Amoo Dodoo. "Reversal of Fortune: Explaining the Decline in Black Women's Earnings." *Gender & Society, 16* (August 2004): 442-464.

Women who experienced life in an alternative family structure (as opposed to a two-parent household) form marriages with characteristics that discourage their success. These unions are associated with early age at marriage, low education of both spouses, premarital fertility, and premarital cohabitation.

Source: Teachman, Jay D. "The Childhood Living Arrangements of Children and the Characteristics of Their Marriages." *Journal of Family Issues, 25* (January 2004): 86-111.

In an analysis of data collected from 11,405 women at age 23 and again at age 33, even after taking into account differences in financial status and the ages of the children in the home, women who were single mothers at age 33 were 1.5 times more likely than married mothers to suffer from significant psychological distress.

Source: Hope, Steven, Chris Power, and Bryan Rodgers. "Does Financial Hardship Account for Elevated Psychological Distress in Lone Mothers?" *Social Science and Medicine, 49* (1999): 1637-1649.

An analysis of a nationally representative sample of over 2,700 mothers found that mothers in their first marriages had higher levels of overall well-being and lower levels of depression than never-married, divorced, and remarried mothers, even after taking into account different income levels.

Source: Demo, David H. and Alan C. Acock. "Singlehood, Marriage and Remarriage: The Effects of Family Structure and Family Relationships on Mothers' Well-Being." *Journal of Family Issues, 17* (1996): 386-407.

An analysis of multiple studies on marriage found that most research indicates that married women fare better on a number of indicators than their unmarried counterparts.

Source: Glenn, Norval D. "The Textbook Story of American Marriages and Families." Publication No.: W.P. 46. New York: Institute for American Values, May 1996.

Based upon an analysis of national census and health data, it was determined that even after controlling for economic status and pre-existing health risk factors, women who live in communities where more than a quarter of the families are headed by unmarried women are more likely to die of heart disease than women who live in neighborhoods with fewer female-headed households. Women who lived in census tracts with the highest female headship rates experienced an 85 percent increase in risk of dying of heart disease when compared to women in tracts with the lowest levels of female-headed households.

Source: LeClere, Felicia B., Richard G. Rogers, and Kimberley Peters. "Neighborhood Social Context and Racial Differences in Women's Heart Disease Mortality." *Journal of Health and Social Behavior, 39* (1998): 91-107.

In a study of 518 single mothers and 502 married mothers living in London, Ontario, Canada, it was found that even after controlling for differences in income, single mothers were almost four times more likely than married mothers to have been depressed in the last year, and were nearly three times more likely to have experienced a major depressive disorder. Single mothers were also found to be more likely to have had recurrent episodes of depression than married mothers.

Source: Davies, Lorraine, William R. Avison, and Donna D. McAlpine. "Significant Life Experiences and Depression Among Single and Married Mothers." *Journal of Marriage and the Family, 59* (May 1997): 294-308.

Using a large community sample of 13,088 pregnant women in the United Kingdom, compared to women in two-parent, married families, women in single-parent families and stepfamilies reported significantly elevated rates of depression even after controlling for levels of social support, stressful life events, and crowding.

Source: O'Connor, Thomas, et al. "Family Type and Depression in Pregnancy: Factors Mediating Risk in a Community Sample." *Journal of Marriage and the Family, 60* (August 1998): 757-770.

Importance of Marriage to Extended Family Support

In a study of family ties and kin networks, newlywed husbands and wives both reported being closer to intact families than to divorced families, whether they were reporting about their own families or their in-laws.

Source: Timmer, Susan G., and Joseph Vernoff. "Family Ties and the Discontinuity of Divorce in Black and White Newlywed Couples." *Journal of Marriage and the Family, 62* (May 2000): 349-361.

Examining data from the 1987-88 National Survey of Families and Households (n = 9,637 households), it was found that one in six married families received a financial gift from the father's side of the family in the last five years, compared to only one in 50 families headed by a divorced mother and no families headed by an unwed mother.

Source: Hao, Lingxin. "Family Structure, Private Transfers, and the Economic Well-Being of Families with Children." Social Forces 75 (1996): 269-292.

VII. Adoption

"When Sam Donaldson said to me, 'Well, what would you say to somebody who just couldn't take care of their children?' If instead of saying orphanages, I had said adoption, we would have had a more profitable debate."

NEWT GINGRICH, FORMER SPEAKER OF THE HOUSE OF REPRESENTATIVES, 1995

Trends in Adoption

In 2001, there were 1.37 million adopted children, down from 1.59 million in 2000. Eighty three percent lived in two parent households, 14 percent lived in single mother households, and 3 percent lived with single fathers.

Source: Kreider, Rose M. and Jason Fields. Living Arrangements of Children: 2001. Current Population Studies, P70-104. Table 4. Washington, D.C.: US Census Bureau, 2005; Kreider, Rose M. Adopted Children and Stepchildren, CENSR-6RV, Table 1, U.S. Census Bureau. Washington, D.C: GPO, 2003.

In 2000 and 2001, about 127,000 children were adopted annually in the United States. Since 1987, the number of adoptions annually has remained relatively constant, ranging from 118,000 to 127,000.

Source: U.S. Department of Health and Human Services. How many children were adopted in 2000 and 2001? Washington, DC: National Adoption Information Clearinghouse, 2004, 7.

Proportion Of All Unwed Mothers Who Gave A Child For Adoption

Before 1973	8.7
1973-1981	4.1
1982-1988	2.0
1989-1995	0.9

Source: Chandra, Anjani, Joyce Abma, Penelope Maza, and Christine Bachrach. "Adoption, Adoption Seeking and Relinquishment for Adoption in the United States." Advance Data, Number 306. Hyattsville, MD: National Center for Health Statistics, May 11, 1999.

It is estimated that between 2% and 4% of all American families have adopted.

Source: Moorman, Jeanne E. and Donald J. Hernandez. "Married-couple Families with Step, Adopted, and Biological Children." *Demography, 26.2* (1989): 267-77; see also Mosher, William D. and Christine A. Bachrach. "Understanding U.S. Fertility: Continuity and Change in the National Survey of Family Growth." *Family Planning Perspectives, 28.1* (1996): 4-12.

It is estimated that between 2% and 4% of all American families have adopted.

As of 1988, there were about 823,000 children living in adopted families in the United States. These children represent about 1.3 percent of all children aged 17 years and under in the country in that year.

Source: Zill, Nicholas. Testimony before the U.S. House of Representatives Committee on Ways and Means Subcommittee on Human Resources. 10 May 1995.

Consequences of Adoption for Child Well-Being

In a longitudinal study of 1,262 New Zealand children from birth to age 16, it was found that children adopted at birth did better than those entering single-parent families at birth on a variety of measures, including standards of health care, family material conditions, family stability, and mother-child interactions. In addition, although children adopted at birth had higher rates of externalizing behavior problems (conduct disorders, juvenile offending, and substance abuse) than those born into two-parent married households, they had fewer problems than those children entering single-parent families at birth.

Source: Fergusson, David, and Horwood, L.J. "Adoption and Adjustment in Adolescence." *Adoption & Fostering 22*(1998): 24-30.

Less than one percent of adopted children receive Aid to Families with Dependent Children, whereas among white children born outside of marriage and raised by their biological mothers, 32 percent were receiving welfare.

Source: Zill, Nicholas. Testimony before the U.S. House of Representatives Committee on Ways and Means Subcommittee on Human Resources. 10 May 1995.

Consequences for the Birth Mother of Placing a Child for Adoption

In a comparison of the consequences of placing a child for adoption versus child rearing for young women who experienced a nonmarital teenage pregnancy, it was found that even after controlling for sociodemographic background factors, resolving a teenage pregnancy through adoption resulted in more favorable outcomes for the mother on a broad variety of sociodemographic and social-psychological outcomes.

Source: Namerow, Pearila Brickner, Debra Kalmuss, and Linda F. Cushman. "The Consequences of Placing Versus Parenting Among Young Unmarried Women." *Marriage and Family Review 25* (1997): 175-197.

ABOUT NATIONAL FATHERHOOD INITIATIVE

National Fatherhood Initiative (NFI) was founded in 1994 to stimulate a society-wide movement to confront the growing problem of father absence. NFI's mission is to improve the well-being of children by increasing the proportion of children growing up with involved, responsible, and committed fathers in their lives.

A non-profit, non-partisan, non-sectarian organization, NFI pursues its mission through a three-E strategy of educating, equipping, and engaging all sectors of society on the issue of responsible fatherhood.

NFI educates and inspires all people, especially fathers, through public awareness campaigns, research, and other resources, publications, and media appearances centered on highlighting the unique and irreplaceable role fathers play in the lives of children. NFI's national public service advertising campaign promoting fatherhood has generated television, radio, print, Internet, and outdoor advertising valued at over $460 million at the time this study was published.

NFI equips fathers and develops leaders of national, state, and community fatherhood programs and initiatives through curricula, training, and technical assistance. Through FatherSOURCE, its Fatherhood Resource Center, NFI offers a wide range of innovative resources to assist fathers and organizations interested in reaching and supporting fathers.

NFI engages all sectors of society through strategic alliances and partnerships to create unique and effective ways to reach all fathers at their points of need. NFI seeks partnerships through the three pillars of culture—business, faith, and government—to create culture change around the issue of fatherhood.

The research in Father Facts, Fifth Edition was compiled by Jamin Warren. For more information on the contents of this report, or for general information about NFI, call 301-948-0599 or visit www.fatherhood.org.

Have you been a dad today?

National Fatherhood Initiative®

www.fatherhood.org

There are 24 million children in the United States today growing up in a home without their father.

America's children need **YOU** to be a Double Duty Dad!

Dad, you can use your unique experiences to do Double Duty!

Mentor TODAY to make a big difference in the lives of children in your community.

Find out more at www.doubledutydad.org.

REWARD GOOD DADS YEAR ROUND!

Buy a Golden Dads™ Kit today to reward good dads in your community!

GOLDEN DAD

Golden Dads™ is a campaign to reward involved, responsible, and committed fathers. With NFI's Golden Dads™ Kit, you get all the goodies you need to reward great dads in your community. Simply purchase your event kit from NFI, fill it with other great NFI resources or your own goodies, and get out there and reward great dads! And, you can use our online resources to help you run a successful and memorable event!

For more information on Golden Dads, visit us online

fatherhood.org/GoldenDads/